How School Principals Use Their Time

Presenting international evidence, from school systems across the globe, this book documents patterns, causes, and effects of school principals' time use, building a case for the implications for school improvement, administration, and leadership. This edited volume offers an unparalleled set of chapters that delve into conceptual and methodological issues in researching principals' time use. Chapters consist of empirical studies that advance fresh perspectives and build empirical ground on how principals use time across different school systems in Africa, Europe, Middle East, Oceania, and North America.

This unique book is a useful resource for researchers and educators, capturing the geographically diverse contexts of principal time use. This work makes a significant contribution to the field of school improvement, administration, and leadership with both theoretical depth and empirical grounding.

Moosung Lee is a Centenary Professor at the University of Canberra in Australia. He also holds professorship at Yonsei University in South Korea. Prior to joining the University of Canberra, he held appointments as associate professor and founding Deputy Director of the Education Policy Unit at the University of Hong Kong. His research areas are educational leadership and administration, social contexts of education, and comparative education. He received the American Educational Research Association's Emerging Scholar Award (Division A—Administration, Organization, and Leadership). He was also chosen as a recipient for the University of Canberra Research Excellence Award in Social Sciences. He currently serves as Senior Associate Editor of the *Journal of Educational Administration*.

Katina Pollock is associate professor of Educational Leadership and Policy in the field of Critical Policy, Equity, and Leadership Studies at the Faculty of Education, Western University. The overall goal of Dr. Pollock's research agenda is to support and improve public education systems; to this effect, her research focuses on supporting school leaders. Specifically, she concentrates on school leaders' work intensification and well-being, policy development and implementation, and knowledge mobilization. Her research with colleagues has been supported by federal granting agencies, provincial governments, and professional associations.

Her current Federal Grants focus on secondary school principals' work intensification (with Dr. Fei Wang) (2016–2023) and the relationship between policy and principals' work (with Dr. Laura Pinto and Dr. Sue Winton) (2015–2023).

Pierre Tulowitzki is a professor of Educational Management and School Improvement at the FHNW University of Applied Sciences and Arts Northwestern Switzerland. In addition, he is a member of the Institute for Educational Sciences at the University of Basel. His research interests revolve around educational leadership, school improvement and networks in education. Pierre serves as the Link Convenor for the EERA Educational Leadership Network and as a Board Member of the International Congress for School Effectiveness and School Improvement (ICSEI).

How School Principals Use Their Time

Implications for School Improvement, Administration and Leadership

Edited by Moosung Lee, Katina Pollock, and Pierre Tulowitzki

LONDON AND NEW YORK

First published 2022
by Routledge
2 Park Square, Milton Park, Abingdon, Oxon OX14 4RN

and by Routledge
52 Vanderbilt Avenue, New York, NY 10017

Routledge is an imprint of the Taylor & Francis Group, an informa business

© 2022 selection and editorial matter, Moosung Lee, Katina Pollock, and Pierre Tulowitzki; individual chapters, the contributors

The right of Moosung Lee, Katina Pollock, and Pierre Tulowitzki to be identified as the authors of the editorial material, and of the authors for their individual chapters, has been asserted in accordance with sections 77 and 78 of the Copyright, Designs and Patents Act 1988.

All rights reserved. No part of this book may be reprinted or reproduced or utilised in any form or by any electronic, mechanical, or other means, now known or hereafter invented, including photocopying and recording, or in any information storage or retrieval system, without permission in writing from the publishers.

Trademark notice: Product or corporate names may be trademarks or registered trademarks and are used only for identification and explanation without intent to infringe.

British Library Cataloguing-in-Publication Data
A catalogue record for this book is available from the British Library

Library of Congress Cataloging-in-Publication Data
A catalog record has been requested for this book

ISBN: 978-0-367-34779-6 (hbk)
ISBN: 978-1-032-00167-8 (pbk)
ISBN: 978-0-429-32790-2 (ebk)

Typeset in Galliard
by KnowledgeWorks Global Ltd.

Contents

List of figures vii
List of tables viii
Acknowledgment ix
Contributors x

Exploring how school principals use their time 1
MOOSUNG LEE, KATINA POLLOCK, AND PIERRE TULOWITZKI

PART I
Theoretical perspectives and methodological issues 7

1 Principals' time use as a research area: Notes on theoretical perspectives, leadership domains, and future directions 9
   MOOSUNG LEE

2 Measurement assumptions in principals' time-use research: Past problems and needed studies 22
   BRIAN ROWAN

3 A framework for evaluating and choosing principal time-use measurement strategies 43
   ERIC M. CAMBURN AND JAMES SEBASTIAN

4 Identifying research opportunities from the methodological history of principal time-use studies 59
   CRAIG HOCHBEIN, ABBY S. MAHONE, AND SARA C. VANDERBECK

5 Principals' direct interaction with individual students: A missing piece in principal leadership research 75
   MOOSUNG LEE, ALLAN WALKER, AND GEOFFREY RIORDAN

vi *Contents*

PART II
Principal time use in Western contexts   93

  6 How principals use their time in Ontario, Canada   95
       KATINA POLLOCK AND FEI WANG

  7 Managing time? Principal supervisors' time use to support principals   110
       LAURA K. ROGERS, ELLEN B. GOLDRING, MOLLIE RUBIN, MICHAEL NEEL, AND JASON A. GRISSOM

  8 How successful school principals balance their leadership and management roles to make a difference   126
       LAWRIE DRYSDALE, DAVID GURR, AND HELEN GOODE

  9 "Wasting time talking to students and parents": Neoliberal efficiency myths about principal discretionary time use in Australia   141
       PHILIP RILEY

10 School business leaders and principal time use in England   157
       PAUL WILFRED ARMSTRONG

11 Out-of-time managers? Educational leaders' use of time in Switzerland   171
       PIERRE TULOWITZKI AND LAETITIA PROGIN

PART III
Principal time use in Africa and the Middle East   185

12 South African school principals' use of time: Learning from a qualitative study   187
       VITALLIS CHIKOKO AND PINKIE MTHEMBU

13 Policy context and time use of primary school head teachers in Kenya: Evidence from the Snapshot of School Management Effectiveness (SSME) survey   201
       PETER MOYI

14 Emotional workload and time use in principalship: Insights from Israeli educational leaders   215
       IZHAR OPLATKA

Index   229

Figures

3.1	Incidence of different strategies for measuring principal practice in volumes 53–55 of *Educational Administration Quarterly*	44
3.2	A framework for evaluating, describing and comparing strategies for measuring principal time use	45
4.1	Principal time use data collection techniques across time	65
5.1	Principals' work hours per week for interaction with individual students across the 34 societies	83
6.1	Time spent on school communication	101
6.2	Percentage of an average day principals spend time in different locations	102
7.1	Principal supervisors' use of time at work	115
7.2	Principal supervisor focus of time with principals	116
7.3	Range of principal-reported school meetings with supervisor in 3 months, by supervisor	118
8.1	Total role concept 1	130
8.2	Total role concept	132
8.3	Balance between management and leadership role	136
9.1	Principal time use by percentage	145
9.2	Principal time use according to the stakeholders with whom they interact	145
9.3	Hours at work per week for catholic primary school principals	146
13.1	Qualification levels of primary school head teachers	208

Tables

4.1	Principal time-use studies with non-unique sampling structures	64
4.2	Sample size and observation periods by school locale	66
4.3	Sample size and observation periods by school level	66
4.4	Sample size and observation periods by time of year	67
5.1	Descriptive statistics of organizational and macro contexts across the 34 education systems	80
5.2	Principals' time used for interaction with students (poisson HLM)	85
6.1	Rotated component matrix	99
6.2	The extent of interactions principals have with people	101
6.3	Hours spent per week and provincial policy	103
7.1	Description of PSI survey and interview participants	113
9.1	Principal health and well-being strategy components	150
12.1	Summary of the core purpose of the South African school principal	189
13.1	Overview of the geographic distribution of the Kenya 2012 Snapshot of School Management Effectiveness data	207
13.2	Responses regarding reviewing teachers' lessons plans and classroom observation	209

Acknowledgment

The editors of this book appreciate the American Educational Research Association's (AERA) funding for a research conference on *Cross-National Exploration of Principals' Time Use* hosted at the University of Canberra in 2016. This edited volume is a major outcome of the AERA-funded conference.

We would like to thank our authors for continuing to work through the global pandemic of 2020. This was an especially difficult time and we are truly grateful for their commitment and dedication.

We would also like to extend a special note of gratitude to Sydney Gautreau for her invaluable editorial expertise. Additionally, we would like to thank the Routledge editorial team for their work in bringing this volume to fruition.

Contributors

Paul Armstrong is a senior lecturer in educational leadership and management at the Manchester Institute of Education, University of Manchester. His main interests and current research agenda concern contemporary forms of educational leadership and management; in particular, he is interested in the means by which schools are managed and resourced organizationally. He is also interested in school-to-school collaboration and support. He has over 15 years experience in educational research on a range of national and international projects across a number of areas of education including educational improvement, collaboration, leadership, management, and policy.

Eric M. Camburn For three decades, Eric Camburn has conducted research on school improvement, school leadership and inequalities in educational opportunity. His research has contributed to the field's understanding of social inequalities in the secondary and post-secondary outcomes of urban students and of factors that promote and impede the progress of urban students at key junctures. His research has also contributed to a better understanding of how schools can structure professional learning experiences for teachers that support the improvement of their practice. Camburn has worked collaboratively with multiple urban school districts to facilitate improvement initiatives with evidence on education practice and organizational conditions.

Vitallis Chikoko is a professor of Educational Leadership at the University of KwaZulu-Natal. He is editor of the books: *Africa Handbook for School Leadership* (2019); *Leadership that Works in Deprived School Contexts of South Africa* (2018); co-editor of the book: *Education Leadership, Management and Governance in South Africa*; and assistant editor of the book: *International Handbook of Leadership for Learning* (2011). His research interests include school leadership, leadership development, school financing, school governance, and education in rural contexts.

Lawrie Drysdale is an associate professor of education in the Melbourne Graduate School of Education, University of Melbourne. Lawrie has an extensive career in teaching and researching principal and middle-level leadership, marketing and innovation, and human resource management. He is a member of several successful international projects, including the International Successful School Principalship Project (ISSPP) and the International School Leadership Development Network (ISLDN). He is a coconvenor in the Leadership Network of ECER and a board member of Victorian Chapter of Australian Council of Educational Leaders (ACEL).

Ellen Goldring is the Patricia and Rodes Hart Professor of Education Policy and Leadership, and Executive Associate Dean, Peabody College, Vanderbilt University. Her research interests focus on the intersection of education policy and school improvement with emphases on education leadership. Her research examines leadership practice, and the implementation of interventions such as professional development, coaching, and performance feedback. A fellow of the American Educational Research Association, she is the recipient of the University Council for Educational Administration's Roald F. Campbell Lifetime Achievement Award.

Helen Goode is a lecturer in the Master of Education program at The University of Melbourne, Australia and a Research Fellow of the Education University of Hong Kong. She is a member of the International Successful School Principal Project (ISSPP), the ISLDN (International School Leadership Development Network), and a convenor of the ECER Network 26 Educational Leadership. Her research interests include sustainability of successful leadership, marketing in schools, and the role of coaching in building leadership capacity.

Jason A. Grissom is Patricia and Rodes Hart Professor of Public Policy and Education at Vanderbilt University's Peabody College and Faculty Director of the Tennessee Education Research Alliance, a research-policy-practice partnership between Vanderbilt and the Tennessee Department of Education that conducts research to inform Tennessee's school improvement efforts. He studies school leadership, educator labor markets, and issues of educational equity, and often the intersections among the three.

David Gurr is an associate professor in educational leadership at the Graduate School of Education, the University of Melbourne. His research is focused on the leadership of schools broadly, and successful school leadership, middle leaders, governance, and accountability in particular. He is a founding member of two of the major international school leadership research projects: The International Successful School Principalship Project and the International School Leadership Development Network. David is editor of *International Studies in Educational Administration* and senior associate editor of the *Journal of Educational Administration*.

Craig Hochbein is an associate professor in the Educational Leadership Program at the Lehigh University College of Education. His research examines factors associated with declining academic achievement, the effectiveness of policies intended to improve school performance, and how school leader time use contributes to educational outcomes.

xii *Contributors*

Moosung Lee is a Centenary Professor at the University of Canberra in Australia. He also holds professorship at Yonsei University in South Korea. Prior to joining the University of Canberra, he held appointments as associate professor and founding Deputy Director of the Education Policy Unit at the University of Hong Kong. His research areas are educational leadership and administration, social contexts of education, and comparative education. He received the Richard Wolf Memorial Award by the International Association for the Evaluation of Educational Achievement (IEA) and the American Educational Research Association's Emerging Scholar Award (Division A—Administration, Organization, and Leadership). He was also chosen as a recipient for the University of Canberra Research Excellence Award in Social Sciences.

Abby Mahone graduated with her doctoral degree from the Educational Leadership Program at the Lehigh University College of Education. She serves as the Assistant Head of Schools and Head of the Early Childhood and Lower School at Harrisburg Academy.

Peter Moyi is an associate professor in the Department of Educational Leadership and Policies at the College of Education, University of South Carolina. His research uses sociological theory to understand school leadership practice in schools. Peter's research agenda is motivated by a keen interest in understanding school leadership as an opportunity to ensure quality education for schools serving poor and marginalized children.

Pinkie Mthembu is a lecturer in the discipline of Educational Leadership Management and Policy at the University of KwaZulu-Natal, South Africa. She has recently graduated with her Ph.D., which focused on the district leadership role in supporting teaching and learning in South African schools. Her research interests are school district leadership, gender and leadership, leading educational change, as well as leading and managing teaching and learning in the context deprived communities.

Michael Neel is a lecturer in the Department of Leadership, Policy, and Organizations at Peabody College, Vanderbilt University. His teaching and scholarly interests focus on professional learning and on the intersection of policy and practice in learning settings.

Izhar Oplatka is a professor of Educational Administration and Leadership at The School of Education, Tel Aviv University, Israel. Prof. Oplatka's research focuses on the lives and career of school teachers and principals, educational marketing, emotions and educational administration, and the foundations of educational administration as a field of study. His most recent books include *Reforming Education in Developing Countries* (2019, Routledge), *Emotion Management in Teaching and Educational Leadership: A Cultural Perspective* (with Arar, EMERALD Publishing Limited), *Project Management in Schools* (2018, with

Yemini and Sagi, Palgrave-Macmillan), and *Higher Education Consumer Choice* (2015, with Jane Hemsley-Brown, Palgrave).

Katina Pollock is associate professor of Educational Leadership and Policy in the field of Critical Policy, Equity, and Leadership Studies at the Faculty of Education, Western University. The overall goal of Dr. Pollock's research agenda is to support and improve public education systems; to this effect, her research focuses on supporting school leaders. Specifically, she concentrates on school leaders' work intensification and well-being, policy development and implementation, and knowledge mobilization. Her research with colleagues has been supported by federal granting agencies, provincial governments, and professional associations. Her current SSHRC Insight Grants focus on secondary school principals' work intensification (with Dr. Fei Wang) (2016–2023) and the relationship between policy and principals' work (with Dr. Laura Pinto and Dr. Sue Winton) (2015–2023). In addition to traditional scholarship, she has also taken on several leadership roles, such as Co-Director of the UCEA Centre for International Study of School Leadership (2011–2014), Director of the Western Centre for Education Leadership (2014–2018), and Co-Director of the Knowledge Network for Applied Education Research (KNAER) (2011–2018).

Laetitia Progin is an associate professor in Leadership at the University of Teacher Education, State of Vaud (Switzerland). Her research examines processes of professional socialization, school culture, the role of head teachers and power dynamics in primary and secondary schools.

Philip Riley holds the chair of education leadership in the Research Centre for Educational Impact at Deakin University in Melbourne, Australia. He researches the overlapping space of psychology, education, and leadership. He began The Australian Principal Occupational Health and Well-being Survey, the first independent research project into principals' occupational health and well-being in 2011. The Principal Health and Wellbeing Survey is now conducted in Australia, Ireland, New Zealand, and, most recently, Finland.

Geoffrey Riordan is an emeritus professor of the University of Canberra where he served for eight years as the Dean of the Faculty of Education. He has undertaken research on a range of topics in educational leadership, student welfare and discipline and teacher collaboration in professional learning.

Laura K. Rogers is an assistant professor in the Department of Educational Leadership and Policy at the University of Utah and a faculty research affiliate at the Utah Education Policy Center. Her research focuses on understanding organizational contributors to principal and teacher effectiveness, including the role of district leadership and policies.

Brian Rowan is an Emeritus Professor in the School of Education and the Department of Sociology at the University of Michigan and also Emeritus

Research Professor at the University of Michigan's Institute for Social Research. A sociologist by training, his research has focused on education as an institution, on school organization and management, and on school and teaching effectiveness. Rowan is a past recipient of the William J. Davis award for outstanding scholarship in educational administration and also an elected member of the U.S. National Academy of Education.

Mollie Rubin is a research assistant professor in the Department of Leadership, Policy, and Organizations at Peabody College, Vanderbilt University. Dr. Rubin's research is focused on improvement of K-12 public education, chiefly the intersection of education policy and the organizational contexts in which reform efforts occur. She is particularly interested in the topics of program implementation and evaluation, professional learning, teacher quality, and the study of school and district leadership.

James Sebastian is an associate professor in the Department of Educational Leadership & Policy Analysis (ELPA) at the University of Missouri-Columbia. He received his Ph.D. in ELPA from the University of Wisconsin-Madison. Before joining the faculty at Missouri-Columbia, he was a senior researcher at the Consortium on Chicago School Research. His research interests include the study of school organizational theory and behavior and organizational learning. Focusing primarily in quantitative methods, he is also interested in the application of mixed-methods in examining school organizations. His work has appeared in the *High School Journal, Education Administration Quarterly*, and the *Journal of Education Administration*.

Pierre Tulowitzki is a professor of Educational Management and School Improvement at the FHNW University of Applied Sciences and Arts Northwestern Switzerland. In addition, he is a member of the Institute for Educational Sciences at the University of Basel. His research interests revolve around educational leadership, school improvement and networks in education. Pierre serves as the Link Convenor for the EERA Educational Leadership Network and as a Board Member of the International Congress for School Effectiveness and School Improvement (ICSEI).

Sara Vanderbeck graduated with her doctoral degree from the Educational Leadership Program at the Lehigh University College of Education. She serves as a Lead Teacher in the High School Program at the Centennial School.

Allan Walker is Chair Professor of International Educational Leadership and Co-director of The Joseph Lau Luen Hung Charitable Trust Asia Pacific Centre for Leadership and Change at The Education University of Hong Kong (EdUHK). He was previously Dean of the Faculty of Education and Human Development at EdUHK. Allan's research interests include the impact of culture on educational leadership and school organization, school leadership in South East Asia, particularly China, leadership development, leading international schools and values and educational leadership.

Fei Wang is an associate professor at the Faculty of Education, the University of British Columbia (UBC). He earned his Ph.D. in educational leadership and administration at Ontario Institute for Studies in Education, the University of Toronto (OISE/UT). His research involves four interrelated areas: (a) the changing nature of school principals' work, particularly, their work intensification and health and well-being in Ontario and British Columbia (funded by SSHRC Insight and UBC SSHRC Explore); (b) principals' subversive strategies in contexts where their day-to-day operation of schools is significantly constrained by policy initiatives and academic standards of educational reform (funded by UBC Hampton Award); (c) principals' strategic leadership through the philosophical teachings of The Art of War to understand school principals' social justice advocacy and activism (funded by SSHRC IDG); and (d) leadership challenges in cross-cultural contexts (e.g., offshore schools) in transnational education (funded by UBC HSS Seed Grant).

Exploring how school principals use their time

Moosung Lee, Katina Pollock, and Pierre Tulowitzki

Background and purpose of the book

In August 2016 we hosted a research conference on *Cross-National Exploration of Principals' Time Use*, funded by the American Educational Research Association (AERA).

Thirty-two leading researchers on school leadership from ten different countries, covering regions such as Africa, Asia, Middle East, Europe, Oceania, and North America, participated in the conference. The researchers presented and discussed their cutting-edge studies aligned to the conference theme. This edited volume is a major outcome of the AERA-funded conference.

This volume aims to deepen our understanding of principal time use from an international perspective and thereby to advance current knowledge of principal leadership across different countries. Specifically, the edited book aims to (1) document common or particular patterns and effects of principal time use across countries, (2) identify common or major causes that shape principal time use across countries, (3) contribute to theorizing the under-researched area of principal time use, and (4) develop a framework of data collection and related analytical tools of principal time use that can be applied to contexts of different countries.

Despite a large body of literature on principal leadership, research focusing on "principal time use" is limited, and a handful of empirical studies exist (see Chapter 1 for details). This relative dearth of studies is surprising given that principal time use is a useful indicator of principal leadership; clearly, principals should spend more time on what is most important for school improvement.

Within this context, this book, as a first of its kind, would be a great resource of principal time use for researchers for several distinctive reasons. First, this book approaches principal time use from an international perspective that broadens our understanding of the research area. The aforementioned research literature has been largely based on Western contexts (mostly in the United States). Through the AERA-funded conference, we learned that research on principal time use has also emerged in non-Western contexts in recent years (e.g., Chile, China, Kenya, Pakistan, South Africa). The emerging line of studies consists of both relatively small-scale qualitative case studies and large-scale quantitative studies. Furthermore, cross-national comparative studies of principal time use, typically including more than a dozen of countries, have also emerged using large international datasets such as PIRLS and TIMSS (e.g., Lee & Hallinger, 2012; Lee, Ryoo, & Walker, 2021; Shin & Slater, 2010; Ten Bruggencate & Luyten, 2010). By encompassing chapters that explore non-western contexts and cross-national comparisons, the edited volume contributes to capturing a fuller picture of principal leadership, given that patterns, causes, and effects of principal time use across different countries are largely uncharted.

Second, this edited volume advances our understanding of principal leadership, given that principal time use is one important way to measure principal leadership; principal time use reflects principals' goal and task prioritization, constituting a fundamental dimension of principal leadership (Dwyer, Lee, Rowan, & Bossert, 1983; Goldring, Huff, May, & Camburn, 2008; Silins & Mulford, 2010).

Third, the book encompasses empirical research on principal time use from various education systems and countries. Specifically, we have secured chapters that cover different societies in Africa, Asia, Europe, Middle East, Oceania, and North America. The geographical diversity of contributing authors would shed light on principal time use in various schooling systems and enable readers to understand (1) principal time use in different school contexts and (2) its implications for school improvement and administration.

Finally, alongside empirical research chapters, we purposively assembled chapters that explore theoretical perspectives and methodological issues in research on principal time use.

Organization of the book

This book consists of 14 research-based chapters, which are divided into three parts. Specifically, Part I explores theories and methods in principal time use studies while Parts II and III provide empirical studies from Western contexts and non-Western contexts, respectively. This combination was designed to comprehensively address the research landscape of principal time use.

Part I begins with Lee's chapter, titled "Principals' Time Use as a Research Area: Notes on Theoretical Perspectives, Leadership Domains, and Future Directions." Lee's chapter charts principal time use as a research area by seeking answers to some key questions such as: (1) Why do we need to research principal time use? (2) What more do we need to know about principal time use? (3) What are theoretical and methodological issues embedded in contemporary research of principal time use? (4) What are the implications of principal time use for school leadership, administration, and improvement?

In his chapter, "Measurement Assumptions in Principals' Time-Use Research: Past Problems and Needed Studies," Rowan offers critical views of 11 theoretical or methodological assumptions that are embedded in data and measures of principal time use. Specifically, his criticisms include (1) researchers' assumptions about the theoretical constructs being measured with time-use data, (2) the ways researchers have established the dimensionality and reliability of time use measures, and (3) the generalizing claims that time-use researchers make about the descriptive results of their studies. In so doing, Rowan makes several suggestions about how these assumptions can be clarified and investigated in future research on principal time use.

Camburn and Sebastian's chapter, "A Framework for Evaluating and Choosing Principal Time Use Measurement Strategies," also delves into the challenges and problems of measuring principal time use by reviewing articles published in *Educational Administration Quarterly*. Based on this, they provide a framework that helps researchers to evaluate and choose the most optimal measurement strategy for different research contexts by concurrently considering measurement validity, financial cost, and respondent burden.

In their chapter, "Identifying Research Opportunities from the Methodological History of Principal Time Use Studies," Hochbein, Mahone, and Vanderbeck provide another comprehensive review of the methodological history of principal time-use studies. Their review traces back to studies in the early 20th century and covers contemporary research literature. The review shows that existing studies have consistently indicated that principals worked extensive hours for brief and unrelated tasks that most often involved managerial obligations. In addition, their review reveals that existing studies tend to rely on similar procedures and types of data collection with limited measurement validity. Hochbein and colleagues, therefore, suggest that future research of principal time use needs to diversify data collection, sampling structures, and observation periods.

Lee, Walker, and Riordan explore a blind spot in principal time-use studies—i.e., principals' direct interactions with individual students that occurs in their daily school life. In their chapter, "Principals' Direct Interaction with Individual Students: A Missing Piece in Principal Leadership Research," they identify that principals across many countries spend a substantial portion of their work time dealing with individual students. Using large-scale international assessment data, they also report macro-societal contexts and organizational factors that are associated with principals' time use for interaction with individual students. Based on their findings, they suggest that future research should pay attention to principals' "direct" effects on student outcomes. This line of research is expected to complement the indirect model of principals' effects (i.e., principals influence student outcomes mainly through teachers' work) theoretically and analytically.

Pollock and Wang begin Part II with their chapter, "How Principals Use Their Time in Ontario, Canada." The authors consider some of the misalignments in principals' time use in the province: between how principals want to spend their time and work and what they actually do, and how different conceptualizations of instructional leadership influence how they use their time. Using survey data from a 2013 study, the authors contend that Ontario principals spend the majority of their time on managerial tasks, despite indicating that they would like to spend more time on instructional leadership.

Next, in their chapter, "Managing Time? Principal Supervisors' Time Use to Support Principals," Rogers, Goldring, Rubin, and Grissom draw upon survey and interview data from the Principal Supervisor Initiative, a four-year effort aimed at improving the quality of the support that principal supervisors provide to principals in six districts, to explore how these supervisors use their time with principals. Specifically, they discuss the frequency and content of meetings between principals and their supervisors, how principals perceive this support, and the barriers supervisors and principals face when finding time to work together. The authors use this data to provide a set of lessons for districts that are seeking to improve both the quality and quantity of the time principals spend with their supervisors.

In "How Successful School Principals Balance their Leadership and Management Roles to Make a Difference," Drysdale, Gurr, and Goode draw on findings from the International School Principalship Project to take a long-term perspective on principal effectiveness. The authors explore how successful Australian principals balance their leadership and management by outlining a model called the *total role concept*, which identifies four key role dimensions (core, expected, augmented, and potential). They ultimately argue that by spending more time on the augmented and potential areas of their work than on the bureaucratic aspects, principals can make a positive difference in their schools.

In his chapter, "Wasting Time Talking to Students and Parents: Neoliberal Efficiency Myths about Principal Discretionary Time Use in Australia," Riley uses Australia as a case study to examine two system-level responses to principals' increasing work demands. In doing so, he reveals two competing silos within the Department of Education with different approaches to school improvement (i.e., the Command and Control model and the Service Delivery model). Ultimately, he critiques the neoliberal contractualism inherent in the first silo and concludes that the Service Delivery model could be the key to positive, significant change for principals.

In his chapter, "School Business Leaders and Principal Time Use in England," Armstrong focuses on a relatively new role within the English educational context: the *school business leader*. Using empirical research, he reflects on the impact and influence of this role, which was introduced in the early 2000s in response to the growing organizational management responsibility associated with the principalship. Armstrong uses the concepts of leadership distribution and values conflict to consider the extent to which school business leaders have changed how English school principals use their time.

In their chapter, "Out-of-Time Managers? Educational Leaders' Use of Time in Switzerland," Tulowitzki and Progin delve into the Swiss education system as well as educational leadership practice and research to consider how Swiss principals use their time. The authors reanalyze data collected over the course of several years (2009–2013, 2015–2017) in the French-speaking cantons of Switzerland to conclude that principals have limited capacity for leadership because they feel overburdened by administrative tasks and that future principals would benefit from time management training being integrated into in-service training programs as well as professional development programs for current principals.

Part III covers research from Africa and the Middle East. In their chapter, "South African School Principals' Use of Time: Learning From a Qualitative Study," Chikoko and Mthembu first lay out the South African Standards for

Principalship in order to provide an orientation regarding the core duties of principals in South Africa. They complement this by synthesizing several pieces of research around the time use of principals. They also draw on interviews from six South African principals to provide insights into how they use their time and how they experience time in their jobs. The findings offer glimpses into hectic work rhythms and provide an extension of the image of principals as "firefighters".

Next, Moyi's chapter, "Policy Context and Time Use of Primary School Head Teachers in Kenya: Evidence from the Snapshot of School Management Effectiveness (SSME) Survey," presents findings from a study of primary school head teachers in Kenya. Using data from the Kenya 2012 Snapshot of School Management Effectiveness survey, Moyi not only demonstrates how head teachers distribute their time across various domains, but also is able to embed the findings into the Kenyan context. The findings show that most head teachers are absorbed by management tasks, leaving little room for instructional support and teaching.

Finally, Oplatka's chapter "Emotional Workload and Time-Use in Principalship: Insights from Israeli Educational Leaders" provides a different perspective on time use by focusing on the emotional workload of Israeli principals through an analysis of 50 interviews. Besides investing considerable time in their manifold responsibilities, Oplatka demonstrates how emotional labor and managing feelings of concern, distress, and worry as well as navigating the emotional concerns of others was tied to the multitude of responsibilities principals faced. Contrary to the "rational" work time, which is usually limited, some principals reported that the emotional workload was theirs to carry day and night. The chapter makes a strong argument for not only looking at observable time use data but also at more latent forms of time use.

Concluding remarks

We wish to note there are research-based books on school leadership and principalship. While some partially touch on the issues of principals' work and time use, we believe that none of them pays special attention to theoretical and methodological issues in principal time use. In addition, there is no existing volume, capturing the geographically diverse contexts of principal time use. In this regard, we believe that the researchers in the field of school leadership, administration, and improvement can benefit from our edited volume. We also wish to note that there is a dozen of "how-to" books such as "Principal's Survival Guide." These are clearly practitioner-oriented and targeted books. We believe therefore that our research-based book of principal time use is unique, important, and timely.

Acknowledgment

The edited volume is an outcome from the research conference hosted by Prof. Moosung Lee at the University of Canberra in 2016. The conference titled "*Cross-National Exploration of Principals' Time Use*" was funded by the AERA's

Education Research Conferences Program. Correspondence concerning this edited book should be addressed to Moosung Lee, University of Canberra and Yonsei University. Email: leemoosung@gmail.com.

References

Dwyer, D., G. Lee, B. Rowan, & Bossert, S. (1983). *Five principals in action: Perspectives on instructional management.* San Francisco, CA: Far West Laboratory for Educational Research.

Goldring, E., Huff, J., May, H., & Camburn, E. (2008). School context and individual characteristics: What influences principal practice? *Journal of Educational Administration*, 46(3), 332–352.

Lee, M., & Hallinger, P. (2012). National contexts influencing principals' time use and allocation: Economic development, societal culture, and educational system. *School Effectiveness and School Improvement*, 23(4), 461–482.

Lee, M., Ryoo, J.H., & Walker, A. (2021). School principals' time use for interaction with individual students: Macro contexts, organizational conditions, and student outcomes. *American Journal of Education*, 127(2), 303–344.

Shin, S.-H., & Slater, C. L. (2010). Principal leadership and mathematics achievement: An international comparative study, *School Leadership and Management*, 30(4), 317–334.

Silins, H., & Mulford, B. (2010). Re-conceptualising school principalship that improves student outcomes. *Journal of Educational Leadership, Policy and Practice*, 25(2) 73–92.

Ten Bruggencate, G., & Luyten, H. (2010). From school leadership to student achievement: Analyses based on TIMSS, 2007. In G. Ten Bruggencate, H. Luyten., & J. Scheerens (Eds.),, *Quantitative analyses of international data: Exploring indirect effect models of school leadership* (pp. 29–46). The Netherlands: University of Twente.

Part I
Theoretical perspectives and methodological issues

1 Principals' time use as a research area

Notes on theoretical perspectives, leadership domains, and future directions

Moosung Lee

Introduction

Principal leadership behaviors and practices have interested researchers of educational leadership and administration for nearly 50 years (e.g., Bridges, 1967; Camburn, Spillane, & Sebastian, 2010; Day, Sammons, Leithwood, Hopkins, Harris, Gu, & Brown, 2010; Dwyer, Lee, Rowan, & Bossert, 1983; Eberts & Stone, 1988; Hemphill, Richards, & Peterson, 1965; Horng, Klasik, & Loeb, 2010; Kmetz & Willower, 1982; Martinko & Gardner, 1990; Martin & Willower, 1981; Peterson, 1977; Wolcott, 1973). Within this context, a line of research on how principals use their time in school has also emerged over the last four decades in particular (e.g., Chung & Miskel, 1989; Goldring, Huff, May, & Camburn, 2008; Grissom, Leob, & Master, 2013; Horng et al., 2010; Kmetz & Willower, 1982; Lee & Hallinger, 2012; Martin & Willower, 1981; Martinko & Gardner, 1990; May & Supovitz, 2011; Shin & Slater, 2010; Spillane & Hunt, 2010; Ten Bruggencate & Luyten, 2010; Wolcott, 1973), although early research on principal time use can be traced further back to the early 20th century (see Hochbein et al.'s chapter in this book).

What we know from the literature, mostly conducted in north American contexts, is that principals' work time in school has continuously increased over the last decades (see McPeake, 2007; Pollock, 2016). Some anecdotal evidence suggests that this pattern may also hold true in non-Western contexts (e.g., Cheng & Szeto, 2016; see also Oplatka's chapter in this book). It appears that there is "so much to do, so little time" in principals' work lives. To capture the changing nature and volume of principals' time use, various methods in terms of data collection and analytical strategies have been developed. Researchers have employed a variety of methods to document how principals spend their time in order to improve their organizations. These include observed work activity analysis (e.g., Kmetz & Willower, 1982; Martin & Willower, 1981), structured observation and reflective interviews (e.g., Dwyer et al., 1983; Martinko & Gardner, 1990), cluster analysis of self-report activity log data (e.g., Goldring et al., 2008), quantitative analysis of combined self-report activity log data and teacher surveys (e.g., May & Supovitz, 2011), ethnography (e.g., Wolcott, 1973), and cluster analysis from an experience sampling method (ESM) log, coupled with data from interviews, observations, and quantitative survey questionnaires (e.g., Spillane & Hunt, 2010), and using large international assessment data (e.g., Lee & Hallinger, 2012; Lee, Ryoo, & Walker, 2021; Shin & Slater, 2010; Ten Bruggencate & Luyten, 2010). All these diverse approaches have their own strengths, limitations, and trade-offs, in that single measurement and analysis is often incomplete (Duckworth & Yeager, 2015). Given that those methodological issues are discussed in depth in the following three chapters (Rowan's chapter, Camburn and Sebastian's chapter, and Hochbein et al.'s chapter), in this chapter I review theoretical issues, leadership domains, and future directions of research on principal time use.

Theoretical perspectives of time use research

Theoretical discussions on principal time use are thin on the ground. There are only a few articles that explicitly discuss theoretical issues in principal time use research (e.g., Eacott, 2018). This is surprising given that principal time use reflects principals' goal and task prioritization and, therefore, constitutes a fundamental dimension of principal leadership (Dwyer et al., 1983; Goldring et al., 2008; Silins & Mulford, 2010). However, beyond the school leadership literature, researchers in the social sciences have long explored time use of people theoretically and empirically in various social dimensions and systems. According to Bauman, Bittman, and Gershuny (2019), the origin of time-diary studies dates back to the 19th century in Russia. These early time-diary studies monitored peasant households with a focus on peasant work. Since then, more systematic approaches to time use research had been conducted in the United States and the United Kingdom during the 20th century. Notably, Taylor's (1911) work "The Principles of Scientific Management" shaped the dominant trend of time use research during the last century. Based on positivism, Taylor viewed time as a quantifiable, linear, and universal unit of analysis. This research tradition (i.e., researching time as "clock time") has been dominant in Western contexts. For example, the contemporary research on time use adopting (post)positivistic research approaches utilizes large survey data such as American Time Use Survey and Australia's Time Use Survey.

At the same time, a diverging epistemological perspective has emerged over the last three decades. Some social scientists (particularly, anthropologists, psychologists, sociologists, education researchers) have paid more attention to understanding how people "perceive and experience" time rather than quantifying how people spend and allocate their time. In other words, researchers have focused on interpretative dimensions of time, because people can perceive and experience time differently due to the socio-cultural contexts within which they are situated. This research approach highlights that time is socially constructed. Therefore, it emphasizes understanding "subjective and diverse temporal experiences that clock time cannot capture" (Duncheon & Tierney, 2013, p. 248). This line of research, in general, camped in social constructivism and/or critical realism, is critical of post-positivistic research approaches to time use. For example, Eacott (2018) points out that clock time should not be the only version of time research. He suggests that focusing on temporality is another way to shed light on time use research, particularly in education research. He also criticizes that research exploring clock time as units of analysis is a case of the commodification of time, given that such research is in line with the capitalist project of economic productivity. Eacott's concern for the dominant time use research has a point, given that most researchers in time use research rely largely on clock time. At the same time, however, his criticism of the commodification of time aligned to capitalist, economic productivity can be trapped in a pitfall that overlooks the contribution of post-positivistic approaches to time use research. Indeed, a body of education research based on the idea of clock time has systematically explored how principals and teachers strive for (1) improving learning outcomes of all students through their time use and allocation (e.g., Gentilucci & Muto, 2007; Robinson & Aronica, 2015), (2) school improvement issues with a focus on educational equity for disadvantaged student groups (e.g., Nettles & Herrington, 2007), and (3) student well-being and sense of belonging to school (e.g., Astor, Benbenishty, & Estrada, 2009; Lee et al., 2021). The wholesale criticism of research using clock time can risk misleading to a fallacious dichotomy. Simply dismissing time use research adopting clock time as (neo-)Taylorism (see Eacott, 2018) is counterproductive and counterintuitive because clock time as a lens captures complex temporal structures and quantities where meanings embedded in diverse temporal experiences are constructed and negotiated. Put differently, an individual's social behavior or conduct is inevitably situated in the world of clock time in which the individual also differently (or similarly) perceives and interprets his/her experienced time. I acknowledge that one's social conduct is not entirely determined by the world of clock time, despite the significant influence of clock time on everyday life. However, it is fair to say that one is not entirely free from the world of clock time in his/her daily life either. Even the moment when one argues that human temporal experiences should be captured primarily by socially constructed time, he/she inextricably exists in the world of clock time, at least, from the eyes of others. The point here is that illuminating principals' perception/experience of time and their relations with time are important issues in education research, but also that principals' structural dependency on clock time in school organization should be neither ignored nor downplayed. In summary, the two approaches (i.e., clock time and socially constructed time) are complementary.

Leadership domains in time use research

Drawing on their review of the leadership literature, Lee et al. (2021, pp. 303-304) reported that "the ways principals use their time in certain task domains plays a significant role in school improvement in general, and student learning in particular." Dozens of studies have proposed similar or different categories to identify leadership domains for which principals use their time in school. Based on my review of those studies, I have identified several common dimensions. Those commonly identified dimensions can be "broadly" categorized as follows: *administration, external relations (parent/community), internal relations (relations with teachers and students), principals' professional development,* and *instructional leadership*. I briefly review those leadership domains below.

First, *administration* has been identified as a common dimension by a majority of prior studies of principals' time use (e.g., Goldring et al., 2008; Horng et al., 2010; Kmetz & Willower, 1982; Lee & Hallinger, 2012; Martin & Willower, 1981; May & Supovitz, 2011; Spillane & Hunt, 2010).[1] In the early 1980s, small-scale case studies using structured observation approaches found that *administration*—including scheduled, unscheduled meetings, and desk work—was the dimension on which principals spent most of their time in U.S. schools (Kmetz & Willower, 1982; Martin & Willower, 1981). Three decades later, Horng et al.'s study confirmed those earlier studies' findings. Using the 2011/12 Schools and Staffing Survey (SASS), Lavigne, Shakman, Zweig, and Greller (2016) also reported that public school principals in the United States spent 59 hours per week for their work and spent most of their time on administrative tasks. This was then found to be applicable on a larger scale to most of the countries in Lee and Hallinger's (2012) cross-national comparisons of principals' time use by using the Progress in the 2006 International Reading Literacy Study (PIRLS). They found that across 34 education systems, elementary school principals spend most of their time for administrative tasks in school.

Second, prior studies have reported *internal relations* (relations with teachers and students) as another common leadership domain for which principals spend their work time (e.g., Astor et al., 2009; Dwyer et al., 1983; Goldring et al., 2008; Horng et al., 2010; Kmetz & Willower, 1982; Lortie, 2009; Martinko & Gardner, 1990; Martin & Willower, 1981; May & Supovitz, 2011; Robinson & Aronica, 2015; Spillane & Hunt, 2010). It should be noted, however, that there is variation in how researchers categorize principals' time spent for interactions or relationships with students. For example, in Goldring et al.'s (2008) study, principals' time use involving students was explored under the category of "student affairs." Goldring and colleagues found that, on average, school principals spend the largest portion of their time on "student affairs." In the case of the study by Horng, Klasik and Loeb (2009), "managing student discipline" and "supervising students (e.g., lunch duty)" were categorized as time spent for administration, instead of internal relations. In contrast, Spillane and Hunt (2010) captured the domain of internal relations under the analytical category of "fostering relationships," with a broader focus on social interactions between principals and students and teachers, rather than on principals' strategic interactions with students and teachers for the purpose of monitoring student academic performance or teachers' instruction.

The literature on transformational leadership (e.g., Leithwood, 2005) confirms the importance of principals' choice to spend time for fostering relationships with teachers, in particular. Specifically, the transformational leadership literature suggests that principals' social and informal interactions with teachers, coupled with principals' interactions with teachers with a focus on instruction and curriculum, play a key role in (re)shaping organizational culture and climate that transform schools. I also wish to note that, unlike principals' interactions with teachers, research knowledge on principals' interactions with individual students has been scarce. The reason for less attention paid to researching principals' time spent for directly interacting with students in daily school contexts is because principals' effects on student outcomes have been predominantly explored through teachers' work. Based on their review of the school leadership literature, Hallinger and Heck (1996) concluded that principals' effects on student learning outcomes (mainly measured by academic achievement scores) are largely indirect through principals' influence on teachers' work and practices. While the indirect model of principals' effects on student learning is valid, the dominant research trend of using the indirect model has led to an unintended consequence—i.e., overshadowing or overlooking the fact that principals spend a fair amount of time for interacting with individual students in school (see Chapter 5 in this book for details). Indeed, early research on principals' time use (e.g., Kmetz & Willower, 1982; Martin & Willower, 1981) showed principals' time use such as "tours" and "monitoring" to be part of relationship building with students. Another early work of Dwyer et al. (1983) clearly illuminated five school principals' allocation of time for developing relationships with individual students (e.g., greeting students as they arrive at school, routinized interactions with students during lunch time, spending time on the playground to speak to students informally). Although Dwyer et al.'s (1983) seminal study does not precisely fit into the type of principal time use research, it demonstrates that principals spend a substantial amount of time interacting with students, apart from the time they spend for developing curriculum and improving teachers' instruction. Relatively recent studies have also shown that principals routinely interact with individual students through various activities, including visiting classrooms, monitoring and guiding individual students' school life, and disciplining students (Gentilucci & Muto, 2007; Lortie, 2009; Waters et al., 2004). Drawing on the 2011/12 SASS, Lavigne et al.'s (2016) found that public school principals in the United States spent 23% of their work time for student interactions. This resonates with Lee et al.'s cross-national analysis (2021) reporting that elementary school principals in the United States from PIRLS 2006, on average, spent 18.4% of their time for interacting with individual students. They also found that U.S. principals tended to spend significantly higher portions of their time than their counterparts in other countries for interacting with individual students. Another study using PIRLS 2006 also demonstrated that principals' time use for interacting with individual students was identified internationally: elementary school principals randomly sampled from 34 societies spent on average 11.4% of their work time (i.e., 4.7 hours per week) interacting with students (see Chapter 5). In other words, school principals across many countries allocate a non-ignorable amount of their work time to dealing with individual students. Given this research evidence, I call for more attention to research on principals' time spent for internal relations, particularly for interacting with individual students.

Another domain of principal time use is *principals' professional development.* The importance of principals' professional development in school improvement has been less examined than that of teachers' professional development (Evans & Mohr, 1999). A few studies have documented how much time principals spend for their own professional development. McPeake (2007) reported that principals, on average, spent 5% of work time for attending conferences, professional readings, and self-improvement planning. Similarly, Lavigne et al. (2016) found that the typical type of principals' professional development was to attend workshops or conferences, whereas only a quarter of principals in the 2011/12 SASS indicated that they attended a university course. This resonates with Rowland's (2017) review showing that principals' professional development was neither systematically planned nor prioritized in most states in the United States. Beyond the United States, international research shows that principals in Asia regularly attend professional development activities. For example, Walker and Qian (2015) reported that principals in China are required to actively engage in professional development in conjunction with school improvement. Buenviaje (2016) found that some principals in the Philippines allocated their time to engage in charitable work at religious or local organizations as part of their professional (and personal) development, given that such engagements enhance their passion and deepen reflections on their school work. Buenviaje's (2016) study offers an important implication for Western leadership development frameworks that focus heavily on "what school principals' roles and responsibilities ought to be" and how those roles can be exercised effectively. The missing piece in this professional development perspective is about questioning why principals should take such responsibilities—i.e., what are the underlying purposes of doing certain tasks and responsibilities that are often externally imposed by central systems? (see also Lee, 2016). This is an important but frequently overlooked question, because questioning certain leadership responsibilities and tasks, externally given and defined, is an important way for principals to stay alert of the negative consequence of externally imposed accountability measures (Lee & Kirby, 2016). Indeed, Lee and Lee's (2020) comparative interrupted time-series analysis using SASS from 1990 to 2012 found that externally imposed accountability measures, such as adequate yearly progress (AYP) under No Child Left Behind (NCLB), pushed principals' perceptions of leadership responsibilities into a particular direction. For example, principals were oriented to improving academic standards, measured by standardized test scores, at the sacrifice of whole-person development of students.

In sum, principals' professional development is one noticeable domain of principals' time use, given that across different education systems principals actively or mandatorily participate in professional development. Research is much needed for this under-researched domain in principals' time use.

The fourth domain is *instructional leadership*. In line with research on *instructional leadership*, which has been placed at the core of school leadership research, there have been studies exploring principals' time use for *instructional leadership*. I wish to note that different studies have employed different terms and scopes in exploring principals' time use on *instructional leadership*. This seems to arise either from different conceptualizations of instructional leadership or from data limitations. For example, the recent study by Chambers, Reyes, Wang, and O'Neil (2014) of the Intensive Partnership (IP) for Effective Teaching Program in the United States, funded by the Gates Foundation, documented the time use of school leaders (i.e., principals and assistant principals) and divided principals' time use into seven dimensions: *administration, instruction, evaluating teachers, providing professional development for staff, receiving professional development, recruitment, and reform.* Notably, "Evaluating Teachers" in the study, referring to a principal's time spent on observing classroom instruction, providing feedback to teachers, and formal evaluation, was conceptualized as instructional leadership. Conversely, Horng et al.'s (2010) study explored the following six dimensions of time use: *administration, organizational management, day-to-day instruction, instructional program, internal relations, external relations, and other tasks.* While "Day-to-Day Instruction" in Horng et al.'s study (referring to classroom observations and coaching teachers) is similar to the dimension of "Evaluating Teachers" in Chambers et al.'s study, the two studies used different terms. Furthermore, in Chambers et al.'s study, "instruction" referred to school leaders' direct teaching of classes.

In addition, the scope of instructional leadership varies across studies of principals' time use. For example, studies by Goldring et al. (2008) and May and Supovitz (2011) operationalized multi-faceted aspects of instructional leadership as a construct which measures "monitoring/observing instruction, school restructuring or reform, supporting teachers' professional development, analyzing student data or work, modeling instructional practices, teaching a class" (Goldring et al., 2008, p. 340). Grissom et al.'s (2013) study of principal time use also incorporated a wider range of principals' behaviors as instructional leadership: coaching teachers, developing the educational program, evaluating teachers, classroom walkthroughs, required and non-required professional development, and other instructional time. In contrast, in Lee and Hallinger's (2012) secondary data analysis of PIRLS, instructional leadership was measured with a single item, representing only one aspect of instructional leadership—i.e., curriculum and pedagogical development. This shows a limitation of using secondary data. A similar issue is identified in studies using the Trends in International Mathematics and Science Study (TIMSS) (i.e., Shin & Slater, 2010; Ten Bruggencate & Luyten, 2010). Although using large-scale international assessment data has various advantages (e.g., representative samples, possibility of cross-national comparisons, possible linkage to other important variables such student learning outcomes), at this stage there are conceptual and analytical limitations in capturing principals' time use for instructional leadership comprehensively.

Future directions of principal time use research

School leadership research can benefit from deepening principal time use research in three distinctive ways: (1) cross-national and/or cross-cultural explorations, (2) addressing methodological limits, and (3) expanding the analytical scope.

16 *Moosung Lee*

Cross-national and/or cross-cultural explorations as a unit of analysis

Cross-national and/or cross-cultural explorations of principal time use can enrich school leadership research. Such comparative studies of principal time use are motivated to achieve the following research goals:

- To identify common and/or particular patterns, causes, and effects of principal time use across countries;
- To navigate and consolidate a new research direction within comparative educational leadership;
- To develop a framework of data collection and related analytical tools of principal time use that can be widely applied to contexts of different countries; and
- To provide insights and guiding principles for policymakers and principals, respectively, in terms of school improvement.

Despite the large body of literature on principal leadership behaviors and practices, cross-national/cultural comparative research is rare. The overwhelming majority of studies have been conducted in individual countries and most involve a small number of principals. The sole comparative study exploring the patterns of principal time use was published more than three decades ago. In that study, Chung and Miskel (1989) compared the way in which South Korean and U.S. principals use their time. Moreover, until recently, there was no cross-national research of principal time use. Still, multiple-society comparative research exploring the effects of principal time use on student achievement remains scarce (Lee et al., 2021; Lee & Hallinger, 2012; Shin & Slater, 2010; Ten Bruggencate & Luyten, 2010).

Notably, cross-national/cultural comparative research on principal time use has the potential to advance our understanding of principal leadership, given that patterns, causes, and effects of principal time use across different countries are largely uncharted. Cross-national/cultural comparative analysis of principal time use can also help illuminate the culturally specific feature of leadership constructs. Specifically, we know that there are various ways and activities principals spend time for instructional leadership. For example, in the U.S. context, principals' time spent for the following activities is regarded as the core part of instructional leadership: "monitoring/observing instruction, school restructuring or reform, supporting teachers' professional development, analyzing student data or work, modeling instructional practices, teaching a class" (Goldring et al., 2008, p. 340), coaching teachers, developing the educational program, evaluating teachers, and classroom walkthroughs (Grissom et al.'s, 2013). However, in some parts of East Asia, principals rarely spend their time on monitoring/observing instruction and classroom walkthroughs and typically do not think that such leadership behaviors are appropriate as instructional leadership. There are two reasons. First, principals in hierarchically structured societies in East Asia assume a more traditional head of school role and delegate instructional leadership activities to others, such as vice principals or department head teachers (Lee & Hallinger, 2012). Second, in some East Asian countries, such as South Korea where teachers have strong egalitarian perceptions of teaching profession regardless of formal leadership positions in school, the aforementioned instructional leadership behaviors can be interpreted as principals' intrusion into the domain of teachers' autonomy and expertise (see Hallinger, 2004; Lee, 2005; Lee & Hallinger, 2012; Walker & Dimmock, 2002). The point here is that cross-national/cultural comparative studies can further shed light on the multifaceted and cultural-diverse aspects of certain leadership constructs.

Currently, cross-national/cultural analysis of principal time use is only available through the use of large international assessment data. As noted above, however, such large international assessment data has limitations in terms of concepts and measures in capturing certain domains of principal leadership. Therefore, future research should focus on creating international collaborative projects through which researchers can develop a framework of data collection and related analytical tools of principal time use to various education systems. This line of research can also help provide insights and guiding principles for policymakers and principals, respectively, in terms of school improvement.

Address methodological limits

Principal time use research needs to address methodological limits, particularly measurement validity issues (see chapters in Part I in this book). In doing so, I propose that future research needs to consider taking opportunities from rapidly developing wearable technology in gathering real-time data longitudinally that can also link various types of data, including principals' emotional and physical well-being. Although there are certain ethnical issues that should be cautiously addressed in using wearable technology, combining big data from wearable technology with traditional data (observation, reflective interviews, self-report activity log data, ESM log, quantitative survey questionnaires) (e.g., Spillane & Hunt, 2010) can possibly improve measurement validity issues. Indeed, a recent study reported the possibility of applying wearable technology to time use research (e.g., Kelly, Thomas, Doherty, Harms, Burke, Gershuny, & Foster, 2015). In addition, I propose to consider using video ethnography in time use research. As Camburn and Sebastian noted in their study (see Chapter 3), interview and one-time self-reporting survey are two most frequently used methods for data collection in time use research published in *Educational Administration Quarterly*. Video ethnography, which has long been used in anthropology, organizational research, and design thinking, enables researchers to delve deeper into activities with complexity in natural settings. Given that both interview and survey are not free from social desirability biases from respondents, video ethnography is an effective method for both researchers and participants to collaboratively review and interpret certain activities of interest.

Expand the analytical scope of principals' work life

Principal time use research needs to further expand the analytical scope. Existing studies of principal time use have focused primarily on principals' time spent "within school boundaries." As mentioned earlier, Buenviaje's (2016) study, conducted in a provincial area in the Philippines, paid special attention to particular spatial (i.e., outside of school) and temporal dimensions (i.e., before/after school) of Filipino principals' lives. Such spatial-temporal dimensions are largely uncharted in the school leadership literature. Buenviaje's (2016) study reported that principals spent time to relax and reflect on daily school work before/after school, and also spent substantial time in engaging in charitable work at community organizations outside of school and after school. This was an integral part of their "work" lives. Buenviaje called such time "therapeutic activities" that maintained and bolstered school principals' passion, spirituality, and well-being. No doubt that principals with spiritual stability and strong passion would lead to working hard for their teachers and students. In a very different context, Ontario in Canada, Pollock (2016) also reported how information and communication technology (ICT) can change the nature and scope of principals' time use for their work. Specifically, Pollock presented that email and social media blurred the line between work and home for principals. In my commentary article on Pollock's work, I interpreted principals' time spent increasingly for email and social media outside of school and before/after office hours for school work as follows:

> ... a sign that principals' work is adopting the characteristics of a 24/7 ubiquitous service, which commonly occurs in business sectors. This somehow resonates with the growing requirement for 24/7 self-management in many professions in late capitalist societies (Crary 2013). In other words, neoliberal discourses in education seem to say that good or successful principals are required to be always in the loop of their work and are asked to go the extra mile for better organisational performance. Indeed, such 24/7 self-management discourses appear a pathological phenomenon to people in leadership positions in public as well as corporate sectors (Lee, 2016, p. 133).

The emerging pathological phenomenon to principals should be further investigated in terms of work intensity and burnout. Further, a common implication from Buenviaje and Pollock is that we need to pay greater attention to principals' time use "before/after school, and outside of school" beyond school hours, given that principals' time use for school work is not limited to 9 a.m. to 5 p.m. during week days. Overall, future research of principal time use can offer fruitful discussions and implications by paving this line of research.

Acknowledgment

An early version of this work was presented as an opening speech at the conference titled "Cross-National Exploration of Principals' Time Use" that was funded by the AERA's Education Research Conferences Program in 2016. This work was also supported by the Ministry of Education and the National Research Foundation of Korea [Grant Number: NRF-2017S1A3A2065967].

Note

1. Some studies did not use the term administration per se. For example, Goldring et al. (2008) used the term "Finances" to be more specific about principals' time use.

References

Astor, R.A., Benbenishty, R., & Estrada, J. (2009). School violence and theoretically atypical schools: The principal's centrality in orchestrating safe schools. *American Educational Research Journal, 46*(2), 423–461.

Bauman, A., Bittman, M., & Gershuny, J. (2019). A short history of time use research; implications for public health. *BMC Public Health, 19*(607), 1–7.

Bridges, E. (1967). Instructional leadership: A concept reexamined. *Journal of Educational Administration, 5*(2), 136–147.

Buenviaje, J. (2016). Embracing work passion: Perspectives of Filipino principals and school heads. *International Studies in Educational Administration, 44*(3), 5–20.

Camburn, E. M., Spillane, J. P., & Sebastian, J. (2010). Assessing the utility of a daily log for measuring principal leadership practice. *Educational Administration Quarterly, 46*(5), 707–737.

Chambers, J. Reyes, I., Wang, A., & O'Neil, C. (2014). How are school leaders and teachers allocating their time in the intensive partnership sites? Santa Monica, CA: RAND Education & Washington DC: American Institutes for Research. Retrieved December 10, 2015 from http://www.rand.org/pubs/working_papers/WR1041-1.html.

Cheng, A.Y-N., & Szeto, E. (2016). Principals' changing work in a time of Hong Kong education reform: Challenges and opportunities. *International Studies in Educational Administration, 44*(3), 21–35.

Chung, K. A., & Miskel, C. G. (1989). A comparative study of principals' administrative behaviour. *Journal of Educational Administration, 27*(1), 45–57.

Crary, J., (2013). *24/7: Late capitalism and the ends of sleep.* London, UK: Verso.

Davis, K., Rogers, D., & Harrigan, M. (2020). A review of state policies on principal professional development. *Education Policy Analysis Archives, 28*(24), 1–22.

Day, C., Sammons, P., Leithwood, K., Hopkins, D., Harris, A., Gu, Q., & Brown, E. (2010). *Ten strong claims about successful school leadership.* Nottingham, UK: The National College for School Leadership.

Duckworth, A. L., & Yeager, D. S. (2015). Measurement matters: Assessing personal qualities other than cognitive ability for educational purposes. *Educational Researchers, 44*(4), 237–251.

Duncheon, J. C., & Tierney, W. G. (2013). Changing conceptions of time: Implications for educational research. *Review of Educational Research, 83*(2): 236–272.

Dwyer, D., Lee G., Rowan B., & Bossert, S. (1983). *Five principals in action: Perspectives on instructional management.* San Francisco, CA: Far West Laboratory for Educational Research.

Eacott, S. (2018). Theoretical notes on a relational approach to principals' time use. *Journal of Educational Administration and History, 50*(4), 284–298.

Eberts, R. W., & Stone, J. A. (1988). Student achievement in public schools: Do principals make a difference? *Economics of Education Review, 7*(3), 291–299.

Evans, P. M., & Mohr, N. (1999). Professional development for principals. *Phi Delta Kappan, 80*(7), 530–532.

Gentilucci, J. L., & Muto, C. C. (2007). Principals' influence on academic achievement: The student perspective. *Nassp Bulletin, 91*(3), 219–236.

Goldring, E., Huff, J., May, H., & Camburn, E. (2008). School context and individual characteristics: What influences principal practice? *Journal of Educational Administration*, 46(3), 332–352.

Grissom, J. A., Loeb, S., & Master, B. (2013). Effective instructional time use for school leaders: Longitudinal evidence from observations of principals. *Educational Researcher*, 42(8), 433–444.

Hallinger, P. (2004). Meeting the challenges of cultural leadership: The changing role of principals in Thailand. *Discourse: Studies in the Cultural Politics of Education*, 25(1): 61–73

Hallinger, P., & Heck, R. H. (1996). Reassessing the principal's role in school effectiveness: A review of empirical research, 1980–1995. *Educational Administration Quarterly*, 32(1), 5–44.

Hemphill, J., Richards, J., & Peterson, R. (1965). *Report of the senior high-school principalship*. Washington, DC: National Association of Secondary School Principals.

Horng, E. L., Klasik, D., & Loeb, S. (2009). *Principal time-use and school effectiveness*. Arlington, VA: National Center for Analysis of Longitudinal Data in Education Research.

Horng, E., Klasik, D., & Loeb, S. (2010). Principals' time use and school effectiveness. *American Journal of Education*, 116, 491–523.

Kelly, P., Thomas, E., Doherty, A., Harms, T., Burke, O., Gershuny, J., & Foster, C. (2015). Developing a method to test the validity of 24 hour time use diaries using wearable cameras: A feasibility pilot, *PLoS ONE*, 10(12), 1–15.

Kmetz, J., & Willower, D. (1982). Elementary school principals' work behavior. *Educational Administration Quarterly*, 18(4), 62–78.

Lavigne, H. J., Shakman, K., Zweig, J., & Greller, S. L. (2016). *Principals' time, tasks, and professional development: An analysis of Schools and Staffing Survey data*. Washington, DC: Institute of Education Sciences & Regional Educational Laboratory at Educational Development Center, Inc.

Lee, M. (2016). The changing nature of school principals' work: Lessons and future directions for school leadership research. *International Studies in Educational Administration*, 44(3), 129–136.

Lee, M., & Hallinger, P. (2012). National contexts influencing principals' time use and allocation: Economic development, societal culture, and educational system. *School Effectiveness and School Improvement*. 23(4), 461–482.

Lee, M., & Kirby, M. (2016). The promises and perils of school leadership for accountability: Four lessons from China, Hong Kong and India. In Easley, J. & Tulowitzki, P. (Eds.), *Educational accountability international perspectives on challenges and possibilities for school leadership* (pp. 129–141). London, UK: Routledge.

Lee, J., & Lee, M. (2020). Is "whole child" education obsolete? Public school principals' priority shifts of educational goals in the era of accountability. *Educational Administration Quarterly*, 56(5), 856–884. https://doi.org/10.1177/0013161X20909871.

Lee, M., Ryoo, J.-H., & Walker, A. (2021). School principals' time use for interaction with individual students: Macro contexts, organizational conditions, and student outcomes. *American Journal of Education*, 127(2), 303–344. DOI: 10.1086/712174.

Lee, S-Y. (2005). Effects of school organizational culture and moral leadership on teachers' professional zone of acceptance. *The Korean Journal of Educational Administration*, 23(1), 71–92 [written in Korean].

Leithwood, K. (2005). A review of transformational school leadership research 1996–2005. *Leadership and Policy in Schools*, 4(3), 177–199.

Lortie, D.C. (2009). *School principal*. Chicago, IL: University of Chicago Press.

McPeake, J. A. (2007). *The principalship: A study of the principal's time on task from 1960 to the twenty-first century.* Unpublished Doctoral Dissertation. Marshall University, Huntington, WV.

Martin, W. J., & Willower, D. J. (1981). The managerial behaviour of high school principals. *Educational Administration Quarterly, 17*(1), 69–90.

Martinko, M. J., & Gardner, W. L. (1990). Structured observation of managerial work: A replication and synthesis. *Journal of Management Studies, 27*(3), 329–357.

May, H., & Supovitz, J. A. (2011). The scope of principal efforts to improve instruction. *Educational Administration Quarterly, 47*(2), 332–352.

Nettles, S. M., & Herrington, C. (2007). Revisiting the importance of the direct effects of school leadership on student achievement: The implications for school improvement policy. *Peabody Journal of Education, 82*(4), 724–736.

Peterson, K. D. (1977). The principal's tasks. *Administrator's Notebook, 26*(8), 1–4.

Pollock, K. (2016). Principals' work in Ontario, Canada: Changing demographics, advancements in information communication technology and health and wellbeing. *International Studies in Educational Administration, 44*(3), 55–74.

Robinson, K., & Aronica, L. (2015). *Creative schools: Revolutionizing education from the ground up.* London, UK: Penguin-Random House.

Rowland, C. (2017). *Principal professional development: New opportunities for a renewed state focus.* Washington DC: American Institutes for Research.

Shin, S.-H., & Slater, C. L. (2010). Principal leadership and mathematics achievement: An international comparative study, *School Leadership and Management, 30*(4), 317–334.

Silins, H., & Mulford, B. (2010). Re-conceptualising school principalship that improves student outcomes. *Journal of Educational Leadership, Policy and Practice, 25*(2), 73–92.

Spillane, J. P., & Hunt, B. R. (2010). Days of their lives: A mixed-methods, descriptive analysis of the men and women at work in the principal's office. *Journal of Curriculum Studies, 42*(3), 293–331.

Taylor, F.W. (1911). *The principles of scientific management.* New York: Harper.

Ten Bruggencate, G., & Luyten, H. (2010). From school leadership to student achievement: Analyses based on TIMSS, 2007. In G. Ten Bruggencate, H. Luyten, & Scheerens, J. (Eds.), *Quantitative analyses of international data: Exploring indirect effect models of school leadership* (pp. 29–46). Enschende, The Netherlands: University of Twente.

Walker, A., & Dimmock, C. (2002). Moving school leadership beyond Its narrow boundaries: Developing a cross-cultural approach. In Leithwood, K., Hallinger, P., Furman, G.C., Riley, K., MacBeath, J., Gronn, P., & Mulford, B. (Eds.), *Second International Handbook of Educational Leadership and Administration* (pp. 167–202). Dordrecht: Springer.

Walker, A., & Qian, H. (2015). Review of research on school principal leadership in mainland China, 1998–2013: Continuity and change. *Journal of Educational Administration, 53*(4), 467–491.

Waters, T, Marzano, R.J., & McNulty, B. (2004). *Balanced leadership: What 30 years of research tells us about the effect of leadership on student achievement.* Aurora, CO: Mid-Continent Research for Education and Learning.

Wolcott, H. F. (1973). *The man in the principal's office: An ethnography.* San Francisco, CA: Holt, Rinehart and Winston Inc.

2 Measurement assumptions in principals' time-use research
Past problems and needed studies

Brian Rowan

Background

My interest in principals' time-use research dates to several studies of education managers' time use conducted in the 1980s (e.g., Peterson, 1977; Martin & Willower, 1981; Pitner & Ogawa, 1981; Sproull, 1981; Kmetz & Willower, 1982). These studies were heavily influenced by Mintzberg's (1973) seminal studies of managerial time use in a wide variety of organizational contexts, work that was, in turn, grounded in even earlier (but small set of) studies of managerial time use conducted in the 1950s and 1960s (for reviews, see Kurke & Aldrich, 1983; Martinko & Gardner, 1985). The distinctive feature of all of these early studies was the use of structured observations to collect time-use data on managers. In the typical study, a single researcher observed a manager performing normal work activities for a day or more at the manager's work site, and during that time, observers took open-ended (or, sometimes, semi-structured) field notes. These field notes were then coded and organized so that researchers could reconstruct the amount of time a manager spent on different kinds of work activities, on the location of these work activities, on the kinds of people with whom the manager spent time, and on the functional purposes of the observed activities.

These early studies were both praised and criticized. On a positive note, this early work produced an important set of stylized facts about managers' work. In all kinds of organizations, including schools, managers engaged in a large number of activities over the course of a day, most of which were initiated by others and of short duration. But early time-use studies were also criticized on a number of counts. The studies were seen as being overly descriptive and largely a-theoretical, as using *ad hoc* coding categories that varied from study to study, as relying on full-day observations as the sole data collection strategy, as failing to address concerns about inter-rater reliability, and as being conducted in very small samples, thereby preventing researchers from drawing trustworthy conclusions about how managerial behavior might vary across settings, people, or roles (Martinko & Gardner, 1985).

Fast forward now to about ten years ago when a new round of managerial time-use studies appeared in education research. In these studies, school principals were the main objects of study (Spillane, Camburn, & Stitziel Pareja, 2007; Goldring, Huff, May, & Camburn, 2008; Camburn et al., 2010; Camburn, Spillane, & Sebastian, 2010; Horng, Klasik, & Loeb, 2010; López, Ahumada, Galdames, & Madrid, 2012; May, Huff, & Goldring, 2012; Grissom, Loeb, & Master, 2013; Grissom, Loeb, & Mitani, 2015). Importantly, these newer studies differed from earlier ones in several important ways. To begin, the newer studies were more intentionally grounded in theory, which produced somewhat more uniformity in the coding schemes used across studies. These newer coding schemes focused squarely on the amounts of time principals' spent on different functional areas of responsibility associated with the role of principal, such as management (of school personnel, finances, and building operations), internal and external relations (with various school constituencies), and activities related to instructional leadership and the improvement of a school's instructional program. The newer studies also were conducted with somewhat larger samples of principals, and this in turn allowed researchers to study how principals' time use varied across principals with different personal backgrounds and commitments, working in different school settings. Moreover, larger sample sizes allowed researchers to begin to explore the connections between the time principals spent on particular behaviors and key organizational outcomes, including student achievement outcomes. And finally, in 2010, several studies began to use self-report strategies to collect time-use data, which in turn encouraged researchers to pay more attention to issues of reliability and validity in time-use research.

The problem

Despite these advances, the newer studies did *not* produce a very sophisticated "validity argument" about how time-use measures can (or should) be used in research. To be sure, the newer studies were more grounded in theory; but as we are about to see, the theoretical rationale for measuring principals' leadership in terms of time spent on particular behaviors was not persuasively justified in the research. Moreover, while newer studies paid attention to the reliability and validity of principal time-use measures, and while they often did so in technically sophisticated ways, many other assumptions about how time-use data were being used to construct measures of principals' leadership were not carefully examined. Finally, although newer research was laudable in trying to connect principals' time use to valued organizational outcomes, researchers rarely discussed how fundamental problems of measurement (such as construct deficiency, poor scale construction, and unreliability) might have attenuated the expected correlations among time-use measures and valued outcomes.

In what follows, I lay out these criticisms and their implications for principals' time-use research in three sections. In the first section, I describe how time-use data are *typically* collected and used by researchers. This sets the stage for my critique of this process, which is advanced in the second section. In a final section, I describe some lines of research that I think could be conducted in the future to address the measurement problems surfaced in this chapter and that could also serve as the basis for developing a better argument about the justified use and interpretation of time-use data in research on school leadership.

How principal time-use data are collected, scored, and interpreted in research

I'll begin by describing how researchers typically collect, score, and interpret time-use data in research on school principals. Obviously, the main focus of principals' time-use research has been on the activities that principals engage in during a work day. Willower and colleagues called these activities "work behaviors" (Martin & Willower, 1981; Kmetz & Willower, 1982), others called these activities "practices" (Spillane et al., 2007; Camburn, Spillane, & Sebastian, 2010; Camburn et al., 2010), and still others called these activities "tasks" (Horng et al., 2010). Whatever word[s] were used to describe principals' work activities, researchers generally classified principals' observed work-day behaviors into a set of functional categories of school management, for example, time spent on instructional leadership, building management, internal and external relations, and so on. Note that the functional categories used in research differed across recent studies, and as a result, the same work behavior/practice/task in which a principal engages can be classified under different headings in different studies.

In recent studies, several methods have been used to collect time-use data on principals. Some studies used direct observation and shadowed principals for a whole day (Horng et al., 2010; Grissom et al., 2013). Other studies (e.g., Camburn, Spillane, & Sebastian, 2010; Camburn et al., 2010) relied on data from principals' self-reports to chart time use. Among self-report studies, some studies used end-of-year surveys, others used end-of-day logs, and still others used an experience sampling method (ESM). As discussed below, some researchers paid attention to the convergent validity (i.e., correlations) of time-use measures derived from different self-report methods (e.g., Camburn, Spillane, & Sebastian, 2010; Camburn et al., 2010). However, less attention has been paid to the convergence of results derived from self-report versus structured observation data. In addition, some studies have combined observation records and interviews to better understand cases where different forms of self-report data diverge (Camburn et al., 2010) and other studies have used interviews as a means of adding clarity to findings on principals' time use (e.g., Grissom et al., 2013).

No matter how time-use data are collected and coded, researchers almost always use the same measurement model when they report scores from the data. In essence, after all the data on principals' behaviors are collected and coded into functional categories, summary statistics are reported about the percentage of time principals spent on tasks/behaviors/practices in a functional area. The measurement model used here is quite simple. Any behavior coded as belonging to some functional category is treated as the equivalent of any other behavior coded into that category. For example, 15 minutes of time spent discussing student work are added to 15 minutes of directly observing classroom teaching so that a principal is reported as having spent 30 minutes on instruction-related activities.

Once data are aggregated into descriptive statistics by categories, the amount of time spent on any one category is divided by total observed time to produce the following form of score reporting, where the quoted example is from Horng et al. (2010, p. 502):

> On average, principals spent [about 30 percent of the school day] on administration activities to keep the school running smoothly, such as managing student discipline and fulfilling compliance requirements. They spent just over a fifth of the day on organization management tasks, such as managing budgets and staff and hiring personnel. On average, they spent 15 percent of their time on the internal relations tasks, such as developing relationships with students and interacting socially with staff, and 5 percent on the external relations tasks, such as fundraising. Principals appear to devote the least total amount of time to instruction-related activities, including day-to-day instruction tasks (6 percent) and more general instructional program responsibilities (7 percent).

Importantly, although researchers typically report basic descriptive data by categories of behaviors/activities/tasks/practices, they almost always give these descriptive data an additional layer of *theoretical* interpretation. Indeed, two theoretical frameworks have appeared in recent research. In one line of work, Grissom et al. (2015) interpreted principal time-use measures in the context of the larger literature on "job performance." In organizational psychology, the job performance construct commonly refers to the array of tasks that job incumbents perform that are assumed to produce valued outcomes in an organization (Motowidlo, 2013). So, in the Grissom et al. (2015) study, the idea was not simply to describe the amount of time principals spent on different work tasks, but also to examine whether principals "allocate adequate time to their job's most important tasks."

More commonly, however, researchers interpret principals' time-use measures as indicators of principals' "leadership" in the particular functional categories of behavior described earlier. For example, Camburn et al. (2010, p. 314) examined survey and daily log measures of what they called "principal leadership practice" and went on to define "principal leadership practice as actions taken by principals to influence people, processes, and organizational structure ... [as exercised in] multiple domains of responsibility" (p. 321). More often than not, time-use researchers also show a special interest in the instruction-related aspects of principals' work and count time spent on various instruction-related behaviors as instructional leadership. As one example, Grissom et al. (2013, p. 433) examined the subset of behaviors they coded as instruction-related tasks and asserted that their time-use data captured "behaviors that count as instructional leadership." The important point here is that descriptive data on principals' time use are not simply interpreted as behaviors within some functional area of responsibility. Instead, time-use data in a particular domain are more frequently interpreted as measures of "job performance" or "leadership" within these areas.

Challenges to the interpretation and use of principals' time-use data

Let's now examine (and challenge) some of the assumptions researchers make as they engage in these standard ways of collecting, scoring, and interpreting principals' time-use data. Some of these assumptions are explicitly discussed by researchers, but many others are "hidden" in the sense that they are rarely (if ever) discussed explicitly. My argument is that most of these assumptions need to be surfaced and closely examined, which is what I am about to do.

The first set of assumptions I want to surface and examine are conceptual in nature. These conceptual assumptions are:

- *The Leadership Assumption*: Time-use data measure principals' leadership.
- *The Job Performance Assumption*: Time-use data measure principals' job performance.
- *The Object of Measurement Assumption*: Principals are the logical object of measurement in research on school leadership.
- *The Agentic Control Assumption*: Principals control how they allocate their time.

The next set of assumptions I want to surface and examine involve scale construction. The scale construction assumptions are:

- *The Dimensionality Assumption*: Observed behaviors have been properly sorted into functional domains of leadership.
- *The Ratio Level of Measurement Assumption*: Leadership is measured by the amount of time a principal spends on behaviors in a given functional domain and, as a result, leadership in a domain can be measured at the interval level of measurement.
- *The Equal Weighting Assumption*: Any behavior classified into a functional domain is an equivalent indicator of leadership in a functional domain as any other behavior classified into that functional domain.
- *The Ignorable Facets of Measurement Assumption*: Data on principals' time-use have been collected across enough days and enough raters to allow for reliable person-level estimates of principals' time use.
- *The Exchangeable Instruments Assumption*: Alternative methods for collecting time-use data are interchangeable.

A final set of assumptions are about the generalizations researchers make from descriptive findings about principals' time use. These claims are:

- *The Replicability Assumption*: The findings on principals' time use obtained from a given study would be replicated if that study were undertaken again in the same or a very similar context.

- *The Generality Assumption*: The findings on principals' time use obtained from a given study would be replicated if that study were undertaken in any other setting and are thus stylized facts about principals' time use.

What I am going to do now is discuss each of these assumptions and assess the extent to which they can be supported by conceptual reasoning or by reference to empirical evidence from existing time-use studies.

The leadership assumption

The leadership assumption holds that time-use data can be used to measure a principal's educational "leadership." Because time-use measures catalog the amount of time principals spend in various behaviors, this assumption implicitly defines leadership as a set of *behaviors*. The problem with defining leadership as a set of behaviors, however, is that it ignores many central features of leadership as defined in social theory. In social theory, leadership is almost always defined as a process of social influence, and that definition opens up the possibility that two people who behave in exactly the same way can exert different amounts of influence and therefore have different levels of leadership. So, measuring leadership simply as a set of behaviors (without also examining whether these observed behaviors exert influence on followers) produces what I see as a serious problem of "construct deficiency," that is, a failure of time-use measures to capture key features of the leadership construct that researchers claim to be measuring with time-use data.

An additional problem with measuring leadership as a set of behavior is that leadership is also seen in theory as a form "action." In social theory, the term action implies that individuals give meaning to their behavior, the most notable component being the intent an actor has in undertaking a behavior (Parsons, 1949). Obviously, intent is not well represented (if at all) in the usual approach to time-use measurement. Take, for example, a study by Spillane et al. (2007), who studied the amount of time principals spent on behaviors in different managerial domains. An important finding from that study was that principals reported "leading" the activities they reported on only about 35% of the time. During the other 65% of time, the activities principals engaged in were being led by others (or the principals was co-leading the activity with someone else). This raises the question of whether principals are "leading" when they engage in behaviors reported as time use, and if they say they aren't leading an activity, should researchers classify that behavior as an observed instance of "leadership?" Consider an additional finding on intentionality of school leaders as reported by Grissom et al. (2013). These researchers conducted a study that tried to understand whether schools where principals spent more time on classroom walkthroughs had better achievement outcomes. What these researchers found was that not all principals intended to use walkthroughs to improve instruction. Moreover, it was not until these researchers took the principals' intentions into account that time spent on walkthroughs had a positive statistical association with student achievement.

The job performance assumption

This same problem of construct deficiency arises when time-use data are interpreted as measuring "job performance." To be sure, behaviors are a part of job performance, but time-use data fails to capture other critical features of job performance as conceptualized in theory. In theory, the job performance construct has been defined as behaviors that *add value* to an organization (Motowidlo, 2013). The problem is that principals' time-use data capture many kinds of task behaviors and research shows that many of these behaviors in fact *don't* add value to the organization (see, for example, May, Huff, & Goldring, 2012; Grissom et al., 2013). Moreover, even if two individuals spend equal amounts of time on behaviors that *potentially* "add value" to the organization, the quality with which they enact these behaviors could differ sharply. Time-use data, however, do not capture the quality of job performance, so once again, time-use measures appear to suffer from construct deficiency. In my view, these problems of construct deficiency could be why efforts to correlate time-use measures of principals' work activities to valued organizational outcomes have produced inconsistent results across studies.

The object of measurement assumption

Yet another assumption worth discussing is what I call the object of measurement assumption, that is, a focus in time-use studies on the principal as the object of measurement. Clearly, if the goal of a study is simply to describe the work activities that principals engage in across a school day, it makes sense for principals to be the object of measurement. However, if the goal is to use principals' time-use data to measure some larger construct like leadership, the use of the principal as the only object of measurement might be problematic.

The main problem with focusing on the principal as the sole object of measurement in school leadership research is that, in theory, leadership tasks/functions/behaviors in a school can be distributed across (and thus performed by) many individuals. Indeed, in an important study of principals' time use conducted by Spillane, Camburn, and Pareja (2013), a central finding was that principals engaged in solo-style leadership on just 35% of observed occasions, which meant they were co-leading or being led by others 65% of the time. This has two important implications for school leadership research: (1) if a researcher wants to use time-use data to measure the amount of leadership exercised in a school, the researcher probably needs to collect time-use data from many different individuals, not just the principal; and (2) because the behaviors that principals engage in during a school day are so often initiated and co-led by others, principals' behaviors might be determined by things like how many other individuals in a school are ready and able to perform leadership tasks, on how work activities are distributed across role occupants in a school, or on variables like school size, staffing, and policies that assign leadership tasks to specific organizational roles. Thus, researchers should be cautious when they use the principal as the exclusive object of measurement in time-use research in school leadership. Indeed, if the interest is describing *school* leadership, the distributed nature of the phenomenon would suggest gathering time-use data from more than just the principal and moving toward a conception of leadership as an organization-level (not person-level) construct (Ogawa & Bossert, 1995; Pounder, Ogawa, & Adams, 1995).

The agentic control assumption

A related assumption arises when time-use researchers argue that the behaviors of principals are under the principal's agentic control. Many time-use researchers appear to make this assumption, especially when they describe how principals "allocate" their time across school leadership functions. For example, Goldring and colleagues (2008) were interested in studying principals' "decisions about how to allocate their attention" to different job responsibilities, and Grissom et al. (2015) set out to study whether principals "allocate adequate time to their job's most important tasks." The theoretical imagery in Goldring et al. (2008) suggests that principals are exercising agentic control over (i.e., "allocating") their time. The imagery in Grissom et al. (2015) takes this assumption one step further by speculating that principals might be able to act as rational decision makers when they allocate scarce time to differently valued managerial behaviors.

The main problem with agentic control assumptions is that they are inconsistent with many findings from principals' time-use research. For example, early time-use researchers frequently observed that managers in education settings have little control over their work behaviors (Sproull, 1981), and this lack of control could be why Grissom et al. (2015) found that principals with good time management skills did not necessarily allocate their time in ways that produced differences in valued organizational outcomes. So, there is little evidence that principals are able to function like rational actors when they "allocate" their time to tasks. Moreover, Goldring and colleagues (2008) found that school context variables had larger effects on how principals' time was distributed across functional tasks than did the personal characteristics of principals, which suggests that principals' ability to "allocate" their time might even be considerably constrained. Further disconfirming evidence comes from Camburn, Spillane and Sebastian (2010, p. 721), who found that only 10–25% of the variance in how much time principals spent on different managerial behaviors was due to persons and that the remaining 75–90% of variance was due to the day of observation. All of this evidence suggests that what principals do on any given day might not actually be under their control, but is rather controlled by external actors and circumstances.

Importantly, if principals *don't* exercise much control over their time (as the agentic control assumption claims), then it could be that what researchers are really measuring when they record principals' time use is not how a particular principal "allocates" his or her time, but rather how people other than the principal are making use of that principal's time. These others might be the people who frequently "interrupt" the principal during the day, or they could be administrative superiors who create organizational structures and policies that channel principals' time use in certain directions. All of this has important implications for interpreting statistical relationships between principals' time use measures and valued organizational outcomes. In particular, a statistical association between principals' time use and valued organizational outcomes could arise, not because a principal chose to engage in certain activities, but rather because people in the organization chose to make particular use of that principal's time or because administrative structures and policies channeled the principal's activities in certain directions. In fact, this was the point made by May, Huff, and Goldring (2012, p. 432–433) as they interpreted the empirical relationships they found between principal time-use measures and student achievement as follows: "Of those leadership activities that we found to be significantly related to student performance ... we believe that the more plausible causal relationship is that school context drives principals' activities." This is not a view of the principal as a leader with "agentic control" over his or her behavior.

The dimensionality assumption

So far, I have been discussing assumptions that are largely conceptual in nature. Let's now move to some assumptions that time-use researchers make as they convert raw time-use data into summary measures. The first of these is what I call the "dimensionality" assumption. In principal time-use research, the dimensionality assumption is typically made at the data collection step. In particular, no matter how time-use data are collected (e.g., from observations, logs, or ESMs), the behaviors that a principal has been observed performing are binned by researchers into one of the functional categories in their coding scheme. The dimensionality assumption is about the structure of this coding scheme. When researchers build coding schemes about functional areas of activity, for example, they assume that each functional area in the coding scheme is analytically distinguishable from every other functional area in the scheme so that as whole, the functional areas are mutually exclusive. Importantly, however, most research studies have not assessed the validity of this dimensionality assumption (e.g., through use of factor analytic or clustering routines), and as a result, the coding systems used in studies might be incorrect on conceptual and empirical grounds.

Consider, as a conceptual matter, the coding scheme used by Camburn, Spillane, and Sebastian, (2010). If I understand that classification system correctly, the act of hiring a new teacher (which would be coded as "personnel" work) might instead be thought of as an act of instructional leadership, especially if the principal makes this appointment to improve instruction It is also possible that several behaviors coded as "school finance" in these researchers' coding schemes could be coded as acts of instructional leadership, for example, time spent budgeting for the purchase of new (and more effective) textbooks or time spent contracting for new instructional interventions. Perhaps that is why at least one prior study found that time spent on personnel issues had a marginally significant, positive association with student achievement (May, Huff,

& Goldring, 2012, p. 428). The larger point, however, is that coding schemes differ from study to study, and researchers have not much attempted to reconcile or adjudicate these differences.

Now consider how the dimensionality assumptions of particular coding schemes might be investigated empirically. One example comes from Camburn, Spillane, and Sebastian (2010), who conducted a study to compare measures of principal's time use derived from an annual survey and end-of-day log. An important finding from that work was that the amount of time principals spent on instructional leadership behaviors was consistently correlated to the amount of time they spent planning for school improvement, both within the same instrument and across the two instruments under study. This finding suggests that the behaviors these researchers classified into these two functional categories might not be two separate constructs because on the basis of the correlational analysis, the two groups of behaviors appear to be (at least partly) measuring the same underlying construct. The larger point is that researchers should carefully investigate the correlations among the scores principals receive in different functional areas and examine whether these correlations are consistent with the kind of strong dimensionality posited by their coding schemes.

The ratio level of measurement assumption

An additional assumption researchers make when they aggregate time-use data into summary measures is that the leadership in any of the functional domains identified in a coding scheme is best measured at the ratio level of measurement, that is, as the "amount" or "percentage" of time spent on leadership activities in that domain. This assumption is pervasive in principals' time-use research, yet as Goldring et al. (2008) pointed out, it might make more sense to think of leadership in terms of "types" rather than amounts, in which case leadership is measured on a nominal scale. For example, using discriminant analysis, Goldring et al. (2008) grouped principals into three leadership types based on the amounts of time they spent on various functional categories of behavior. The three types of leaders in that study were "eclectic" leaders, who distributed their time about across all types of activities, "instructionally focused" leaders, who spent more time on instructional leadership behaviors than behaviors in any other functional category, and "student-centered" leaders, who spent more time on student affairs activities than any other class of behavior. In this approach, two principals might spend the same amount of time on instructional leadership but differ on the amounts of time they spend on other tasks, so that the distribution of time spent across *multiple* tasks defines types of leadership.

The equal weighting assumption

Yet another assumption researchers make when they aggregate time-use data into summary measures is that any behavior coded into a functional category of behavior is an equivalent indicator of the "strength" of leadership (or job performance) in that category as any other behavior coded into that category. In the typical research study, for example, 30 minutes of classroom walkthroughs are given the same weight in calculating the "amount" of instructional leadership exercised by a principal as 30 minutes of reviewing student work or 30 minutes of classroom observation with feedback. However, this equal weighting assumption might not be warranted. For example, suppose that classroom walkthroughs are only sometimes used to exercise instructional leadership and at other times used to improve relationships with students, whereas discussions about student work are *always* about instructional leadership. In this case, the amount of time a principal spends on classroom walkthroughs provides a fuzzy signal about instructional leadership, whereas the amount of time a principal spends discussing students' work sends a stronger signal. In this situation, researchers might want to assign some type of "weight" to the amount of time spent on different behaviors in building a measure of instructional leadership, giving more weight to time spent on behaviors that send a strong signal about leadership and less weight to behaviors sending a fuzzy signal. Readers familiar with formal measurement theory will immediately see that such weights are often estimated as factor loadings in factor analytic models and as item discrimination parameters in item-response-theory (IRT) measurement models.

To date, I know of only one study that examined the equal weighting assumption of time-use research. In that study, Camburn et al. (2010) calculated Cronbach's *alpha* (a measure of internal consistency) for several multi-item scales constructed from an end-of-year time-use survey given to principals. In the analyses, the researchers implemented the equal weighting assumption by calculating scores on each multi-item scale as a simple average of scores for each item in the scale. Importantly, the statistical packages researchers typically use to calculate *alpha* provide three pieces of information that can be used to evaluate the equal weighting assumption. The first is the *alpha* coefficient itself, which becomes larger as the correlations among items on a multi-item scale increase. So, a high *alpha* is one indicator that items on a scale are measuring the same underlying construct (with little error, and hence to the same degree). However, the value of Cronbach's *alpha* also increases as the number of items in a multi-item scale increases, so researchers often examine two additional pieces of information provided by statistical packages: the correlation of each item to the total scale score and the *alpha* for a scale if an item is deleted. Looking at these additional *item* statistics allows a researcher to examine whether some specific items provide more or less signal to the measurement of a construct, and this is a more specific test of the "equal weighting" assumption. Unfortunately, Camburn and colleagues (2010) did not report this item-level information, and instead provided only an *alpha* coefficient for scales in their study. Thus, this was an incomplete examination of the "equal weighting" assumption.

Note that the Camburn et al. (2010) were reporting on end-of-year survey data. However, it would also be possible to examine the "equal weighting" assumption using Cronbach's *alpha* in cases where researchers used log, ESM, or structured observation instruments. For these instruments, specific behaviors would become the "items" to be analyzed, and researchers could then examine the extent to which minutes spent on particular behaviors were correlated to one another and to the total (or average) amount of time spent on the underlying functional category being measured. To be sure, reporting on specific behaviors would make log and ESM instruments longer (and increase respondent burden), and as a result, in current studies, principals using log and ESM instruments are not asked to directly code their behaviors (e.g., working with student data) but rather to code what they are doing into one of the coding scheme's functional categories (i.e., instructional leadership). Reporting at the behavior level is possible, however (cf. Rowan, Camburn, & Correnti, 2004), and if codes were entered at the behavior level, researchers could use factor analytic or IRT models to directly assess their dimensionality assumptions. The same is true of studies using structured observation data. These studies almost always record time spent on specific behaviors as part of the observation record (e.g., Grissom et al., 2013), but to date, I am not aware of any structured observation studies that examine the extent to which time on specific behaviors are correlated to one another or "load" onto specific scales. In the future, however, I recommend that researchers pay more attention to these kinds of "item-level" analyses. This would not only allow for more explicit testing of the dimensionality assumptions now used in time-use research, but also could serve as the basis for weighting time-spent on particular behaviors in the construction of time-use scales.

The ignorable facets of measurement assumption

The arguments made in the last two sections showed that time-use researchers often treat items as "ignorable" features of their measurement protocol (i.e., by failing to report how these items affect measurement reliability). In this section, I want to discuss two additional features of time-use data that researchers often ignore but that also can affect the reliability of time-use measures: the number of days on which a principal's time use was observed and the number of observers who gathered/reported on that principal's time use. Here, time-use researchers most often pay insufficient attention to how these features of data collection affect time-use measurement and especially measurement reliability. As a result, I will now briefly describe Generalizability (G) theory (for an overview, see Shavelson & Webb, 1991) and show how this statistical approach to measurement analysis can be used to analyze how the number of observation days and the number of raters used in a study can affect the reliability of time-use measures.

G theory is a statistical framework that views the score obtained from a measurement instrument as one of a many possible alternative scores that might be obtained from using that instrument, where alternative scores could come from, for example, measurements collected at a different time points, or perhaps from measurements recorded by different raters. In G theory, each of these features of a measurement procedure is called a "facet" of measurement, and each facet has the potential to produce error in observed scores. The goal of G theory is to calculate the degree to which these various facets of measurement produce error and to use that to understand score reliability. Although not used very much in principals' time-use research, G theory could be used to address what I am calling the "ignorable facets of measurement assumption."

The ignorable facets of measurement assumption arise in time-use research when time-use data come from multiple days of observation or are gathered by multiple observers. A problem for principals' time-use researchers is thus to understand the extent to which these facets of measurement affect overall scale reliability. As an example, researchers often collected time-use data on principals on multiple days of observation, and an interesting question is how this affects the reliability of summary measures of principals' time use reported in studies. Obviously, if principals spend exactly the same amount of time on each charted activity each day, a researcher can estimate a principal's time use without error from a single day of observation. But, if principals' time use varies across days (as research strongly suggests), more than one day of observation will be needed to get a precise estimate of each principals' time use, in which case a researcher will have to average over days. What G theory allows a researcher to do is decide on the basis of evidence how many days of observation are needed to obtain a measure of principals' time use with a desired level of reliability. It does this in the present case by decomposing the variance in principals' scores into two components: variance lying among principals (denoted as τ) and variance lying within principals due to differences in time use across observation days (denoted as $\sigma 2$). Then, if time is the only varying facet of measurement, the reliability of any time-use measure would be calculated from G theory as $\tau/[\tau + (\sigma 2/n)]$, where n is the number of days of observation. Most time-use studies of principals that I read did not calculate this reliability coefficient for the number of days over which they collected data, which is why I am arguing that days have been treated as an "ignorable" facet of measurement in past research on principals' time use.

One time-use study of principals did supply the kind of information needed to examine how days of observation might affect reliability. This was a study conducted by Camburn, Spillane, and Sebastian (2010), who used end-of-day logs collected over 15 total days spread out across a single school year to obtain estimates of principals' time use. Using these log data, the authors decomposed the variance in time-use scores into variance due to principals [τ] and variance within principals ($\sigma 2$), which represents variance due to days of data collection. Those variance components are shown in Table 2 of the paper (Camburn, Spillane, & Sebastian, 2010, p. 729). Using those published variance components, I calculated how the reliability of a time-use measure of instructional leadership based on *log data* would be expected to vary if instructional leadership scores were based on 5, 10, and 15 days of log data. Applying the G theory formula just above shows that if a researcher were to use the end-of-day log used in the study under discussion, and if that researcher used that log in the same (or a very similar) sample of principals, the researcher could expect to obtain a reliability coefficient of .63 for an estimate of time spent on instructional leadership based on 5 days of log data, .78 for an estimate based on 10 days of log data, and .84 with 15 days of log data. Importantly, Table 2 in Camburn, Spillane, and Sebastian (2010, p. 729) also showed that the variance components (τ and σ^2) were different for different functional categories of managerial behavior (and were also different in data taken from the log versus an ESM instrument). So, G theory claims about the reliability of measures apply only to circumstances that very closely resemble the original research conditions.

The Camburn, Spillane, and Sebastian (2010) paper makes a very good contribution to the literature on the reliability of time-use estimates based on log and ESM data and shows that the number of days of observation undertaken in a study has observable effects on measurement reliability (which means days are not an ignorable facet of measurement). Unfortunately, I am unaware of similar analyses conducted with structured observation data, which is also collected across multiple days. Moreover, structured observations have an additional facet of measurement: observers. For this reason, it is important for researchers using structured observations to decompose score variance from their studies into *three* components—variance due to principals, variance due to observation days, and variance due to observers. Using these variance components (and formulas from G Theory), researchers would then be able to know just how dependable their estimates are when they come from a particular structured observation protocol collecting data with a given number of raters across a given number of days, and they could use these results to plan for future studies. Lacking G studies of structured observation data, however, principals' time-use researchers currently treat days and raters as ignorable facets of measurement.[1]

The exchangeable instruments assumption

There is yet one more facet of measurement that could be examined using G theory: the different instruments researchers use to measure principals' time use. Here, G Theory could be deployed to examine whether estimates of principals' time use are similar across different kinds of instruments (the "exchangeable instruments" assumption). This question, it should be noted, was posed by Camburn et al. (2010) when they compared time-use scores obtained from the same sample of principals using two different measuring instruments: an end of day log and an end-of-year survey. These researchers constructed a multi-trait, multimethod (MTMM) correlation matrix to examine convergence and divergence among scores, where the "traits" in the MTMM matrix were the functional categories of leadership practice measured in the study and the "methods" were the two approaches to gathering time use data (logs and end-of-year surveys). What I am going to do now is re-conceptualize this MTMM analysis using G Theory. In G Theory, the traits and methods would be considered "facets" of measurement. Using G Theory, a researcher could then conceptualize variance in principals' time-use scores as a function of: (a) a principal's "true" time use; (b) the leadership dimension for which time use is being measured; and (c) the instrument being used to measure that leadership dimension. A researcher could then estimate a multi-level model and obtain the same "trait" and "method" correlations reported in the MTMM analysis, and in addition, use the variance components from the multi-level model to estimate how the reliability of time-use estimates would be improved if time use was measured with more than one instrument. A worry researchers should have is that the correlations among time-use measures of the same leadership dimension might be low across different measurement instruments, because this would suggest a great deal of method variance in time-use estimates. If that is the case, then the instruments used to collect time use data aren't perfectly exchangeable and there might be a need to use more than one data collection method to construct reliable estimates of principals' time use.

How likely is such a finding? In the paper by Camburn et al. (2010), the correlation between instructional leadership scores using a log and annual survey was .63 (after correction for measurement error).[2] If we consider .63 to be an intra-class correlation, then about 37% of the variance in principals' observed time spent on instructional leadership would be due to the instrument in use, which further suggests that if a researcher averaged principals' scores across these two instruments, the reliability of this averaged score would be about .77. If we then added a third data collection instrument and assumed that this new instrument produced an estimate with roughly the same correlation to log and survey measures as the log and survey measures have to one another, reliability with three methods of measurement would increase to .84. This suggests that instrumentation is *not* an ignorable facet of measurement and that different instruments are imperfectly exchangeable. Note, furthermore, that this finding *should not* be generalized to the use of structured observation methods as the third data collection method. Recall that log and surveys measures are both based on principal self-reports. If we added a measure derived from third-party observations, the intra-class correlation might be much lower than that reported by Camburn et al. (2010), meaning that the reliability of any score averaged across measures from these different instruments might also be lower. The larger takeaway is this. The data collection instruments that researchers use almost certainly introduce measurement error into time-use measurements, and as a result, researchers should not necessarily conclude that one instrument can be exchanged for another. Rather, researchers should consider the advantages of using more than one instrument to measure time use, weighing the advantages of increased precision of measurement gain through this practice against the costs of additional data collection.

The replicability and generality assumptions

The use of G theory to explore the facets of measurement and exchangeable instruments assumptions is important because G theory provides information about the precision (i.e., reliability) of person-level estimates of time use. But it is also useful to think about the precision of time-use estimates for sample means—the main descriptive statistic provided in most time-use research. In what follows, I will argue that principals' time-use researchers have too frequently failed to provide readers with a sense of this latter kind of precision and I will show how attention to placing confidence intervals around sample-wide estimates can help researchers and readers understand the warrant for two additional classes of assumption often found in time use research: the replicability assumption and the generality assumption.

The replicability assumption

The "replicability" assumption as I use it refers to a narrow claim that the findings from any given study, if conducted again in a similar sample (using similar instruments and facets of measurement), would be replicated. The assumption is most often made implicitly, for example, when a research paper concludes that "principals in this study" spent a certain percentage of time on some functional activity, like instructional leadership. An example can be found in Horng et al. (2010, p. 518) who state that, "The data cover all high schools in the Miami-Dade County Public School District [and show that] on average, the activities on which principals spent the most time were overseeing student services, managing budgets, and dealing with student discipline issues." Note how this statement is offered as a good faith qualification about the extent to which the findings from that particular study can be generalized beyond the study. But as it turns out, even a very limited statement of the sort offered by these researchers will be subject to the uncertainty of sampling error. As a result, such a statement should be qualified by calculating the standard error of estimate for the sample-wide means being reported and those standard errors can then be used to place a confidence interval around those estimated means. Using that procedure, the replicability assumption now would become something like, "there is a 95% chance that the principals in our study spent between x% and y% of their time on instructional leadership."

Importantly, many studies that I read did not report these kinds of confidence intervals for their descriptive statistics on time use. However, I have every reason to believe that such confidence intervals are surprisingly large in many studies. For example, two studies that I read presented enough data for me to construct confidence intervals around the estimates of principal time use provided in the papers (Horng et al., 2010; May, Huff, & Goldring, 2012). One of these (May, Huff, & Goldring, 2012) collected data on the same principals across three years of study, and should have had precise, person-level estimates of principals' time use. Using the data published in that study (and assuming n = 55 principals), however, the data from the May, Huff, and Goldring (2012) suggest that the 95% confidence intervals for sample means of time spent on particular functional categories of behavior are surprisingly large. For example, my very approximate calculation of the 95% confidence interval for the percent of time principals spent on instructional leadership in that study was ± 7.5%, which implies that if the study were re-done, perhaps with a different sample from the same population of principals, there would be a 95% chance that the average time on instructional leadership would be somewhere between 12% and 26%.

The generality assumption

A generality assumption is even more ambitious than a replicability assumption. As I define it in this chapter, a generality assumption holds that previous studies of principals' time use have produced a set of highly general findings that are also true in the current study. As one example of a generality assumption, consider the statement in Goldring et al. (2008, p. 336) that, "Research has long characterized … [the principal's day].as … dominated with managerial issues unrelated to instruction." Even assuming that this claim is meant to apply only to principals in schools in the United States, the claim seemingly encompasses *all* principals, no matter what their specific school setting, as well as all "days" without regard to when in the school year data were collected. But I would argue that evidence to support this broad claim is not as clear as time-use researchers seem to assume. To begin, I am unaware of any nationally representative principals' time-use study, so there are *no* national estimates on principals' time use. Instead, there is simply a limited number principal time-use studies conducted in a very small number of school systems (Mahone, Hochbein, & Vanderbeck, 2016). To be sure, each of these studies would probably have large confidence intervals around their time-use estimates (if such intervals were published), and for that reason, one might be tempted to assume if one tested the assumption that there are no statistically significant sample-to-sample differences in principals' patterns of time use. Instead, investigating differences among samples probably requires larger sample sizes than are present in many current studies. In any case, it is also very difficult to generalize estimates of principals' time use across current studies since current studies often use different coding schemes and thus have incomparable time-use estimates to compare (as also noted by May, Huff, & Goldring (2012). More to the point about generalizing assumptions, studies conducted with larger samples of principals who work in diverse contexts have found a great deal of variability in principal activities across community, organizational, and student contexts (see, especially, Goldring et al., 2008). So, I would like to see a greater empirical warrant for broad generalizing claims about principals' time use.

Lacking national samples, how can researchers studying principals' time use make generalizing claims about similarities of their findings to populations different from their particular samples? One approach to building up generalizations would be to establish what I call a series of "linking" claims. This approach to generalization has been well described by Shadish (1995). He argued that where studies are conducted in distinctive samples, generalization occurs as researchers: (a) carefully replicate their study findings in very similar settings; (b) then replicate findings in settings that are quite different from original study findings; (c) then carefully specify the exact features of settings that are producing variation; and finally (d) build and test a strong theory of variation in principal time use. From this perspective, the relatively casual claims (that are often made in passing) by time-use researchers about the universal nature of principals' time use need to be tempered and larger, generalizing claims need to be advanced with better empirical warrants.

Implications for future research

I have offered a number of criticisms of principals' time-use research, criticisms related to researchers' assumptions about the theoretical constructs being measured with time-use data, criticisms of how education researchers typically transform time-use data into quantitative measures of these constructs, criticisms about the ways researchers have established the dimensionality and reliability of time-use measures, and criticisms about the generalizing claims that time-use researchers make about the descriptive results of their studies. These criticisms were not advanced as an argument against time-use data *per se*, or about the potential for time-use data to advance research about school leadership. Rather, I presented these criticisms to signal a path forward for principals' time-use research, and it is to that path that I now turn.

One way to improve research on principals' time use would be to put more effort into aligning time-use data collection efforts to the definitions social researchers typically give to terms such as "leadership" and "job performance." There are several ways this could be done. As an initial step, it would be good to get principals' perspectives on their own observation records, perhaps by interviewing principals at the end of the day, reviewing their log, ESM, or structured observation record, and then asking principals to reflect on the behavioral record, not so much to identify or clarify coding inconsistencies (as was done in Camburn et al., 2010), but rather to gain a better understanding of how a principal classifies observed behaviors in terms of the usual leadership functions that appear in time-use coding schemes, what the principal's intentions might have been in these enacting these behaviors, what the meaning for and potential influence on others is that he or she thinks these behaviors have, what the temporal context is within which the behaviors occurred (e.g., part of a continuing set of actions or a one-time action), and whether or not the principal thought the action was under his or her agentic control. Setting the coded behavioral record beside a principal's interpretations of the actions might go a long way toward clarifying how coding categories typically used in leadership theory are (or are not) represented by the coded record of behavior.

In my view, the data gathered from these qualitative studies would be a useful first step in building better time-use observation instruments, especially self-report instruments. In particular, these newer instruments could be used to code not only the specific behaviors a principal was doing during some time interval, but also whether it was self- or other-initiated, an interruption or planned, an act of leadership or followership, part of a continuing series of interactions or a one-off interaction, whether it was an influence attempt or not, and more. Such instruments would, in my view, lessen the potential for construct deficiencies in time-use measurement, and perhaps provide more potential for identifying empirical relationships between principal behaviors and valued organizational outcomes. As I envision this data collection strategy these enhanced observation instruments would be coded at the behavior-level, with each recorded behavior being associated with a set of additional codes about function, intention, projected influence, and other variables surfaced at the initial step, and with these data in hand, researchers could then use empirical methods (like factor analysis, cluster analysis, discriminant analysis) to probe the dimensionality in time-use data and to development measurement models that perhaps assign "weights" to particular items (or clusters of items) composing scales developed from the data.[3] If sample sizes were large enough, and budgets were sufficient, researchers could also begin to correlate these new measures to valued organizational outcomes in an effort to assess the "predictive validity" of richer instruments.

Many readers might view the kind of data collection procedures I just described as overly burdensome for principals. After all, if a given principal was observed (or was recording his or her behaviors) across a full day, reviewing a day-long observation record, or filling out an ESM or log record that had multiple reporting elements at each observed time interval, that principal would definitely spend more time on data collection compared to existing methods. But this is where G theory might prove useful. For example, given that there is a great deal of day-to-day variance in principals' behaviors, it might be more convenient and less burdensome on principals if researchers observed more days (but fewer time intervals per day); moreover, this kind of observation schedule might also produce measures with the same (or even more) reliability than existing data collection schedules. Moreover, time-use instruments that recorded a rich set of data on principals' behaviors, intentions, and potential influence might obviate the need to combine instruments, such as logs with surveys (e.g., as was done by Camburn et al., 2010), or observation instruments with surveys (e.g., Grissom et al., 2013), although a G study of the sort I described earlier in this chapter would probably be needed to assess this claim. In such a study, it might also be useful to supplement time-use data on the educational leadership of a school's principal with assessments of leadership coming from other sources, for example teachers or supervisors (perhaps using the VAL-ED instrument developed by Porter, Polikoff, Goldring, Murphey, Elliot, & May, 2010).

Once researchers have developed better ways of using time-use data to measure key dimensions of principals' leadership actions, there will be a need to pay more attention to the replicability and generality assumptions I discussed in this chapter. All future studies, in my view, should publish means and standard deviations for descriptive data on time-use and related variables, and researchers should use these data to engage in sample size planning. In descriptive studies of local samples, sufficient sample sizes will produce smaller confidence intervals around estimated sample means, thereby placing more precise bounds around claims about how often principals in that sample engage in particular actions. Moreover, if time-use researchers begin to do the kinds of systematic "linking" studies that I discussed earlier, larger sample sizes will improve statistical power for independent samples comparisons.

Finally, there is a need in principals' time-use research to thoroughly examine what I called the "agentic control" assumption: the idea that the observed behaviors of principals are under the control of principals and not simply a reflection of the contexts in which they operate. One way to test the agentic control assumption would be to follow principals who changed schools and to examine stability and change in a single principal's behaviors as they change contexts. Another way to examine the "agentic control" assumption would be to develop intervention programs that targeted change in principals' behaviors and then examine whether principals indeed changed their leadership actions as a result of training.

The reader should note that what I have described just now is a long-term agenda for conducting research on principals' time use. That long-term agenda would be grounded in the solid foundation of studies on principals' time use in the 1980s (e.g., Spillane et al., 2007; Goldring et al., 2008; Camburn et al., 2010; Camburn, Spillane, & Sebastian, 2010; Horng et al., 2010; López et al., 2012; May, Huff, & Goldring, 2012; Grissom et al., 2013), but it would also learn from that body of research and make refinements to time-use data collection instruments, measurement models, and study designs moving forward.

Notes

1. A few additional notes about structured observations are in order. Based on my experience using structured observation instruments to observe and measure teacher behavior, I suspect that observer error might be relatively low in principals' time-use research. This is consistent with the inter-rater reliability statistics reported in the Horng et al. (2010) who used multiple observers to record time-use data. However, even if there is a relative lack of rater error, there are still good reasons to use multiple raters in principals' time use research and to observe the same principal with more than one observer on at least a few occasions. If only one observer records data on a principal, rater error and principal "true" scores are completely confounded. The appropriate procedure for conducting a study with structured observation is therefore to observe principals across multiple days, randomly assign raters to principal observation days, and assign two observers to observe the same principal on about 10–20% of all days. In that design, researchers can estimate how much observer error is present in principals' score estimates, report the reliability of their estimates given different numbers of occasions and observers, and disconfound observer and principal effects on time-use scores.
2. The correction used by Camburn et al. (2010) to dis-attenuate these correlations did not adjust for correlated measurement error. However, correlated measurement error was almost certainly present in their analyses because the same respondent completed both time-use instruments. Moreover, this correlated measurement error probably inflated the magnitude of their "corrected" correlations. Despite this, we use these researchers' reported correlations in what follows.
3. These techniques were used to good effect in work I have done with colleagues in developing teacher logs (e.g., Rowan et al., 2004; Correnti & Rowan, 2007).

References

Camburn, E. M., Huff, J. T., Goldring, E. B., & May, H. (2010). Assessing the validity of an annual survey for measuring principal leadership practice. *The Elementary School Journal, 111*(2), 314–335.

Camburn, E. M., Spillane, J. P., & Sebastian, J. (2010). Assessing the utility of a daily log for measuring principal leadership practice. *Educational Administration Quarterly, 46*(5), 707–737.

Correnti, R., & Rowan, B. (2007). Opening up the black box: Literacy instruction in schools participating in three comprehensive school reform programs. *American Educational Research Journal, 44*(2), 298–339.

Goldring, E., Huff, J., May, H., & Camburn, E. (2008). School context and individual characteristics: What influences principal practice? *Journal of Educational Administration, 46*(3), 332–352.

Grissom, J. A., Loeb, S., & Master, B. (2013). Effective instructional time use for school leaders: Longitudinal evidence from observations of principals. *Educational Researcher*, 42(8), 433–444.

Grissom, J. A., Loeb, S., & Mitani, H. (2015). Principal time management skills. *Journal of Educational Administration*, 53(6), 773–793.

Horng, E. L., Klasik, D., & Loeb, S. (2010). Principal's time use and school effectiveness. *American Journal of Education*, 116(4), 491–523.

Kmetz, J. T., & Willower, D. J. (1982). Elementary school principals' work behavior. *Educational Administration Quarterly*, 18(4), 62–78.

Kurke, L. B., & Aldrich, H. E. (1983). Note—Mintzberg was right!: A replication and extension of the nature of managerial work. *Management Science*, 29(8), 975–984.

López, V., Ahumada, L., Galdames, S., & Madrid, R. (2012). School principals at their lonely work: Recording workday practices through ESM logs. *Computers & Education*, 58(1), 413–422.

Mahone, A., Hochbein, C., & Vanderbeck, S. (2016). Examining the construct validity of principal time use studies. In *Annual conference of the University Council for Educational Administration, Detroit, MI*.

Martin, W. J., & Willower, D. J. (1981). The managerial behavior of high school principals. *Educational Administration Quarterly*, 17(1), 69–90.

Martinko, M. J., & Gardner, W. L. (1985). Beyond structured observation: Methodological issues and new directions. *Academy of Management Review*, 10(4), 676–695.

May, H., Huff, J., & Goldring, E. (2012). A longitudinal study of principals' activities and student performance. *School Effectiveness and School Improvement*, 23(4), 417–439.

Mintzberg, H. A. (1973) *The nature of managerial work*. New York: Harper & Row.

Motowidlo, S. J. (2003). Job performance. In *Handbook of psychology*. Hoboken, NJ: Wiley.

Ogawa, R. T., & Bossert, S. T. (1995). Leadership as an organizational quality. *Educational Administration Quarterly*, 31(2), 224–243.

Parsons, T. (1949). *The structure of social action* (Vol. 491). New York: Free Press.

Peterson, K. D. (1977). The principal's tasks. *Administrator's Notebook*, 26(8), 1–4.

Pitner, N. J., & Ogawa, R. T. (1981). Organizational leadership: The case of the school superintendent. *Educational Administration Quarterly*, 17(2), 45–65.

Porter, A. C., Polikoff, M. S., Goldring, E., Murphy, J., Elliott, S. N., & May, H. (2010). Developing a Psychometrically Sound Assessment of School Leadership: The VAL-ED as a Case Study. *Educational Administration Quarterly*, 46(2), 135–173. https://doi.org/10.1177/1094670510361747

Pounder, D. G., Ogawa, R. T., & Adams, E. A. (1995). Leadership as an organization-wide phenomena: Its impact on school performance. *Educational Administration Quarterly*, 31(4), 564–588.

Rowan, B., Camburn, E., & Correnti, R. (2004). Using teacher logs to measure the enacted curriculum: A study of literacy teaching in third-grade classrooms. *The Elementary School Journal*, 105(1), 75–101.

Shadish, W. R. (1995). The logic of generalization: Five principles common to experiments and ethnographies. *American Journal of Community Psychology*, 23(3), 419–428.

Shavelson, R. J., & Webb, N. M. (1991). *Generalizability theory: A primer* (Vol. 1). Thousand Oaks, CA: Sage.

Spillane, J. P., Camburn, E. M., & Stitziel Pareja, A. (2007). Taking a distributed perspective to the school principal's workday. *Leadership and Policy in Schools*, 6(1), 103–125.

Sproull, L. S. (1981). Managing education programs: A micro-behavioral analysis. *Human Organization*, 40(2), 113–122.

3 A framework for evaluating and choosing principal time-use measurement strategies

Eric M. Camburn and James Sebastian

Introduction

Researchers studying principal time use have a wide array of measurement strategies at their disposal. But what strategies do they actually use? Researchers have documented a variety of different strategies including observations, one-time self-report surveys, daily instruments, and experience-sampling methods (ESMs) (Camburn, Spillane et al., 2010; Gronn, 2003). To get a better sense of the frequency with which different strategies are used, we reviewed abstracts of all articles in volumes 53–55 of the journal *Educational Administration Quarterly* (EAQ) that empirically examined some aspect of principal practice. These volumes approximately correspond with the years 2017–2019. We identified all articles in which some aspect of principal practice was measured. We then identified the strategy used to measure principal practice. Most of the respondents in these studies were principals, though in a small number of studies, measures of principal practice came from teachers and students. If the measurement strategies could not be determined from the abstract, we reviewed the entire article. We found 24 articles that met these criteria. We then classified the measurement strategies used in the articles to measure principal practice. EAQ was chosen because it is a leading journal of education leadership that publishes studies from a wide range of contexts and that use a wide range of methods. With this limited sample, we wanted to provide a snapshot of the most common methods used in recent school leadership research. We found that interviews (44 percent) and one-time, self-administered questionnaires (32 percent) were by far the most common strategies used by education leadership scholars in EAQ (Figure 3.1). Fifteen percent of all studies used observations to measure principal practice. We found only two studies that utilized document analysis and one study that used daily questionnaires.

Despite the wide range of choices available to researchers, we believe there is room for improvement in the guidance that researchers use to choose among measurement strategies. When choosing a strategy, researchers must often consult multiple, disparate sources which often are not purposefully designed to provide guidance in choosing among available options. There are very few resources that discuss a full range of measurement strategies, in a side-by-side, comparative

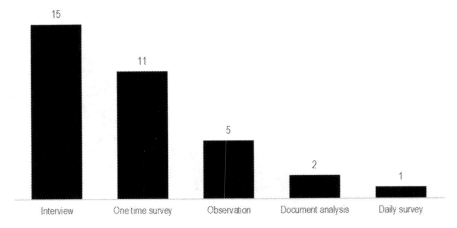

Figure 3.1 Incidence of different strategies for measuring principal practice in volumes 53–55 of *Educational Administration Quarterly*

format as we do here. And among such resources, very few focus specifically on the measurement of principal time use or even the broader domain of principal leadership practice. A second motivation for this chapter is our belief that the field may be over reliant on a small number of measurement strategies, particularly, one-time self-administered questionnaires and interviews. Our own research indicates that emerging, but very rarely used strategies like daily questionnaires can serve as a useful complement to other measurement strategies or can even have greater validity than more frequently used strategies such as one-time surveys (Camburn, Spillane et al., 2010). Therefore, one of our goals in developing this framework is to promote greater heterogeneity in the measurement approaches used in the field, thereby strengthening the validity of the knowledge base on principal time use.

Framework

Our framework holds that when a measurement strategy is implemented, three outcomes occur, all of which depend on the choice of strategy: First, data are produced and those data have a certain degree of validity. Second, the implementation of a measurement strategy results in varying financial costs to researchers. And third, measurement strategies impose a burden on respondents. When we measure principal time use, our goal should be to maximize validity and minimize financial cost and respondent burden. A visualization of our framework can be found in Figure 3.2.

Our framework uses a standard input, process, output format (Curry et al., 2006). Broadly speaking, the measurement stage of research involves measuring some trait (a phenomenon being measured) of a population. Thus, the "inputs" in our model are the population of interest to be measured and the phenomenon

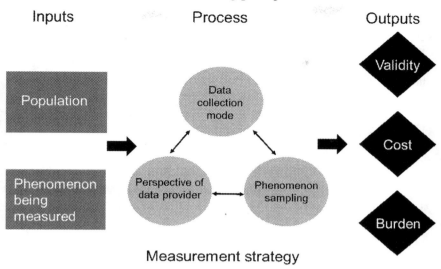

Figure 3.2 A framework for evaluating, describing and comparing strategies for measuring principal time use

being measured. The outcomes of validity, cost, and burden depend greatly on a measurement process in which a data collection mode is implemented. This mode will be more or less sensitive to the perspective of the person who provides the evidence, and represent the phenomenon more or less well given the way in which the phenomenon of interest is sampled. These components of a measurement strategy are all aspects of research design that researchers have control over and therefore represent leverage points on which researchers can exercise the greatest amount of influence on validity, cost, and burden. In summary, the framework holds that the extent to which choices about mode, perspective, and phenomenon sampling maximize validity and minimize cost and respondent burden will depend on the degree to which they respond to the needs of the population being measured, and represent well the population and phenomenon being measured.

Population

One of the main purposes of quantitative research is to discover "truths" about a population of interest. Our framework posits that for a measurement strategy to maximize validity and minimize burden, it must reflect a good understanding of the population, particularly of optimal modes of accessing and communicating with population members. This is because measurement, regardless of mode, involves interaction and communication between researchers and members of the population. Bradburn et al. (2004) and others, for example, have likened the process of participating in a survey to a conversation between respondent and researcher. This analogy even holds for self-administered surveys in which researchers are not physically present. With such surveys, researchers still "converse" with respondents through their written communication in the questionnaire. Similarly, even though researchers and research participants might not be communicating during an observation, observations will clearly be more valid to the extent to which researchers understand the target population being observed. Our framework thus posits that for a measurement strategy to be valid, it needs to effectively access and communicate with members of the target population of interest. Doing so requires an understanding of nuances like population members' education and literacy levels (this will determine validity of different communication modes), how they can be accessed (technologically, physically, and socially), and the ways in which population members' social, cultural, and political contexts might affect the measurement process.

Principals are a distinctive population that have been likened to executives and administrators in other fields. Principals are busy, autonomous individuals who are often difficult to reach. Relative to members of the general population they are very literate and it is safe to assume that most will have ready access to technology. Principals navigate complex social and political spaces in their work, having to work effectively with parents, teachers, the community, and district leaders. The political complexity of principals' work means that some topics will be highly sensitive, especially those in which principals are discussing one of their many constituent groups, or those which might potentially cast themselves in a negative light. We found collecting valid data on principal time use at scale to be challenging and resource intensive (Camburn, Spillane et al., 2010). Beyond education, there is evidence in the literature about unique challenges of conducting research with executives. Cycyota and Harrison (2006), for example, found that survey response rates for executives are generally low and have been declining over time, and that non-response follow-up strategies that are effective in other populations were ineffective with executives. In our own research, we found that substantial participant contact time, strategic follow-up, and $100 incentive payments (US dollar, 2005–2007) yielded a response rate of 78 percent (Camburn, Spillane et al., 2010). The incentive payment was provided for completing 15 daily questionnaires, one end of the year questionnaire, and completing an experience sampling instrument.

Phenomenon measured

In studying principals, researchers measure a range of principal attributes which fall into three general categories: knowledge, attitudes, and behavior. Principal time use can be best thought of as comprising a range of behaviors. When we measure principals' time use, we are generally asking questions like: What did principals do? When did they do it? How frequently did they do it? Who did they collaborate with? The survey methods literature identifies two significant challenges in measuring behavior: recall problems and socially desirable reporting. The likelihood that either of these problems will affect the measurement process depends greatly on what is being measured. In the case of principal time use, some behaviors will likely be easy to remember (for example, giving remarks at the start of the year convocation) while remembering others may be difficult (for example, speaking with a parent about a disciplinary matter last Thursday afternoon). Groves et al. (2009) identify four factors that determine the likelihood that respondents will provide error-prone reports of their behavior:

- The time of the occurrence (the further back in the past behaviors occurred the more difficult they are to report accurately)
- The proximity of the event to temporal boundaries (for example, the beginning or end of a week or year—behaviors occurring more closely to a temporal boundary are easier to report accurately)
- The distinctivess of the behavior (more distinctive behaviors are easier to report accurately)
- The importance and emotional impact of the behavior (important, more emotionally significant behaviors are easier to recall)

As Bradburn et al. (2004) note, when a measurement strategy places respondents in a situation where information they share might be socially embarrassing or worse, research participants are placed in a dilemma. On one hand they want to be good respondents and give accurate reports, but at the same time they also want to appear to be good people in the eyes of the researcher. There are many aspects of principal time use that might be socially sensitive and therefore engender socially desirable reporting. For example, principals will understandably be motivated to report they are spending time on initiatives that leaders in their district expect them to spend time on.

We highlight a third characteristic of the phenomenon being measured that is particularly salient when studying principal time use—the complexity of principals' work. Studies conducted in the late 70s and early 80s found that principals' work was characterized by many different, brief tasks that unfolded at a hectic pace (Kmetz & Willower, 1982; Martin & Willower, 1981; Peterson, 1977). These studies also found that principals participated in a wide range of activities in single day with most lasting for very brief periods of time. Sebastian et al. (2018) argue that the work of principals has become even more complex in the years since those studies were conducted. Pollock and Hauseman (2019) note that challenges to leadership work include "high volume of e-mail messages, extended workdays, increased workload, increased expectations of shorter response times, and blurred boundaries between work and home." (p. 387). The complexity of principals' work has two implications for our framework. First, the complex nature of principals' work will make it more difficult for principals to accurately report their time use in self-report instruments and interviews. Second, this complexity makes it difficult if not impossible to exhaustively measure every aspect of principals' work. This presents challenges for measurement strategies like self-administered questionnaires which require that all measurement categories be specified ahead of time. We discuss this issue further in the section on phenomenon sampling.

Data collection mode

As discussed previously, researchers have used a range of different data collection modes to measure principal time use, including interviews, observations, one-time self-report surveys, daily surveys, and ESMs (Camburn, Spillane et al., 2010). The choice of data collection mode can have direct bearing on the validity of data captured, the cost of data collection, and the burden placed on research participants.

There is a substantial literature on how data quality is impacted by the researchers' choice of data collection mode. The literature identifies three characteristics of modes which have major implications for measuring principal time use: the nature of communication used during data collection, the degree of respondent privacy during data collection, and the degree of researcher involvement (and inversely, the degree of respondent autonomy) (Groves et al., 2009).

Communication

The nature of communication during data collection has significant consequences for data validity. There are two key aspects of communication to consider—the channel of communication (visual or auditory), and literacy and language requirements (Groves et al., 2009). All data collection requires respondents to react to either visual or auditory stimuli. People's ability to accurately process visual and auditory information varies, and when people struggle to process either visual or auditory information, data quality can be diminished. The literacy and language skills required for participation in data collection can also affect data quality. Clearly, research participants need to understand what is printed in questionnaires and also the questions asked by interviews in order for their answers to be valid. When written and spoken questions require literacy or language skills respondents do not possess, data quality will suffer.

Degree of privacy

If research topics are sensitive, providing respondents with privacy can increase the validity of data by helping respondents feel more comfortable giving answers that potentially cast them in an unflattering light (Groves et al., 2009). Self-administered surveys offer the most privacy and therefore are best suited for sensitive topics. Surveys or interviews conducted over the phone offer some privacy in that researcher and participant are not in the same physical location. However, because respondents are not completely private with these modes, social pressures induced by the intimacy of a phone call could in turn induce socially desirable responding. In-person interviews and observations offer the least amount of privacy for research participants and are, therefore, not well suited to the collection of evidence on activities or beliefs that have the potential to be socially embarrassing to research participants.

Researcher involvement

The aspect of data collection mode receiving the most attention in the literature is the degree of direct researcher involvement with research participants during data collection. Researcher involvement can be viewed as running on a continuum from no involvement (as with self-administered questionnaires) to high involvement (as in interviews in which the researcher reads the questions and records the answers). Interviewer involvement in data collection has multiple advantages, perhaps chief among them being that interviewers can react to respondents in the moment and ask probing and clarifying questions (Groves et al., 2009). This kind of responsive, real-time interaction can yield data that provide more nuanced, in-depth understanding of respondents' behaviors and experiences than is possible with self-administered questionnaires (Patton, 2005). Interviewers can also potentially encourage participation which may have positive benefits such as reducing item non-response. Using interviewers to collect data also has multiple disadvantages. It is more expensive than data collection modes for which researchers are not on site. There is also considerable research documenting how interviewers can adversely affect respondents' answers, thus undermining data validity (see discussion of interview bias below). As previously discussed, sensitive questions will also be more difficult to answer in the presence of an interviewer.

Self-administered instruments are most commonly used to collect quantitative data from large samples of individuals, and they are well suited for this purpose. Self-administered instruments can be relatively less expensive to administer, therefore being more affordable for large samples. And unlike data from interviews, data from self-administered instruments are well suited to describing regularities and patterns in behaviors, attitudes, and knowledge for large groups of people. Many of the advantages of interviewer presence during data collection correspond with comparative disadvantages of self-administered instruments. In particular, with the lack of direct interaction between researcher and research participant, researchers have no "real-time" influence over data content and quality with self-administered instruments as they do with interviews (Groves et al., 2009). Another disadvantage is that self-administered instruments must be self-explanatory and are therefore prone to errors arising from unclear meaning of questions and instructions and instrument formatting which impede respondents' understanding of questions (Schaeffer & Presser, 2003). Unlike interviews, with self-administered instruments, researchers have only one chance to communicate the meaning of questions to respondents, since follow-up, probing, and clarifying questions are not possible.

Perspective of data provider

Imagine that a principal and a researcher spend the first hour of a principal's day together. Further imagine that during that hour, both people periodically take notes about what the principal is doing and at the end of the hour, they compare notes. Prior research suggests that while they may agree on some aspects of what the principal did, the principal and researcher are likely to have quite different perceptions of other aspects (Camburn & Barnes, 2004; Sebastian et al., 2018). In this section, we discuss how such differences are rooted in part, in differences in the perspectives of those who provide data on principal time use.

In principal time-use studies, data have historically come from one of two sources—researchers or the principals themselves. One-time questionnaires, daily questionnaires, and experience-sampling instruments are all self-administered instruments in which principals provide data about their work. With observations, researchers are the sole providers of data on what principals do. With interviews, data are the product of an in-person interaction between principal and interviewer. Even though interview data are based on what principals tell interviewers, researchers have substantial influence over the data through processes like notetaking and transcription. Indeed, some studies have shown that interviewers can have a significant impact on the data. In interviews, respondents have been shown to be less likely to answer sensitive questions, more likely to provide answers they perceive will be acceptable or pleasing to the interviewer, and more reluctant to answer questions related to observable traits of the interviewer (for example, answering questions about race when the interviewer is of a different race than the respondent) (Groves et al., 2009).

As previously discussed, a series of influential studies conducted in the 70s and 80s found the principal's workday to be characterized by long hours, multiple tasks, frenetic pace, brevity, and fragmentation (see, for example, Kmetz & Willower, 1982; Martin & Willower, 1981; Peterson, 1977; Wolcott, 1973). More recent studies did not find principals' work tasks to be as brief and constantly shifting as the earlier studies (Sebastian et al., 2018; Spillane & Hunt, 2010). Sebastian et al. (2018) explained these differences as stemming in part from differences in the perspectives of the people providing the data. In the earlier studies, which were largely observation-based, researchers provided the data. The more recent studies relied on direct reports from principals themselves. Reflecting on the differences between the two sets of studies, Sebastian et al. (2018) noted:

> It is possible that to an external observer, a principal may be moving rapidly from one activity to the next, but from the principal's perspective these different activities may be part of the same larger domain. Another possibility is that principals encounter many interruptions but they tend to deal with them as minor disruptions during work on a larger functional domain … principals might also be more likely to remember activities that spanned greater durations and overlapped more than a single time block, while they might also forget rare events. (p. 77).

This example shows how the perspective of the data provider can affect fundamental understanding of the nature of principals' work. What has long been accepted as a defining characteristic of principal time use—brevity and fragmentation—were brought into question when a different perspective was used for measuring time use.

While observation data are not prone to respondent biases such as socially desirable reporting, they are prone to different sources of error. Self-reports can be more valid sources of data on work done outside of school hours and can be better suited to capturing linkages between activities that are spread over time. These aspects of principals' work are either completely hidden from researchers, or at least difficult for researchers to access, yet are clearly understood by principals themselves. Camburn and Barnes (2004) documented errors such as these. Specifically, they saw errors in observers' reports of teachers' instructional practices that were ultimately attributed to observers' misunderstanding of teachers' intentions and purposes, and prior history within the classroom. Teachers' self-reports on daily questionnaires were grounded in these intentions, purposes, and prior history; however, these features of instruction were inaccessible to observers. Many features of principals' work are likewise hidden from observers, therefore undermining the validity of observation data.

Phenomenon sampling

Like many constructs, principal time use is many-faceted and highly variable from one instance to the next. When constructs have this sort of complexity, exhaustive measurement of all facets of the construct is not feasible. This leads researchers to sample phenomena, measuring some aspects of the phenomena but not others. Cook et al. (2002) describe this process of sampling, noting how it has a major impact on the construct validity of a measurement:

> Construct validity is fostered by (1) starting with a clear explication of the person, setting, treatment, and outcome constructs of interest; (2) carefully selecting instances that match those constructs; (3) assessing the match between instances and constructs to see of any slippage between the two occurred, and (4) revising construct descriptions accordingly (p. 66).

Given the complexity of principal time use as a construct, all measurement strategies are prone to invalidity associated with incompleteness in representing the construct with sampled instances. Self-administered instruments have a distinctive disadvantage in this area compared to researcher-administered instruments. With the former, researchers must commit to a pre-determined set of "instances" ahead of time whereas researcher-administered instruments allow for a flexible, adaptive identification of salient "instances" during data collection, thus opening up the possibility of a deeper coverage of the construct.

Just as it is impossible for researchers to measure all facets (instances) of principal time use, it is also practically infeasible to measure all occurrences of principal time use for a given sample member. One solution to this conundrum is to "sample" occurrences through a time sampling strategy. Different measurement strategies employ very different ways of sampling time, each of which have implications for validity, cost, and burden. For example, it would be difficult for a researcher to observe a principal's time use across multiple hour blocks in a day, over several days, at multiple points throughout a semester, across an academic year. However, with colleagues, we have collected such data from principals using daily self-report questionnaires (Camburn, Spillane et al., 2010; Sebastian et al., 2018). A combination of placing the responsibility for data reporting in the hands of principals and sampling work days throughout an academic year made the representation of principal time use across such long expanses of time feasible. Earlier observation-based studies examined principal time use over much narrower ranges of time, and a heavy reliance on this data collection strategy may have constrained the field's understanding of principal time use.

With the commonly used method of one-time questionnaires, respondents have to retrospectively recall events that occur over long periods of time. The downside of this form of time sampling is that recall over such long stretches of time can be highly inaccurate. Daily instruments and experience sampling instruments are believed to be more accurate in part because they greatly reduce the amount of time that elapses between when an event occurs and when a respondent reports on the event. These instruments rely on time sampling strategies in which days, or moments within days, are selected for measurement. Just as samples of people imperfectly represent populations, samples of days and moments in a principal's work life imperfectly represent their work overall. Observations are prone to similar kinds of errors as researchers typically sample relatively small "slices" of time such as a class period, or a single day or small number of days.

Validity

Each mode used to measure principal time use comes with its own unique profile of validity and invalidity. Direct observations of principals can have greater validity than self-report methods when observers record events that principals fail to remember or are not aware of (Gronn, 2003). Observations conducted by independent observers may also mitigate invalidity related to principal biases to which self-reports are more susceptible. At the same time, however, we have already discussed examples where observation data are fallible because aspects of principals' work are hidden to researchers. We have also discussed how daily questionnaires are better suited at capturing principal practice over broader expanses of time, but how self-report instruments, even those that reference a single day, are susceptible to errors of faulty recall and socially desirable reporting.

In our view, and that of others (see, for example, Denzin, 1978; Patton, 1980), no method can be described as a gold-standard. Instead, each data collection strategy can provide distinctive and useful insight into different facets of principal work. While classic definitions of triangulation stress consistency, elimination of bias, and convergence of results for greater validity, other conceptions stress multiplism and complementarity—where methods can be used to study "overlapping but also different facets of a phenomenon, yielding an enriched, elaborated understanding of that phenomenon" (Greene et al., 1989, p. 258, see also Duckworth & Yeager, 2015). Our own efforts to assess the validity of measures of principal time reflect these ideas of multiplism and complementarity (Camburn, Huff et al., 2010; Camburn, Spillane et al., 2010; Sebastian et al., 2018). In these studies, validity was assessed by comparing evidence from multiple instruments and seeing how it converged or diverged.

We have conducted multiple studies on the validity of a daily questionnaire for measuring principal time use called the "end of day log" (Camburn, Spillane et al., 2010; Sebastian et al., 2018). Some of the advantages of this mode were described earlier including capturing principal time use across greater expanses of time including throughout the day, across multiple days, and at different points in an academic year. Innovative use of a web interface also allowed us to ask principals to provide fine grained information on who principals worked with for different tasks (see Camburn, Spillane et al., 2010, for a description of this web interface). In examining its validity, we compared data from three sources: the end of day log, an ESM instrument, and observations. In the ESM design, we prompted principals throughout their workdays at random times using a smart device or pager to complete a brief survey regarding the practice or activity that there were engaged in (see Camburn, Spillane et al., 2010). Compared to annual surveys or EOD logs, this approach reduces memory recall bias and collects data from respondents' natural work settings. Data from all three sources were collected on the same work days. We found that estimates from the daily log and ESM instruments were very similar. "In general, the daily logs and experience-sampling instruments yielded very similar estimates of the portion of time principals devote to the six leadership domains. In fact, the estimates produced by the two instruments rank order the six domains nearly identically." (Camburn, Spillane et al., 2010, p. 721). The observation data were then used to explain remaining discrepancies between the EOD and ESM instruments, Camburn, Spillane et al. (2010) described four factors that led to reporting errors: errors associated with brief events, noncontinuous events—those that occur in 'fits and starts', events that occur in the edges of time-blocks, and events that are overshadowed by other, more dramatic events. These provide an extension of Gronn's (2009) typology of errors in measurement instruments for principals, specific to the use of EOD instruments.

With colleagues, we have also assessed the validity of data from an annual survey by comparing it to evidence from a daily log (Camburn, Huff et al., 2010). With an instrument such as annual survey where the time gap between event occurrence and reporting is much greater than the daily log, errors due to faulty recall are more likely to undermine the validity of time-use reports. The results showed that the surveys were less accurate in measuring irregular or less frequently occurring events. Still, the study found considerable evidence for the validity of the survey instrument.

Financial cost

Researchers of course will endeavor to measure principal time use in the most cost effective way possible. There are some financial costs that are unique to particular data collection modes. With strategies utilizing an in-person researcher presence such as observations and interviews, there are researcher labor costs that do not exist with self-administered modes. This labor includes not only wages for conducting data collection activities, but also travel costs, and costs for developing and delivering observer or interviewer training. Within self-administered data collection modes, there are also distinct cost differences. With mail questionnaires there are costs for the printing of materials and postage that do not exist with web surveys. With web surveys there may be costs associated with programming that are not incurred with mail surveys.

Groves et al. (2009) report that "very few studies provide a detailed reporting of costs" (p. 173). Summarizing existing research, they report that data collection strategies that involve an in-person researcher presence are estimated to cost roughly twice as much as interviews or surveys conducted by phone. Groves et al. (2009) also report that phone surveys are estimated to cost between 1.2 and 1.7 times as much as self-administered mail surveys. Because researchers studying principal time use very rarely collect data over the phone, a comparison of the costs of in-person versus self-administered modes is of greater interest. Using the range of cost differentials reported by Groves et al. (2009) suggests that in-person data collection methods might exceed self-administered methods by a factor of 2.4–3.4. While the proliferation of readily accessible, and full featured web survey tools like Qualtrics and Survey Monkey have likely driven down the costs of conducting web surveys, data on how the costs of such surveys compare to other modes are relatively scarce. One of the few studies conducted by Cobanoglu et al. (2001) not surprisingly showed that web-based surveys are significantly less expensive than mail or fax-based survey methods.

There is little research that examines cost and data quality differences by mode within the confines of a single study. One of the few such studies was conducted by Pruchno and Hayden (2000) who compared costs and quality of data collected by interviews, telephone, and self-administered questionnaires. They found that the cost of data collection was 25 percent to 30 percent lower for the self-administered mode than for other modes. However, the quality of information collected, as measured by response rates and rates of missing data, was the poorest for self-administered questionnaires compared to other modes. The authors also compared respondents completing each mode on a range of background and demographic characteristics and found no significant differences.

Incentive payments to participants are often a major portion of total data collection costs. As we discuss below, incentive payments will be more effective to the degree that they are responsive to the burden data collection places on research participants. Teisl et al. (2005) note that including appropriate incentives can actually be cost effective, noting that a number of studies have found that "a small monetary incentive provides a more cost-effective approach compared to no incentives or relatively large incentives." (p. 365).

Burden

Different strategies for measuring principal time use place different amounts of burden on research participants. It is important to pay attention to the burden imposed by a study because it may be a factor in how seriously participants engage in a study, or whether they choose to participate at all.

Bradburn (1979) described four dimensions of respondent burden: survey or interview length, respondent effort required by data collection, respondent stress, and the frequency of data collection. Length refers to the total amount of time required to participate in all facets of the study including recruitment, consent, and data collection. The obvious implication regarding study length is that respondents may be less likely to participate in all or any study activities if the time commitment feels overly burdensome. The frequency of data collection is closely related to the issue of data collection length and indeed will inevitably a determinant of participation length. Effort refers to the challenge or difficulty of the data collection experience for respondents. Answering straightforward questions that one does not have to think about very deeply would translate into low effort while questions that are more cognitively taxing, or that require a respondent to search their records, are examples of high-effort experiences. Stress refers to the amount of personal discomfort a respondent experiences, either resulting from interview or survey questions, or from the social situation within which data are collected. Potentially embarrassing or sensitive questions could lead to respondent stress, as could observation of activities in which a respondent might be embarrassed by their actions.

The act of data collection has been productively described as a social exchange between research participants and researchers (Bradburn, 1979; Bradburn et al., 2004; Childers & Skinner, 1996). As such, data collection is governed by the kinds of social norms that govern other types of social interactions. The Childers and Skinners (1996) conceptual model of mail survey response behavior provides an instructive way of considering how burden might affect participation in data collection. Their model posits that decisions to participate in surveys are governed by the constructs of cooperation, trust, and commitment. They argue that with interviews and surveys, which involve cooperative mutual effort, there is an expectation of a "balanced exchange" in which both parties receive some benefit. They go on to argue that the decision to participate in research is governed by a cost/benefit calculation in which the "cost" or burden of participation is weighed against potential benefits. According to this model, burden is thus a major determinant of whether, and how, earnestly someone participates in research.

Research on the impact of respondent burden on willingness to participate and data quality is quite modest and of mixed quality. In one of the more robust examinations, Sharp & Frankel (1983) conducted a study in which interview length and effort were experimentally manipulated. In the length factor, respondents were assigned to participate in either 25- or 75-minute interviews. The "effort" factor contained two conditions: one in which respondents were asked to provide estimates based exclusively on their memory (low effort) and another where they were asked to consult their checkbooks or other records to answer questions (high effort). The researchers found a number of detrimental effects of greater interviewer length—respondents in the long interview group were more likely to be preoccupied during the interview, were less willing to be re-interviewed in the future, were more likely to characterize the interview as too long, and were more likely to characterize effort put into answer questions as "not well spent." The deleterious effects of burden were not universal however, as there no significant differences in unit non-response rates and no significant effects associated with the "effort" factor.

In our own research we have modest evidence about the association between study burden, participation rates, and data quality. With colleagues, we conducted a study of an executive training program for school principals which involved the collection of data from four sources: one-time questionnaires, daily questionnaires, ESM instruments, and shadowing observations. All principals in the participating district were asked to participate in the first three study components while only a subset of principals were observed. As previously mentioned, we provided a $100 incentive payment per year (US dollar, 2005–2007) for completing 15 daily questionnaires per year, 1 end of year questionnaire, and completing an ESM instrument. The study also involved substantial participant contact time and substantial strategic follow-up for non-response. With these field procedures, we achieved good principal participation with this substantially burdensome research design. Across seven data collection waves, the percentage of daily questionnaires completed by principals ranged from 67 to 93 percent, with an average of 78 percent (Camburn, Spillane et al., 2010) and the response rate for the end of year questionnaire was 75 percent (Camburn, Huff et al., 2010). We suspect that this combination of regular principal contact and incentive payment might have made participation in this study feel like something approaching a "balanced exchange," thus inducing the participation of sizeable percentages of principals.

Conclusion

We have presented a framework for evaluating, describing, and comparing data collection strategies that we have applied to the problem of measuring principal time use. The framework is grounded in survey research methodology literature, empirical research, and our experience with measuring and studying principal time use. The framework is intended to help researchers choose measurement strategies that maximize the validity of measures of principal time use while minimizing financial costs and respondent burden. A potential application of the framework might be for researchers to devise rubrics based on the framework's elements that they use to evaluate different measurement strategies. An example of such a rubric can found in Sudman (1983) who provides a "credibility scale" for evaluating small samples. Other chapters in this volume highlight the growing array of options available to researchers measuring principal time use. It is our hope that this framework might encourage the use of a more diverse set of measurement strategies than is currently in use.

Author note

This research was funded through a grant from the Institute of Education Sciences, award number R305E040085. Correspondence concerning this article should be addressed to Eric M. Camburn, Urban Education Research Center,

UMKC School of Education, Volker Campus 615 E 52nd St. Kansas City, MO 64110. Email: camburne@umkc.edu

References

Bradburn, N. M., Sudman, S., & Wansink, B. (2004). *Asking questions: The definitive guide to questionnaire design–for market research, political polls, and social and health questionnaires.* Hoboken, NJ: John Wiley & Sons.

Camburn, E., & Barnes, C. A. (2004). Assessing the validity of a language arts instruction log through triangulation. *The Elementary School Journal, 105*(1), 49–73.

Camburn, E. M., Huff, J. T., Goldring, E. B., & May, H. (2010). Assessing the validity of an annual survey for measuring principal leadership practice. *The Elementary School Journal, 111*(2), 314–335.

Camburn, E. M., Spillane, J. P., & Sebastian, J. (2010). Assessing the utility of a daily log for measuring principal leadership practice. *Educational Administration Quarterly, 46*(5), 707–737.

Cobanoglu, C., Moreo, P. J., & Warde, B. (2001). A comparison of mail, fax and web-based survey methods. *International Journal of Market Research, 43*(4), 1–15.

Cook, T. D., Campbell, D. T., & Shadish, W. (2002). *Experimental and quasi-experimental designs for generalized causal inference.* Boston, MA: Houghton Mifflin.

Curry, A., Flett, P., & Hollingsworth, I. (2006). *Managing information and systems: The business perspective.* Abingdon: Routledge.

Cycyota, C. S., & Harrison, D. A. (2006). What (not) to expect when surveying executives: A meta-analysis of top manager response rates and techniques over time. *Organizational Research Methods, 9*(2), 133–160.

Denzin, N. K. (1978). *The research act: A theoretical introduction to sociological methods* (2nd ed.). New York, NY: McGraw-Hill.

Duckworth, A. L., & Yeager, D. S. (2015). Measurement matters: Assessing personal qualities other than cognitive ability for educational purposes. *Educational Researcher, 44*(4), 237–251.

Greene, J. C., Caracelli, V. J., & Graham, W. F. (1989). Toward a conceptual framework for mixed-method evaluation designs. *Educational Evaluation and Policy Analysis, 11*(3), 255–274.

Gronn, P. (2003). *The new work of educational leaders: Changing leadership practice in an era of school reform.* London, UK: Sage/Paul Chapman.

Groves, R. M., Fowler Jr, F. J., Couper, M. P., Lepkowski, J. M., Singer, E., & Tourangeau, R. (2009). *Survey methodology* (2nd ed.). Hoboken, NJ: John Wiley & Sons.

Kmetz, J. T., & Willower, D. J. (1982). Elementary school principals' work behavior. *Educational Administration Quarterly, 18,* 62–78.

Martin, W. J., & Willower, D. J. (1981). The managerial behavior of high school principals. *Education Administration Quarterly, 17,* 69–90.

Patton, M. Q. (1980). *Qualitative evaluation methods.* Beverly Hills, CA: Sage.

Patton, M. Q. (2005). Qualitative research. *Encyclopedia of statistics in behavioral science.*

Peterson, K. D. (1977). The principal's tasks. *Administrator's Notebook, 28*(8), 1–4.

Pollock, K., & Hauseman, D. C. (2019). The use of e-mail and principals' work: A double-edged sword. *Leadership and Policy in Schools, 18*(3), 382–393.

Pruchno, R. A., & Hayden, J. M. (2000). Interview modality: Effects on costs and data quality in a sample of older women. *Journal of Aging and Health, 12*(1), 3–24.

Schaeffer, N. C., & Presser, S. (2003). The science of asking questions. *Annual Review of Sociology*, *29*(1), 65–88.

Sebastian, J., Camburn, E. M., & Spillane, J. P. (2018). Portraits of principal practice: Time allocation and school principal work. *Educational Administration Quarterly*, *54*(1), 47–84.

Sudman, S. (1983). Applied sampling. In Peter H. Rossi, James D. Wright & Andy B. Anderson (Eds.), *Handbook of survey research*. Orlando FL: Academic Press.

Teisl, M. F., Roe, B., & Vayda, M. E. (2005). Incentive effects on response rates, data quality, and survey administration costs. *International Journal of Public Opinion Research*, *18*(3), 364–373.

4 Identifying research opportunities from the methodological history of principal time-use studies

Craig Hochbein, Abby S. Mahone, and Sara C. Vanderbeck

Introduction

For more than 100 years, educators, policymakers, and researchers have been concerned with how principals spend their time. Understanding the relationships between how principals allot their time and educational outcomes could inform principal training, selection, development, performance, and evaluation. Historically, researchers have described the principal workday as an extensive schedule filled with numerous, intense, and fragmented activities (English, 1927; May & Supovitz, 2011; McAbee, 1958; Peterson, 1977). In addition to commonalities among the configuration of principals' schedules, researchers have consistently discovered that administrative tasks consume a greater percentage of principals' activities than instructional tasks (Bates, 1925; Buttram et al., 2008; Davis, 1953; Scott 1990). Although knowledge about principal time use has been derived from decades of studies, limited data research designs could weaken the validity of these claims. For instance, researchers often sampled small numbers of principals and observed limited periods of activity (Dwyer et al., 1983). Recognizing the implications stemming from such issues, Kmetz and Willower (1982) cautioned, "The small sample sizes that characterized all of the studies employing the method can easily lead to false generalizations" (p. 76). The purpose of this study was to identify principal time-use research opportunities. To achieve this purpose, we examined the methodologies of studies identified by a systematic review of principal time-use research and asked three research questions:

1 What data collection techniques have researchers employed to measure principal time use?
2 What is the sample composition of principal time-use studies?
3 What observation periods have researchers used to study principal time use?

Background

Principal responsibilities and influence

The roles and responsibilities of principals usually do not include teaching students. Yet, only students' socioeconomic characteristics and classroom teachers have accounted for more variance in student outcomes than principals. (Reynolds et al., 2014). Most researchers have investigated indirect means by which principals contributed to student outcomes (Hallinger & Heck, 1996). Examples of principal activity that scholars have hypothesized influence the effectiveness of teaching and learning include, but are not limited to, establishing trust between constituents (Pogodzinski et al., 2012), implementing efficient organizational procedures (Bossert et al., 1982), cultivating positive school culture (Dupper & Meyer-Adams, 2002), supervising classroom instruction (Grissom et al., 2013), fostering community relationships (Khalifa, 2012), and utilizing data to make decisions (Levin & Datnow, 2012).

In addition to contributing to effective schools, principals have also been identified as a primary factor responsible for successful school improvement (Duke & Salmonowicz, 2010). Researchers have demonstrated that principals exert indirect influence on school conditions that contribute to instructional improvement (Leithwood & Montgomery, 1982). In their recommendations for turning around persistently low-achieving schools, Herman and colleagues (2008) identified capable principals as a necessary, but insufficient factor. As a result of principals' influence, researchers have attempted to better understand how principals use their time to lead effective and improving schools (Lee & Hallinger, 2012).

Principal time-use findings

Decades of research have described the configuration of the typical day of a principal as an extensive schedule consisting of a substantial number of brief and unrelated engagements (Morris et al., 1984). Wolcott's (1973) ethnography demonstrated how extracurricular and community-oriented commitments extended the workday of the principal beyond the hours that school was in session. From structured observations of five female high school principals for 147.9 hours, Berman (1982a) calculated a mean of 84 daily activities and noted, "Many of these activities were started, interrupted, and resumed" (p. 76). Although Spillane and Hunt (2010) acknowledged these common findings about principals' schedules, they warned, "… the empirical knowledge-base on the practice of the school principal is relatively small and much of the literature predates the standards and accountability movement" (p. 294).

In addition to the configuration the principals' time use, researchers have also examined the content, focus, and purpose of principals' activities. For decades, researchers have reported that the majority of principals' time has not involved activities related to instruction (Sebastian et al., 2018; McClure, 1921). From the daily time logs of 112 principals working in Detroit, Bates (1925) estimated that the sample spent 51% of their time engaged in administrative duties, with 36% dedicated to instructional supervision. More than eight decades later, Horng and colleagues (2010) reported from single day observations of 65 principals working in Miami that the sample spent 48% of their time engaged in administrative duties, with 13% dedicated to instructional activities. Camburn et al. (2010) concluded, "The consistent finding that principals spend substantial time running the building and attending to student affairs suggests to us the existence of persistent structural constraints on principals' time that press them to attend to such issues rather than instructional leadership" (p. 730).

Although the majority of studies have attempted to describe the configuration and content of principal time use, some research designs have exploited differences to compare how principals use their time. For example, English (1927) compared the time use of ten rural principals with nine urban principals, discovering that the rural sample spent less time supervising instruction. Attempting to derive lessons about effective principal time use, Martinko and Gardner (1983) compared 25 principals identified as "high performing" against 19 peers identified as "moderately performing." Despite the differences they identified between their comparisons of high and moderately performing principals the researchers cautioned, "The large number of significance tests conducted compared to the relative paucity of significant differences found suggests the possibility that the results relating to performance level may be a function of chance" (Martinko & Gardner, 1983, p. 551).

Even fewer studies have attempted to associate principal time use with educational outcomes. For example, Horng and colleagues (2010) examined associations between principal time use and four distinct measures of school effectiveness and concluded, "The results show that time on organization management activities is associated with positive school outcomes" (p. 519). Relying on data collected within the same school district as Horng et al. (2010), Grissom et al. (2013) discovered an inverse relationship between informal principal observations and student achievement. In contrast, May and Supovitz (2011) found a correlation between teacher reported instructional changes and frequency of interactions with their principals. From the same sample as May and Supovitz (2011), May et al. (2012) utilized longitudinal data to further examine the link between principal activity and student performance. Although they discovered statistically significant relationships between leadership activities and student achievement, the researchers hypothesized that "… the more plausible causal relationship is that school context drives principals' activities" (May et al., 2012, p. 433).

Principal time-use methodologies

The accurate interpretation of findings from principal time-use studies compels consideration of the methodologies employed to collect and analyze data. Collecting valid time-use data requires numerous methodological considerations by researchers (Zirkel et al., 2015). The variety of tasks, multiple locations, and variable times of principal activity further challenge the capabilities of researchers to accurately capture principal time use (Hochbein et al., 2018). To address the challenges of studying principal time use, researchers have employed four types of collection methods: observation, daily instruments, event sampling methodology (ESM), and one-time surveys (Camburn et al., 2010).

Since at least 1913, researchers have conducted observational studies to collect data about how principals allocated their time (McMurry, 1913). Although observational studies provide rich and continuous data, shadowing principals requires extensive resources, which limits sample sizes (i.e., Wolcott, 1973). As a cost-effective means of gathering data from large samples, researchers have implemented one-time surveys, but this methodology often gathers principals' generalized estimation or categorization of time use (Lavigne et al., 2016). To mitigate the recall or recency bias of principals, as well as accurately capture the continuous daily experiences of principals, researchers have implemented daily instruments (i.e., Sebastian et al., 2018). Researchers have used ESM to reduce the burden of principals completing time diaries or daily logs (Hochbein et al., 2018), but the results from ESM might not accurately represent the prevalence of principals' activities (Camburn et al., 2010). To reduce the limitations of any single collection method, researchers with sufficient resources have utilized multiple forms of these data collection techniques (i.e., Barnes et al., 2010).

Several authors have provided further details about the advantages and disadvantages of these data collection techniques to study principal time use (Camburn et al., 2010; Gronn, 2003; Spillane & Zuberi, 2009). Researchers have implemented these various techniques to collect data across the numerous settings of principal activity, as well as during the extensive principal work schedule (Hochbein et al., 2018). Researchers have not only used a variety of techniques to capture data on principal time use, but they also have cited common methodological limitations, including small sample size and abbreviated observation periods (Martin & Willower, 1981). Although individual studies might suffer validity threats imposed by limited sample sizes and observation periods, consistent findings across a historical collection of principal time-use research that included multiple forms of data collection, heterogeneous sampling, and representative periods of observation could mitigate such threats.

Methodology

To examine the distribution of data collection techniques, sample composition, and observation periods of principal time studies, we conducted a systematic review of principal time-use research. Our initial attempts to systematically identify principal time-use research revealed that pertinent research was interspersed among studies exploring the relationship between principal leadership and school outcomes. To avoid biasing our sample through the exclusion of pertinent studies, we applied a "snowball" sampling technique to the cited references of five contemporary articles that specifically focused on principal time use: Camburn et al. (2010), Grissom et al. (2013), Horng et al. (2010), Lee and Hallinger (2012), and May et al. (2012).

Many of the referenced works offered conceptual or theoretical estimations of appropriate principal time use (Hallinger & Murphy, 1985). Another subset of articles empirically gathered perception or opinion data on principal time use, but did not directly measure principal time use (Lavigne et al., 2016). In addition, we located numerous studies that examined (Gaziel, 1995; López et al., 2012; Rosenblatt & Somech, 1998) or compared (Calder & Shibles, 1974; Lee & Hallinger, 2012) school leader time use from various international contexts.

Given the breadth of works related to principal time use, we developed two criteria that guided the inclusion of studies for the review.

First, we required sampling structures that exclusively sampled principals leading schools that operated in the United States. Although many high-quality studies examined school leaders working in international contexts (Lee & Hallinger, 2012; Rosenblatt & Somech, 1998), our concern with the external validity of findings compelled us to exclude international studies. This inclusion requirement further excluded non-empirical works, as well as surveys that sought non-principals' perceptions of principal time use. Second, we required that the collection of data includes a measurement of time. Requiring time measurement eliminated studies that surveyed principals to estimate the percentage of time they allotted to specified tasks.

Beginning our review with the references cited in the original five articles, we independently reviewed article references. When we identified a study for inclusion in the review, we subsequently searched its cited references for additional studies. Once we exhausted the review of cited references, we initiated a similar process of reviewing all studies that cited a study included in our sample for review. At intermittent points throughout the process, we compared our independent identification of studies, using the two criteria to resolve disagreements.

Our sampling technique identified 5746 distinct references. To locate references, we utilized a variety of internet databases, made interlibrary loan requests, and contacted authors. From reviewing the titles and abstracts of the references we obtained, we identified 517 manuscripts for more thorough review of methodological procedures. After applying our inclusion criteria, we identified 55 manuscripts that empirically examined principal time use. The identified manuscripts spanned publication between 1920 and 2015, which comprised of both qualitative and quantitative methodologies, and encompassed a variety of formats, including books, journal articles, dissertation studies, and papers presented at peer-reviewed conferences.

However, for the purposes of examining methodologies, we did not include all 55 manuscripts in our analytic sample. Twenty-four of the manuscripts relied on eight non-unique sampling structures (Table 4.1). For instance, our systematic review identified a dissertation by Ariranta (2000) and paper presented by Blendinger et al. (2000), which both reported findings from data collected on a rural elementary school principal during a 16-day observation period. To avoid bias in our analysis, we included just one study from each of the eight non-unique samples. For each of the eight non-unique groupings, we selected the study with the largest sample size. In cases of identical sample sizes, we prioritized the most recently published articles, and then those in peer-reviewed outlets.

After including only a single manuscript from the non-unique groupings, our sample consisted of 39 manuscripts. Several of the manuscripts included more than one data collection procedure, but relied on the same sampling structure (i.e., Spillane & Zuberi, 2009). When researchers applied the multiple methods to the same sample for the same observation period, we counted the sample and observation period just once. However, for manuscripts with multiple sampling

64 *Craig Hochbein, Abby S. Mahone, et al*

Table 4.1 Principal time-use studies with non-unique sampling structures

Location	Authors	Sample size	Study included
Two northeast states	Kmetz and Willower (1982)	5	Yes
	Kmetz (1982)	5	
Chicago area	Krug, Scott, and Ahadi (1989)	81	
	Scott (1990)	81	Yes
Chicago city	Morris et al. (1981)	16	
	Morris et al. (1982)	24	
	Morris et al. (1984)	24	Yes
Cloverville	Barnes et al. (2010)	48	
	Camburn et al. (2006)	38	
	Camburn et al. (2010)	48	
	Goldring et al. (2008)	46	
	May and Supovitz (2011)	51	Yes
	May et al. (2012)	39	
	Spillane and Hunt (2010)	38	
	Spillane et al. (2008)	42	
	Spillane et al. (2007)	42	
Metropolis	Berman (1982a)	5	
	Berman (1982b)	5	Yes
Northeast Mississippi	Ariratana (2000)	1	
	Blendinger et al. (2000)	1	Yes
Northeast state	Martin (1980)	5	
	Martin and Willower (1981)	5	Yes
Oregon	McAbee (1957)	62	
	McAbee (1958)	62	Yes

strategies (Grissom et al., 2015), we only included the sample size from procedures that satisfied our three inclusion criteria.

With the sample of manuscripts systematically identified, we examined their methodologies, focusing on the type of data collection, sample composition, and observation periods. For the type of data collection, we specifically assessed the frequency with which researchers employed the methods, as well as the publication data. We analyzed the composition of samples and periods of observation by the same three criteria: school level, school locale, and time of the year that the observation occurred.

Results

Among the sample of 39 manuscripts, researchers sampled 2271 principals and reported 976 days of observations. Mean statistics demonstrated that manuscripts averaged a sample of 58 principals observed for 28 days. However, calculations of the median sample and observed days identified 24 principals observed for six days. The manuscripts included principals leading elementary, middle, and high schools that operated in rural, suburban, and urban locales. In addition, the manuscripts also included observation periods during the fall, winter, and spring, as well as throughout the academic and calendar year.

Methodological history of time use studies 65

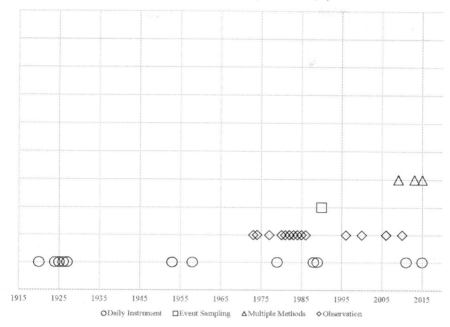

Figure 4.1 Principal time use data collection techniques across time

Data collection

Analysis of the data collection techniques implemented in the studies revealed four types: daily instrument, event sampling, multiple methodologies, and observation. The earliest studies of principal time use collected data through daily instruments and researchers have continued to rely on this technique (Figure 4.1). Collecting data via observation began during the 1970s, yet researchers have implemented observation more often than the other techniques. However, since 2000, researchers have begun applying a combination of data collection techniques to capture principal time-use data, which has included ESM, observation, daily instrument, and one-time surveys.

School locale

In studying principal time use, researchers have more frequently sampled principals from urban schools or a combination of locales (Table 4.2). We identified three manuscripts that focused specifically on rural (2) or suburban (1) schools. The 13 manuscripts that sampled principals from a combination of locales accounted for 71% of the total sample of principals and 64% of observation days. Despite the prevalence of manuscripts that sampled principals from more than one locale, only three have occurred since 1985 (Buttram et al., 2006; Goldring et al., 2015; Turnbull et al., 2009).

Table 4.2 Sample size and observation periods by school locale

| | Sample size |||| Observation period ||||
| | Manuscripts || Principals || Manuscripts || Days ||
	N	%	n	%	n	%	N	%
Population	39		2271		35		976	
Rural	2	5	4	<1	2	6	31	3
Urban	16	41	529	23	14	40	257	26
Suburban	1	3	1	<1	1	3	10	1
Combination	14	36	1635	72	12	34	633	65
Total	33	85	2169	96	29	83	931	95

In contrast, half of the 16 manuscripts that focused on urban locales have been conducted since 1986. These eight more recent studies accounted for 84% of the sample of principals working in urban locales and 20% of the overall sample of principals. Further examination of the manuscripts that examined urban locales also revealed that the sampling involved a limited number of urban settings. For instance, Miami-Dade County Public Schools accounted for the research sites of three studies (Grissom et al., 2013; Grissom et al., 2015; Horng et al., 2010), with one other manuscript situated in another large urban area (Scott, 1990).

School level

Unlike the trend toward focusing on schools from a single locale, researchers have more recently sampled principals from multiple school levels. Half of the 14 samples that included principals from multiple levels have occurred since 2009. In contrast, 21 of the 24 manuscripts that focused on elementary or high school principals were published prior to the adoption of the No Child Left Behind Act. Finally, none of the 38 manuscripts that specified school level exclusively examined principals leading middle schools (Table 4.3).

Table 4.3 Sample size and observation periods by school level

| | Sample size |||| Observation period ||||
| | Manuscripts || Principals || Manuscripts || Days ||
	N	%	n	%	N	%	N	%
Population	39		2271		35		976	
Elementary	15	38	335	15	15	43	362	37
High	9	23	856	38	7	20	173	18
Combination	14	36	1075	47	13	37	441	45
Total	38	97	2266	99	35	100	976	100

Table 4.4 Sample size and observation periods by time of year

	Sample size				Observation period			
	Manuscripts		*Principals*		*Manuscripts*		*Days*	
	n	%	n	%	n	%	n	%
Population	39		2271		35		976	
Fall	5	13	38	2	5	14	37	4
Winter	7	18	136	6	7	20	66	7
Spring	8	21	662	29	7	20	27	3
Academic	7	18	199	9	7	20	457	47
Calendar	1	3	373	16	1	3	319	33
Total	28	72	1408	62	27	77	906	93

Observation periods

Twenty-seven of the 39 manuscripts specified the time of year when researchers measured principal time use, which accounted for 62% of the total sample of principals and 93% of observed days (Table 4.4). The researchers reported five common observation periods: fall, winter, spring, academic year, and calendar year. Yet, we could not discern any longitudinal trends among the implementation of observation periods. Each of the five observation periods included a manuscript from within the last three decades and all five observation periods are represented among the nine manuscripts released since 2000.

Although manuscripts demonstrated similar distribution across the observation periods, sample sizes and days observed exhibited substantial differences by time of year. For instance, manuscripts specifying a spring data collection accounted for 30% of the total sample of principals, yet 3% of the observed days. Unsurprisingly, manuscripts focused on data collection throughout the academic and calendar year averaged longer observation periods than seasonal collections. The seven manuscripts that collected data across the academic and calendar year accounted for 23% of the total sample of principals, but 78% of the total number of observed days.

Synthesis

From the results of the examination of the methodologies employed by researchers across the history of studies that examined the time use of principals leading schools in the United States, we identified three systematic limitations. First, researchers relied on a limited number of data collection techniques. Although these data collection techniques might have best aligned with capturing principal activity, they also suffer from limitations such as recall bias, estimation errors, and observer influence (Shadish et al., 2002). In addition, researchers' reliance on self-report and observational methodologies have likely narrowed the factors and measurements used to study principal time use. For example, every study identified in this review examined either the configuration or content of principal time use.

Second, the sampling structures of principal time-use studies have lacked adequate representation of principals. Of the original 55 empirical manuscripts identified by our systematic review, we discovered that 24 relied on eight non-unique sampling structures. Nine different manuscripts reported findings from a sample of the same principals leading schools in "Cloverville," an urban district operating 42 schools in the southeastern United States. Multiple reports of findings from a single sample could contribute to bias in generalizations about how principals use their time. For example, in a subsequent study of principal time use, Grissom et al. (2015) cited five of the nine manuscripts derived from the Cloverville sample.

Third, observation periods have not captured the full extent of the expectations and responsibilities of principals. Similar to the gaps identified in the sampling of locale and school level, we also identified a need for a greater variety of observation during the year. Although manuscripts were evenly distributed across five common observation periods, the number of sampled principals and observed days were not. The greatest number of principals was observed during the spring, but for the least number of days. Moreover, despite the extensive preparation needed to lead an efficient and effective school year, only a single study examined the time use of principals during summer months.

Together these results indicated that researchers have derived knowledge about principal time use from self-report and observational data collected during common observation periods from samples of principals working in similar contexts. These systematic limitations have exposed plausible threats to the validity of claims about principal time use. For example, common sampling structures have constrained the knowledge about the time use of principals working in different contexts. However, the identification of these limitations indicates future research opportunities.

Recommendations

Nearly a century of empirical studies have reported consistent findings about principal time use. Yet, our examination of data collection, sample selection, and observation periods indicated plausible threats to the validity of claims about principal time use. These systematic limitations provide opportunities for researchers interested in principal time use. To facilitate the development of future principal time-use research, we suggest recommendations and cite examples that exhibit the potential to address the identified limitations.

Identify different data collection opportunities

Although researchers have begun to mitigate validity threats by implementing multiple forms of data collection, existing datasets provide researchers of principal time use with opportunities to employ data collection techniques that do not rely on self-report or observation. For example, Drake (2015) collected the timestamps from principals' access of a data warehouse. These timestamps enabled analyses of the frequency, timing, and duration of principals' data use. For principals' duties that rely on digital access, researchers could employ similar strategies to collect data on principal time use. Rather than rely on principals' perceptions (Pollock & Hauseman, 2019), Hochbein (2020) analyzed the timestamps of email communications to assess the contribution of email to principal time use.

Technological advancements have provided opportunities to expand not only data collection techniques, but also measures of principal time use. For instance, Riley (2014) used survey measures to record data on principal time use and associated it with critical factors like well-being and attrition. To complement these self-report measures, researchers could employ activity trackers to independently record measurements such as heart rate, distance traveled, and even amount of sleep.

Diversify sampling strategies

To add diversity to the literature on principal time use, researchers should purposefully sample principals from different contexts. The sampling of principals from large urban school districts has facilitated sophisticated quantitative analysis and research designs (i.e., Grissom et al., 2013). However, rural and suburban principals might encounter challenges, resources, and other unobserved factors that compel them to use their time differently (Stewart & Matthews, 2015). Recruiting principals from multiple settings, such as different districts, geographic locations, and performance levels, will enhance researchers' abilities to examine the contribution of context to principal time use. For instance, Goldring et al. (2019) evaluated the influence of a professional development initiative on the time use of 16 principals working in four school districts. Specifically focusing on non-metropolitan contexts, Mahone (2018) analyzed the time use of 62 principals from 20 districts. Similarly, Vanderbeck's (2020) study of principal time use during the summer months included 12 principals from eight school districts.

In addition to studying schools from different locales and levels, researchers might also examine how principals in different types of schools spend their time. Researchers could examine the time use of principals leading vocational, charter, independent, and Catholic schools. For instance, Mulvaney Hoyer and Sparks (2017) analyzed data from the Schools and Staffing Survey to compare the time use of principals from private and public schools. Similarly, Sun and Ni (2016) analyzed principal practices to compare principal turnover in traditional and charter schools. Such comparisons further address validity threats that stem from plausible contextual influences on principal time use.

Expand observation periods

Similar to diversifying principal sampling, researchers might also expand the times when they observe principal time use. The majority of principal time-use studies have observed principals during "typical" periods during the academic year. Researchers could observe principals as they engage less frequent, but annual activities. Examples of such examinations could include principal time use during the summer months or first weeks of school. Additionally, researchers might examine principal time use during activities, such as teacher evaluation or selection.

In addition, longitudinal studies present opportunities for researchers of principal time use. Several studies utilized extended observations or conducted multiple samples throughout the year (Turnbull et al., 2009). However, observing the same sample of principals during the same period across multiple years could inform knowledge about the stability and predictability of principal time use. Moreover, such studies would enable analyses of how principals allocate their time as they gain leadership experience.

Concluding remarks

Although researchers across the history of principal time-use studies have reported similar findings, their studies also tend to rely on similar data collection, sampling, and observation protocols. As scholars have highlighted the influence of school context on principal time use (May et al., 2012), future research needs to sample contexts and collected data not sufficiently represented in prior research. Such work might not only fill obvious gaps, but also expand to contexts such as charter schools (i.e., Ni et al., 2015). To increase knowledge of how principals effectively use their time in complex contexts, future research can seize opportunities to diversify data collection, sampling structures, and observation periods.

Author note

Correspondence concerning this chapter should be addressed to Craig Hochbein, Lehigh University, College of Education, Bethlehem, PA 18015.
Email: craig.hochbein@lehigh.edu. Phone: 610-758-6249. Fax: 610-758-3227

References

Ariratana, W. (2000). *Field investigation of on-the-job behavior of an elementary school principal*. [Unpublished doctoral dissertation]. Mississippi State University, Starkville, MS.

Barnes, C. A., Camburn, E., Sanders, B. R., & Sebastian, J. (2010). Developing instructional leaders: Using mixed methods to explore the black box of planned change in principals' professional practice. *Educational Administration Quarterly, 46*(2), 241–279.

Bates, G. (1925). Functions of the elementary school principal. *Journal of Educational Method, 4*, 178–184.

Berman, J. (1982a). *The Managerial behavior of female high school principals: Implications for training*. [Unpublished doctoral dissertation]. Columbia University, New York, NY.

Berman, J. (1982b). *The Managerial behavior of female high school principals: Implications for training*. Paper presented at the Annual Meeting of the American Educational Research Association, New York, NY.

Blendinger, J., Ariratana, W., & Jones, L.T. (2000). *Field investigation of on-the-job behavior of an elementary school principal.* Paper presented at the Annual Meeting of the Mid-South Educational Research Association, Bowling Green, KY.

Bossert, S. T., Dwyer, D. C., Rowan, B., & Lee, G. V. (1982). The instructional management role of the principal. *Educational Administration Quarterly, 18*(3), 34–64.

Buttram, J. L., Mead, H., Loftus, D., & Wilson, J. O. (2008). *Allocation of school leaders' time.* Paper presented at the Annual Meeting of American Educational Research Association, New York, NY.

Calder, C. R., & Shibles, M. (1974). The British Headmaster and the American Principal: A comparison of roles. *The Elementary School Journal, 74*(7), 393–398.

Camburn, E. M., Spillane, J. P., & Sebastian, J. (2006). *Measuring principal practice: Results from two promising measurement strategies.* Paper presented at the Annual Meeting of the American Educational Research Association, San Francisco, CA.

Camburn, E. M., Spillane, J. P., & Sebastian, J. (2010). Assessing the utility of a daily log for measuring principal leadership practice. *Educational Administration Quarterly, 46*(5), 707–737.

Davis, H. C. (1953). Where does the time go? *California Journal of Secondary Education, 28*(6), 347–361.

Drake, T. A. (2015). *How technology, strategic decision making, and school context influence principals' use of a data warehouse: A latent class growth analysis.* [Unpublished doctoral dissertation]. Vanderbilt University, Nashville, TN.

Duke, D. L., & Salmonowicz, M. J. (2010). Key decisions of a first-year 'turnaround' principal. *Educational Management, Administration, & Leadership, 38*(1), 33–58.

Dupper, D. R., & Meyer-Adams, N. (2002). Low-level violence a neglected aspect of school culture. *Urban Education, 37*(3), 350–364.

Dwyer, D., Lee, G., Rowan, B., & Bossert, S. (1983). *Five principals in action: Perspectives on instructional management.* San Francisco, CA: Far West Laboratory for Educational Research.

English, M. (1927). A comparative study of the time distribution of rural and urban principals. *National Education Association Bulletin, 7*(1), 4–19.

Gaziel, H. (1995). Managerial work patterns of principals at high-and average-performing Israeli elementary schools. *The Elementary School Journal, 96*(2), 179–194.

Goldring, E., Huff, J., May, H., & Camburn, E. (2008). School context and individual characteristics: What influences principal practice? *Journal of Educational Administration, 46*(3), 332–352.

Goldring, E., Grissom J., Neumerski, C. M., Murphy, J., & Blissett, R. (2015). *Making time for instructional leadership. Volume: 1: The evolution of the SAM process.* New York, NY: The Wallace Foundation.

Goldring, E., Grissom, J., Neumerski, C. M., Blissett, R., Murphy, J., & Porter, A. (2019). Increasing principals' time on instructional leadership: exploring the SAM® process. *Journal of Educational Administration, 58*(1), 19–37.

Grissom, J. A., Loeb, S., & Master, B. (2013). Effective instructional time use for school leaders: Longitudinal evidence from observations of principals. *Educational Researcher, 42*(8), 433–444.

Grissom, J. A., Loeb, S., & Mitani, H. (2015). Principal time management skills: Explaining patterns in principals' time use, job stress, and perceived effectiveness. *Journal of Educational Administration, 53*(6), 773–793.

Gronn, P. (2003). *The new work of educational leaders: Changing leadership practice in an era of school reform.* Thousand Oaks, CA: Sage/Paul Chapman.

Hallinger, P., & Heck, R. H. (1996). Reassessing the principal's role in school effectiveness: A review of empirical research, 1980–1995. *Educational Administration Quarterly*, *32*(1), 5–44.

Hallinger, P., & Murphy, J. (1985). Assessing the instructional management behavior of principals. *The Elementary School Journal*, *86*(2), 217–247.

Herman, R., Dawson, P., Dee, T., Greene, J., Maynard, R., & Redding, S. (2008). *Turning around chronically low performing schools*. Washington, DC: United States Department of Education.

Hochbein, C. (2020). You've got email. *Educational Leadership*, *77*, 42–45.

Hochbein, C., Dever, B. V., White, G., Mayger, L. K., & Gallagher, E. (2018). Confronting methodological challenges in studying school leader time use through technological advancements: A pilot study. *Educational Management Administration & Leadership*, *46*(4), 659–678.

Horng, E. L., Klasik, D., & Loeb, S. (2010). Principal's time use and school effectiveness. *American Journal of Education*, *116*(4), 491–523.

Khalifa, M. (2012). A re-new-ed paradigm in successful urban school leadership: Principal as community leader. *Educational Administration Quarterly*, *48*(3), 424–467.

Kmetz, J. T. (1982). *The work behavior of elementary school principals*. [Unpublished doctoral dissertation]. The Pennsylvania State University, University Park, PA.

Kmetz, J. T., & Willower, D. J. (1982). Elementary school principals' work behavior. *Educational Administration Quarterly*, *18*(4), 62–78.

Krug, S., Scott, C., & Ahadi, S. (1989). *An experience sampling approach to the study of principal instructional leadership I: Results from the principal activity sampling form*. Champaign, IL: University of Illinois at Urbana-Champaign University High Laboratory School.

Lavigne, H. J., Shakman, K., Zweig, J., & Greller, S. L. (2016). *Principals' time, tasks, and professional development: An analysis of Schools and Staffing Survey data* (REL 2017–201). United States Department of Education, Institute of Education Sciences, National Center for Education Evaluation and Regional Assistance, Regional Educational Laboratory Northeast & Islands.

Lee, M., & Hallinger, P. (2012). National contexts influencing principals' time use and allocation: economic development, societal culture, and educational system. *School Effectiveness and School Improvement*, *23*(4), 461–482.

Leithwood, K. A., & Montgomery, D. J. (1982). The role of the elementary school principal in program improvement. *Review of Educational Research*, *52*, 309–339.

Levin, J. A., & Datnow, A. (2012). The principal role in data-driven decision making: Using case-study data to develop multi-mediator models of educational reform. *School Effectiveness and School Improvement*, *23*(2), 179–201.

López, V., Ahumada, L., Galdames, S., & Madrid, R. (2012). School principals at their lonely work: Recording workday practices through ESM logs. *Computers & Education*, *58*(1), 413–422.

Mahone, A. S. (2018). *Principal behaviors outside large metropolis school districts: Exploring the relationships between time use and school context*. [Unpublished doctoral dissertation]. Lehigh University, Bethlehem, PA.

Martin, W. J. (1980). *The managerial behavior of high school principals*. [Unpublished doctoral dissertation]. The Pennsylvania State University, University Park, PA.

Martin, W. J., & Willower, D. J. (1981). The managerial behavior of high school principals. *Educational Administration Quarterly*, *17*(1), 69–90.

Martinko, M. J., & Gardner, W. L. (1983). *An executive summary of the behavior of high performing educational managers: An observational study*. Tallahassee, FL: Department of Management, College of Business, Florida State University.

May, H., & Supovitz, J.A. (2011). The scope of principal efforts to improve instruction. *Educational Administration Quarterly, 47*, 332–352.

May, H., Huff, J., & Goldring, E. (2012). A longitudinal study of principals' activities and student performance. *School Effectiveness and School Improvement, 23*(4), 417–439.

McAbee, H. V. (1957). *The Oregon secondary school principal and his job*. [Unpublished doctoral dissertation]. University of Oregon, Eugene, OR.

McAbee, H. V. (1958). Time for the job. *NASSP Bulletin, 42*(236), 39–44.

McClure, W. (1921). The functions of the elementary-school principal. *The Elementary School Journal, 21*(7), 500–514.

McMurry, F. M. (1913). *Elementary school standards*. New York, NY: World Book Company.

Morris, V. C., Crowson, R., Hurwitz, E., & Porter-Gehrie, C. (1981). *The urban principal: Discretionary decision-making in a large educational organization*. Washington, DC: National Institute of Education.

Morris, V. C., Crowson, R., Hurwitz, E., & Porter-Gehrie, C. (1982). *The urban principal: Middle manager in the educational bureaucracy*. Phi Delta Kappan, 689–692.

Morris, V. C., Crowson, R., Porter-Gehrie, C., & Hurwitz, E. (1984). *Principals in action: The reality of managing schools*. Princeton, NC: Merrill.

Mulvaney Hoyer, K., & Sparks, D. (2017). *How principals in public and private schools use their time: 2001–12*. Washington, DC: United States Department of Education.

Ni, Y., Sun, M., Rorrer, A. (2015). Principal turnover: Upheaval and uncertainty in charter schools? *Educational Administration Quarterly, 51*(3), 409–437.

Peterson, K. D. (1977). The principal's tasks. *Administrator's Notebook, 26*(8), 2–5.

Pollock, K., & Hauseman, D. C. (2019). The use of e-mail and principals' work: A double-edged sword. *Leadership and Policy in Schools, 18*(3), 382–393.

Pogodzinski, B., Youngs, P., Frank, K. A., & Belman, D. (2012). Administrative climate and novices' intent to remain teaching. *The Elementary School Journal, 113*(2), 252–275.

Reynolds, D., Sammons, P., De Fraine, B., Van Damme, J., Townsend, T., Teddlie, C., & Stringfield, S. (2014). Educational effectiveness research: A state-of-the-art review. *School Effectiveness and School Improvement, 25*(2), 197–230.

Riley, P. (2014). *Australian principal occupational health, safety and wellbeing survey: 2011–2014 data*. Brisbane: Australian Catholic University.

Rosenblatt, Z. & Somech, A. (1998). The work behavior of Israeli elementary school principals: Expectations versus reality. *Educational Administration Quarterly, 34*(4), 505–532.

Scott, C. (1990). *An experience sampling approach to the study of principal instructional leadership II: A comparison of activities and beliefs as bases for understanding effective school leadership*. Project Report.

Sebastian, J., Camburn, E., & Spillane, J. (2018). Portraits of principal practice: Time allocation and school principal work. *Educational Administration Quarterly, 54*(1), 47–84.

Shadish, W. R., Cook, T. D., & Campbell, D. T. (2002). *Experimental and quasi-experimental designs for generalized causal inference*. Boston, MA: Houghton Mifflin.

Spillane, J. P., & Hunt, B. R. (2010). Days of their lives: a mixed-methods, descriptive analysis of the men and women at work in the principal's office. *Journal of Curriculum Studies, 42*(3), 293–331.

Spillane, J. P., & Zuberi, A. (2009). Designing and piloting a leadership daily practice log: Using logs to study the practice of leadership. *Educational Administration Quarterly*, 45(3), 375–423.

Spillane, J. P., Camburn, E. M., & Pareja, A. (2007). Taking a distributed perspective to the school principal's workday. *Leadership and Policy in Schools*, 6(1), 103–125.

Spillane, J. P., Camburn, E. M., & Pustejovsky, J. (2008). Taking a distributed perspective: Epistemological and methodological tradeoffs in operationalizing the leaderplus aspect. *Journal of Educational Administration*, 46(2), 189–213.

Stewart, C., & Matthews, J. (2015). The lone ranger in rural education: The small rural school principal and professional development. *The Rural Educator*, 36(3), 1–13.

Sun, M., & Ni, Y. (2016). Work environments and labor markets: Explaining principal turnover gap between charter schools and traditional public schools. *Educational Administration Quarterly*, 52(1), 144–183.

Turnbull, B. J., Haslam, M. B., Arcaira, E. R., Riley, D. L., Sinclair, B., & Coleman, S. (2009) *Evaluation of the school administration manager project*. New York, NY: The Wallace Foundation.

Vanderbeck, S. C. (2020). *The content and configuration of principal time use during the summer and fall*. [Unpublished doctoral dissertation]. Lehigh University, Bethlehem, PA.

Wolcott, H. F. (1973). *The man in the principal's office: An ethnography*. New York, NY: Rinehart and Winston.

Zirkel, S., Garcia, J. A., & Murphy, M. C. (2015). Experience-sampling research methods and their potential for education research. *Educational Researcher*, 44(1), 7–16.

5 Principals' direct interaction with individual students
A missing piece in principal leadership research

Moosung Lee, Allan Walker, and Geoffrey Riordan

Introduction

Over the last three decades, school leadership research exploring principals' effects on student learning outcomes clearly indicates that principal leadership is the second most significant in-school factor shaping student learning outcomes (see Bryk, Sebring, Allensworth, Luppescu, & Easton, 2010; Heck & Hallinger, 2009; Leithwood & Louis, 2012; Robinson, Lloyd, & Rowe, 2008; Scheernes, 2012). Prior studies also suggest that principals' effects on student learning are indirect (Hallinger & Heck, 1996) suggesting that principals affect student learning outcomes by influencing teaching practices such as instruction, curriculum development, and collaboration. The indirect model of principals' effects on student learning has not only been empirically demonstrated by accumulated studies, but it also makes sense conceptually, given that principals rarely teach students in classroom settings.

However, the research focus on the indirect effect of principals' work has had the effect of masking the fact that principals spend time interacting with individual students. We know that principals routinely interact with individual students (Waters, Marzano, & McNulty, 2004). This interaction comprises various activities, including visiting classrooms, monitoring student work, acknowledging and promoting academic achievement, disciplining, guiding and reviewing individual cases of academic failure (Gentilucci & Muta, 2007). Drawing on his data of 83 school principals in Chicago, Lortie (2009) reported that 18% of those school principals indicated relational tasks involving students, mainly for disciplinary issues, were part of their daily routine with these tasks judged to be their least enjoyable leadership responsibility.

We aim to extend our current knowledge of school principals' behaviors by providing empirical findings on principals' time use when interacting with individual students. Specifically, we address the following questions: *Do school principals spend time for interaction with individual students? If so, how much time do school principals spend time for interaction with individual students?* In addition, to identify how organizational and macro contexts are associated with principals' time use for interacting with individual students, we explore the following supplementary question: *What organizational and macro contexts are significantly associated with principals' time use for interaction with individual students?*

Our study is conceptually and analytically informed by Lee and Hallinger's (2012) cross-national study that explored national contexts that shape principals' time use and allocation in key leadership domains, including curriculum and pedagogical development, administration and parent and community relations. That study did not investigate principals' interaction with individual students. Therefore, our investigation contributes to expanding the area of cross-national studies that we hope will contribute to the further development of the field of comparative school leadership. Finally, our empirical findings will provide a foundation for future research aiming to investigate principals' direct effects on student outcomes.

Principals' interactions with individual students

Principals' effects on student outcomes have been viewed as indirect in the mainstream research literature (Hallinger & Heck, 1996) as principals influence student outcomes mainly through teachers' work. As a result, little attention has been paid to principals' interaction or direct involvement in student outcomes. There are only a handful of studies that illuminate principals' interactions with individual students. Specifically, two distinctive groups of studies are found. The first set of studies examine principals' direct involvement in student learning. The studies have commonly reported that there is a direct effect of principals on student academic achievement through principals' spending a substantial amount of time in engaging in student learning process (e.g., Gentilucci & Muta, 2007; Nettles, 2005; Nettles & Herrington, 2007; Silva, White, & Yoshida, 2011). For instance, Silva et al. (2011) conducted an experimental study and found that students' reading achievement was significantly and directly impacted by principals' one-to-one support for low-achieving students. Similarly, Nettles and Herrington (2007) reported an improvement in student learning outcomes as a result of principals' interaction with individual students especially when principals provided clear goals, monitoring processes and high expectations directly for individual students. Furthermore, this was particularly true for high-risk students. Likewise, Gentilucci and Muta (2007) reported that students who believed that principals were actively engaged in student life via individual conversations and contacts had a tendency to have higher levels of academic motivation and achievement in their schools.

Another group of studies has documented how principals' interaction with individual students contributes to improving the quality and safety of the learning environment in school (e.g., Astor, Benbenishty, & Estrada, 2009; Dwyer, Lee, Rowan, & Bossert, 1983; Lortie, 2009; Robinson & Aronica, 2015). This research shows that principals' interactions with individual students are primarily intended to address school safety, problem behavior, student well-being, and disciplinary matters, rather than having a direct impact on student learning. For example, a case study conducted by Astor et al. (2009) of nine Israeli schools showed that principals' direct interaction with individual students was a major organizational feature in shaping and maintaining safe learning environments.

Notably, about three decades ago, Dwyer et al.'s (1983) seminal work already reported a similar observation about how school principals in the United States develop relationships with students through their daily interactions:

> An important component of Delling's [school principal] leadership derives from her desire to keep her finger on the pulse of the school ... she greets students as they arrive for the day, moving up and down the jagged lines of smiling faces, laughing, greeting, scolding, praising, making sure that no egos are stepped on and that order prevails. Lunchtime provides another opportunity to interact with youngsters. After the last child has been fed, she spends time on the playground, where she can "handle problems immediately" and "speak to the children informally" (p. 35).

Robinson and Aronica's (2015) interviews with a principal leading a school facing the challenges of student absences, discipline referrals, and low academic achievement revealed that the principal's reason for individual student interaction was to address school safety and problem behavior:

> [the school principal] spent a great deal of time in her initial year getting kids out of each other's faces and, more often than she wanted, sending them home on suspension. .... By the end of that first year, she'd put enough ground rules in place for the students to begin to understand what kind of behavior was expected of them (p. 2).

Drawing on his multi-site case study, Lortie (2009, p. 36) reported similarly that given their "standing at the peak of the control system," the range or nature of principals' interactions with students are usually boiled down to disciplinary actions, which "carry more serious consequences" for students. In sum, all this suggests that principals' interactions with individual students may potentially bring different effects on student development and student school life in a broader term, which is frequently overlooked by previous research focusing on the indirect effects of principal leadership on student academic outcomes.

These aspects of the literature reveal several important points of principals' leadership behaviors that are largely ignored in the research on school principals. First, principals' interactions with individual students occur routinely in school while they go about their daily tasks. Second, such direct interactions can possibly have effects on student academic outcomes (e.g., Nettles & Herrington, 2007; Silva et al., 2011), safe school environments (e.g., Astor et al., 2009; Robinson & Aronica, 2015), and student school life in a broader term (e.g., Dwyer et al., 1983; Lortie, 2009). Notably, these possible impacts are not reflected in the indirect effect model where principal leadership has a significant effect on student achievement by influencing teachers' instructional capacity. Third, the literature illuminating principals' interactions with individual students for supporting students' school life through a safer and better learning environment, for example, suggests that our current knowledge of principal leadership is still limited. We know that effective principal leadership is often assessed in terms of student learning outcomes, commonly measured by test scores, even though a principal's efforts to improve test scores are only a small part of a principal's role. Otherwise excellent principals who improve students' non-academic outcomes such as well-being and behavior cannot be recognized by current, narrow accountability metrics. Given that the underlying purpose of principals' daily interactions with individual students is largely related to making better and safer school environments and addressing disciplinary issues (Astor et al., 2009; Dwyer et al., 1983; Lortie, 2009; Robinson & Aronica, 2015), principals' direct involvement in students' school life may possibly bring impacts on students' well-being, sense of belonging, and sense of safety.

In summary, we think that looking closely at principals' time use for interaction with individual students warrants a rigorous investigation; it would be an important step toward understanding a fuller picture of principals' leadership behaviors, not explored by the indirect effect model. In so doing, we extend the scope of our investigation to provide an international perspective. By using a large-scale international database, we aim to investigate this overlooked area of inquiry in the existing literature.

Use of large international assessment data

There are two major datasets, administered by the International Association for the Evaluation of Educational Achievement (IEA), available for cross-national explorations of principals' time use. Both Progress in International Reading Literacy Study (PIRLS) 2006 and Trends in International Mathematics and Science Study (TIMSS) 2007 provide relevant variables of principals' time use. In terms of examining principals' time allocation to instructional leadership behaviors, TIMSS 2007 seems better than PIRLS 2006, given that TIMSS 2007 provides two relevant variables (i.e., developing curricula and pedagogy and supervising and evaluating teachers) while PIRLS 2006 offers a single variable of curriculum and pedagogical development. However, as far as principals' time for interacting with individual students, PIRLS 2006 is the only large international dataset that researchers can utilize. In addition, PIRLS 2006 measures principals' time use not just as the percentage of time allocated to particular leadership tasks but also as actual hours whereas TIMSS 2007 measured principals' time use as a categorical variable based on the percentage of principal time allocated to particular work domains (i.e., 1 = 25% or less, 2 = 26–50%, 3 = 51–75%, 4 = 76–100%). Therefore, PIRLS has a better feature of measurement validity than TIMSS 2007 (see Chapter 1 in this book for details). For the current study we thus used PIRLS 2006.

PIRLS 2006 includes principal survey data drawn from 47 participating societies from 39 countries since some countries included more than one participating jurisdiction to represent different regions (e.g., England and Scotland, five Canadian provinces). The principal survey data were gathered from randomly selected principals by using probability-proportional-to-size sampling (Martin,

Mullis, & Kennedy, 2007). On average 169 elementary school principals were randomly sampled per country.

As a follow-up study of Lee and Hallinger's (2012) work, this study targets 34 societies from 28 countries, which were also investigated by Lee and Hallinger (2012). As such, the dataset used in the final analysis includes the same samples of Lee and Hallinger's (2012) study—i.e., 5,927 principals from 34 education systems.

Measures and analytical strategies

Two broad groups of independent variables were used: organizational level characteristics, representing school organizational settings, and macro-level characteristics, reflecting broader societal settings, respectively. We used Poisson hierarchical linear modeling (HLM) to identify how organizational and macro contexts are associated with principals' time use for interacting with individual students. Principals' time use for interaction with individual students was used as the dependent variable in the main analysis. These variables are defined below. For more information about independent measures, see Lee and Hallinger (2012) as we use the same set of measures.

Organizational level characteristics (level-1)

Organizational-level characteristics consisted of variables representing internal organizational conditions and external organizational contexts (see Table 5.1 for details). All organizational level variables were used as level-1 predictors in the analysis of HLM.

School-level SES was measured by taking the proportion of students participating in free or reduced-price lunch programs, as reported by principals (reversely coded as 1 = none, 2 = some, and 3 = all). A measure of *the percentage of immigrant students* enrolled in the sample schools was also included in the level-1 model. As reported by Nettles (2005), the mix of at-risk and/or ethnic minority students is a key organizational condition in forming the working environment of principals. Considering principals are highly alert to the scarcity of school resources for supporting teaching and learning (Arikewuyo, 2007; Spillane, Diamond, Walker, Halverson, & Jita, 2001), we used an index of *school resources* offered by the PIRLS 2006. This index was based on the extent to which a lack of resources impacted the school's capacity to provide instruction as reported by principals. High values (on a 3-point scale) point to the lack of school resources as being a serious problem.

School climate was included as it has been shown as a predictor of various organizational outcomes (see Anderson, 1982). Specifically, *negative school climate* was included in our analytical model where high values indicate that school climate is seriously negative. Principals play an important role in managing a safe school environment (Astor et al. 2009); therefore, we also included *school safety* in our analysis. Based on the literature (Goldring, Huff, May, & Camburn, 2008; Hallinger & Murphy, 1985) showing relationships between school size and leadership behaviors, *school size* was also used for the analytical model.

Table 5.1 Descriptive statistics of organizational and macro contexts across the 34 education systems

Societies	Number of schools	Immigrant students	Lack of school resources	Negative school climate	Lack of school saftey	Home-school involvement	School size	Suburban (%)	Rural (%)	Urban (%)	PDI	System Standardization	GPD (PPPs)
AUS	158	1.9	1.2	1.6	1.4	2.1	4.9	20	51	28	11.0	2.0	10.46
BEL-FL	137	1.5	1.2	1.7	1.2	2.8	5.7	34	44	22	65.0	1.0	10.39
BEL-FR	150	1.5	1.6	1.3	1.4	2.5	5.7	23	33	45	65.0	0.0	10.39
BUL	143	1.9	1.8	1.9	1.5	1.6	5.8	8	26	66	70.0	3.0	9.21
CAN-A	150	1.4	1.2	1.3	1.3	3.0	5.7	27	29	44	39.0	2.0	10.95
CAN-BC	148	1.7	1.2	1.4	1.2	2.9	5.8	42	22	36	39.0	2.0	10.60
CAN-NS	201	1.3	1.3	1.4	1.3	2.9	5.6	21	57	2	39.0	2.0	10.38
CAN-O	180	1.9	1.3	1.5	1.3	2.9	5.8	31	18	52	39.0	2.0	10.70
CAN-Q	185	1.6	1.3	1.6	1.4	2.8	5.9	36	20	44	39.0	0.0	10.50
DEN	145	1.4	1.1	1.5	1.3	2.4	6.0	30	35	35	18.0	2.0	10.49
ENG	148	1.5	1.3	1.4	1.2	2.1	5.6	34	22	45	35.0	2.0	10.36
FRA	169	1.2	1.4	1.7	1.3	2.4	5.0	22	49	28	68.0	2.0	10.32
GER	405	1.7	1.3	1.8	1.5	2.2	5.4	18	40	42	35.0	1.0	10.36
HK	144	1.1	2.4	1.6	1.1	2.3	6.5	37	6	57	68.0	2.0	10.47
HUN	149	1.2	1.4	1.9	1.6	2.2	5.9	38	34	29	46.0	1.0	9.83
IND	168	3.0	1.6	1.6	2.1	1.3	5.2	14	73	13	78.0	3.0	8.47
IRA	236	2.2	2.3	1.5	1.1	2.2	5.1	13	31	57	58.0	3.0	9.04
ISR	149	2.0	1.8	1.5	1.6	2.6	6.0	19	32	49	13.0	3.0	10.10
ITA	150	1.2	1.5	1.7	1.4	2.4	6.2	16	15	69	50.0	2.0	10.30
KUW	149	1.2	2.4	1.7	1.9	2.7	6.5	57	14	29	80.0	1.0	9.72
MOR	159	2.0	2.4	1.8	2.3	1.6	6.1	19	40	41	70.0	2.0	8.48
NET	139	1.5	1.1	1.7	1.6	2.8	5.6	31	42	27	38.0	2.0	10.38
NOR	135	1.4	1.3	1.5	1.4	2.2	5.6	30	45	25	31.0	2.0	10.70
POL	148	1.2	1.3	1.8	1.6	1.6	5.7	5	41	55	68.0	1.0	9.53
RF	232	1.6	2.5	1.8	1.2	2.2	6.1	6	33	60	93.0	3.0	9.38
ROM	146	1.4	1.6	1.8	1.6	1.9	5.9	5	47	47	90.0	3.0	9.15
SA	397	1.8	2.0	1.9	1.8	2.3	6.1	20	6	16	49.0	2.0	9.46

Table 5.1 (Continued)

Societies	Number of schools	Immigrant students	Lack of school resources	Negative school climate	Lack of school saftey	Home-school involvement	School size	Suburban (%)	Rural (%)	Urban (%)	PDI	System Standardization	GPD (PPPs)
SCO	130	1.1	1.2	1.4	1.2	2.3	5.5	34	35	32	35.0	1.0	10.36
SIN	178	3.0	1.4	1.4	1.2	2.7	7.3	0	0	100	74.0	3.0	10.29
SLO	167	1.3	1.4	2.0	1.7	1.9	5.7	8	42	50	104.0	3.0	9.75
SPA	152	1.7	1.5	1.7	1.3	2.5	6.0	18	24	57	57.0	2.0	10.22
SWE	147	1.6	1.2	1.4	1.4	2.5	5.5	53	20	27	31.0	2.0	10.35
TAI	150	1.4	2.0	1.3	1.2	2.1	7.1	15	6	79	58.0	2.0	10.28
USA	183	1.6	1.2	1.3	1.3	2.9	6.1	42	27	31	40.0	2.0	10.67
Total	5927	1.7	1.6	1.6	1.4	2.3	5.8	23	35	42	52.7	1.9	10.06

Note: $N = 5,927$ principals from 34 societies (based on the imputed data).

Austria (AUS), Belgium-Flemish (BEL-FL), Belgium-French (BEL-FR), Bulgaria (BUL), Canada-Alberta (CAN-A), Canada-British Columbia (CAN-BC), Canada-Nova Scotia (CAN-NS), Canada, Ontario (CAN-O), Canada, Quebec (CAN-Q), Denmark (DEN), England (ENG), France (FRA), Germany (GER), Hong Kong SAR (HK), Hungary (HUN), Indonesia (IND), Iran, Islamic Republic (IRA), Israel (ISR), Italy (ITA), Kuwait (KUW), Morocco (MOR), Netherlands (NET), Norway (NOR), Poland (POL), Russian Federation (RF), Romania (ROM), South Africa (SA), Scotland (SCO), Singapore (SIN), Slovak Republic (SLO), Spain (SPA), Sweden (SWE), Tai Pei (TAI), United States (USA).

We utilized the index of *home-school involvement*, developed by the IEA. Higher values in the measure of *home-school involvement* indicate that teacher-parent conferences and events at school are held four or more times per year and that these are attended by more than half of the parents (Martin et al., 2007). Lastly, *school location* was included as representing an external organizational context. Dummy codes were used to group areas into three categories: urban (urban = ref. group), suburban, and rural.

Macro-level characteristics (level-2)

Informed by Lee and Hallinger's (2012) study, we focused on three macro-contextual variables. They were used as level-2 predictors (see Table 5.1 for details). *GDP per capita based on Purchasing Power Parities (PPPs)* was used to indicate the level of economic development. The data were drawn from International Monetary Fund (IMF).[3] The values were converted into the natural logarithm. *Hofstede's power distance index (PDI)* was used to capture a key dimension of broad societal culture closely related to social relationships in an organizational context (Hofstede, 1997, 2001). Information regarding the level of standardization in the education system of each society, assessed by the presence of national curriculum, national testing, and mandated textbooks, was provided by the PIRLS 2006.

Dependent variable

The number of hours principals spent interacting with individual students each week was used as the dependent variable.

Reflecting the nested structure of the data, a two-level Poisson hierarchical linear model (HLM) was utilized (Raudenbush & Bryk, 2002). Prior to the HLM analysis, we imputed the level-1 dataset to address missing values based on Little's MCAR test. We employed the imputation model that is compatible with the analytical model used in this study (Allison, 2002).

Using the imputed dataset, we first set up a random-effects ANOVA model which was followed by Model 1 with school-level variables and Model 2 with macro-level variables. The final HLM model was constructed using a random-coefficient model (Raudenbush & Bryk, 2002). We used this approach for two reasons. First, we assumed that parameters representing key school characteristics would vary across schools in the level-2 model, which was analytically supported by deviance statistic tests. Second, significant cross-level interaction was not identified.

A Poisson HLM analysis was conducted to investigate principals' time spent interacting with individual students since the dependent variable substantially followed a Poisson distribution. Specifically, we used constant exposure given that the expected number of hours each principal i within each society j (Υ_{ij}) would be the number of hours spent during a typical week. In other words, we regarded the number of hours as count data in the HLM analysis. In addition, to detect the overall model fit through deviance statistics, we utilized Laplace estimation. Finally, we used a school weight variable and also checked multicollinearity among the variables in the model.

Results

Our investigation indicated that principals across 34 education systems had an average work week of 41 hours.[1] Also, on average principals allocated 11.4% of their work time for interaction with students. Based on the combined information of the overall work hours and the percentage of time principals spent for interacting with individual students, we computed principals' work hours spent for interacting with individual students across the 34 societies, presented in Figure 5.1. The international average number of work hours for interacting with individual students was 4.7 hours per week (41 hours per week × 0.114); see the horizontal dotted line in Figure 5.1.

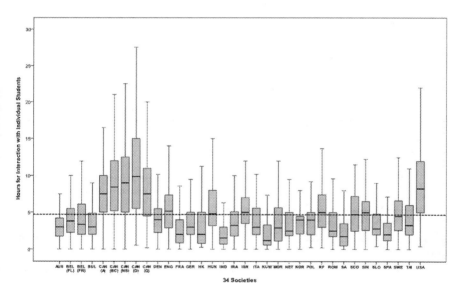

Figure 5.1 Principals' work hours per week for interaction with individual students[a] across the 34 societies[b]

[a] The figure is constructed from the dataset with the imputation (5,927 principals from 34 societies). Outliers are included in the figure, yet they are not visualized.

[b] Austria (AUS), Belgium-Flemish, (BEL-FL), Belgium-French (BEL-FR), Bulgaria (BUL), Canada-Alberta (CAN-A), Canada-British Columbia (CAN-BC), Canada-Nova Scotia (CAN-NS), Canada, Ontario (CAN-O), Canada, Quebec (CAN-Q), Denmark (DEN), England (ENG), France (FRA), Germany (GER), Hong Kong SAR (HK), Hungary (HUN), Indonesia (IND), Iran, Islamic Republic (IRA), Israel (ISR), Italy (ITA), Kuwait (KUW), Morocco (MOR), Netherlands (NET), Norway (NOR), Poland (POL), Russian Federation (RF), Romania (ROM), South Africa (SA), Scotland (SCO), Singapore (SIN), Slovak Republic (SLO), Spain (SPA), Sweden (SWE), Tai Pei (TAI), United States (USA).

Figure 5.1 illustrates that there is a notable within-society variation in principal time use for interacting with individual students in several societies (e.g., five provinces in Canada and the United States) whereas there is a relatively less within-society variation in countries such as Austria, Indonesia, Kuwait, Norway, South Africa, and Spain; in the figure, the longer the vertical length of tinted boxes and the vertical distance between the top/bottom edges and the upper/lower lines, the more the within-society variation.

In addition, the wide range of medians (i.e., thicker horizontal lines in the tinted boxes in each box plot) indicates a salient variation in principals' time use for interacting with individual students across the 34 education systems. While there is a fluctuation of the median work hours across the 34 societies, a majority of principals in North America (i.e., the five provinces of Canada and USA) spent more time than their counterparts in the other societies for interacting with individual students. Conversely, most of the principals in India, Kuwait, South Africa, and Spain spent less time for interacting with individual students, compared to their counterparts in the rest of other societies.

The notable between-society variation in principals' time use for interacting with individual students led us to assume that macro-societal conditions have different associations with principals' time use for interacting with individual students. Table 5.2 further illustrates how macro-context factors predicted the striking fluctuation of principals' time used interacting with individual students across the 34 societies. The results indicate that two macro contexts were significantly associated with principal time usage in this domain when other predictors are held constant. Specifically, principals in higher PDI countries tended to spend less time interacting with their students than counterparts in lower PDI countries. If two countries differ by one standard deviation in PDI (sd_{PDI} = 22.66, the range of PDI is 1 to 104), one would expect that principals' interaction time with students in the higher PDI country would be a decrease of 11% times that of principals in the lower PDI country, when other predictors are held constant: $\exp\{(22.66) \times (-.005)\} = 0.89$. In other words, principals in societies with greater status differentiation tended to spend less time interacting with individual students, compared to principals in low PDI societies.

Greater standardization was also negatively associated with time use for interacting with individual students. If two countries differ by one standard deviation in standardization of education system ($sd_{EDU.SYS}$ = .814, the range of the predictor is 0 to 3), the expected difference in principals' time spent interacting with individual students in the country with greater standardization would be a decrease of 6% times that of principals in the country with lower standardization, when other predictors are controlled for: $\exp\{(.814) \times (-.076) = 0.94\}$. In sum, principals in more structured systems spent less time on interaction with individual students than their counterparts in less standardized systems.

However, there was no significant association between GDP per capita (ppps) and principals' time spent for interacting with students. Put differently, there was no significant difference in time used interacting with individual students by the level of economic development.

Table 5.2 Principals' time used for interaction with students (poisson HLM)

Fixed effects	Model 1 (Unconditional model) Coefficient	(se)	exp(coeff)	p-value	Model 2 (Level-1 predictors added) Coefficient	(se)	exp(coeff)	p-value	Model 3 (Level-2 predictors added) Coefficient	(se)	exp(coeff)	p-value
Overall mean γ_{00}	1.283***	.184	3.608		1.471***	.128	4.352		1.532***	.113	4.625	***
PDI γ_{01}									−.005***	.001	0.995	***
Standardization γ_{02}									−.076*	.034	0.926	***
GDP per capita (ppps) γ_{03}									−.048	.031	0.953	
Students in free/reduced-price lunch γ_{10}					.026	.071	1.026		.027	.072	1.027	
Immigrant students γ_{20}					.010	.027	1.010		.011	.027	1.011	
Lack of school resources γ_{30}					−.085**	.023	.919	***	−.081**	.025	0.922	***
Negative school climate γ_{40}					.033	.032	1.034	***	.034	.032	1.035	***
Lack of school safety γ_{50}					−.054	.076	.947	**	−.054	.076	0.947	**
Home-school involvement γ_{60}					.084	.066	1.088	***	.083	.066	1.086	***
School size γ_{70}					.030	.060	1.030	***	.029	.060	1.029	***
Suburban γ_{80} (urban as the reference)					−.090	.098	.914	***	−.087	.099	0.916	***
Rural γ_{90}					−.082	.045	.921	**	−.080	.046	0.923	**
Random effects	v.c.	d.f.		p-value	v.c.	d.f.		p-value	v.c.	d.f.		p-value
Students in free/reduced-price lunch u_{1j}					.033	32		***	.033	32		***
Immigrant students u_{2j}					.009	32		***	.008	32		***
Lack of school resources u_{3j}					.006	32		***	.006	32		***
Negative school climate u_{4j}					.008	32		**	.007	32		**
Lack of school safety u_{5j}					.025	32		***	.025	32		***
Home-school involvement u_{6j}					.024	32		***	.024	32		***
School size u_{7j}					.019	32		***	.019	32		***
Suburban u_{8j} (urban as the reference)					.043	32		***	.043	32		***
Rural u_{9j}					.009	32		**	.009	32		**

Note: $N = 5,927$ principals from 34 societies, effect = coefficient; *$p<.05$. **$p<.01$. ***$p<.001$, v.c. = variance component, d.f. = degree of freedom.

In summary, the hierarchical poisson regression modeling confirmed the impression of substantial cross-national variance in terms of principals' time used in interacting with individual students. Approximately 54% of the between-society variance in principals' time used for interacting with students was explained by the macro-context factors where PDI and the standardization of education systems signficantly predicted principals' time use for interaciton with individual students.

Regarding the substantial within-school variance, we note that unexpectedly, most of the organizational variables which have been found previously to predict principal leadership behaviors or time use in previous studies turned out to be insignificant. The only exception to this was the level of school resources (−.081, $p < .01$). Principals in schools lacking school resources tended to spend less time in interacting with individual students than their counterparts in schools with more resources (Table 5.2).

Discussion

Principals spend a substantial portion of time interacting with individual students

The results from the PIRLS reveal a number of important features of principals' time use for interaction with individual students. The results support our argument that principals' interaction with individual students is part of their daily work life. Not surprisingly, principals tended to allocate less time for interaction with students, compared to time spent on other traditional leadership domains (e.g., curriculum development, staff management, administration). However, allocating 11.4% of their work time for interaction with students suggests that despite the pressing nature of other demands on their time, principals' actions suggest that this aspect of their work is critical to their role. Given that the average work hours per week is cumulated throughout the academic year, principals' time for interaction with individual students is substantial.

Principals' time for interacting with individual students varies across the 34 societies

Principals' interaction with individual students appears to be perceived and performed differently across the 34 societies. The results show that macro-societal settings are significantly associated with the way elementary school principals spend their time interacting with individual students. Particularly, we found that macro-societal culture and the institutional arrangements of educational systems appear to substantially influence principals' time use for meeting with and talking to individual students. The status of economic development was not significantly associated with principal time use for interacting with individual students. This result is in contradistinction with Lee and Hallinger's (2012) study, which also used PIRLS, reporting that *the overall hours per week* principals spent for other more traditional activities mentioned above are significantly associated with the status of economic development such as GDP per capital (ppps). Specifically, Lee and Hallinger (2012) found that principals from economically advanced societies tend to spend more time working than their counterparts in developing countries. This relationship implies that as societies develop economically the institutional features of school organizations appear to be more complex (Scott & Meyer, 1994), which in turn appears to demand more work hours from principals in economically developed societies. Taken together, it can be said that while the status of economic development has a significant association with the overall principal work hours, the level of economic development has no significant association with principals' time spent for interacting with individual students. This result suggests that other macro-contextual features may play a more important role in principals' time usage in dealing with individual students. Indeed, results indicate that principals working in less status-differentiated organized societies tended to spend more time in such interactions than principals from more hierarchical societies (i.e., societies with higher PDIs). Notably, the United States was one of the top three societies in terms of principal-individual student interaction. This finding resonates with Nettles and Herrington's (2007) study. They reported that principals tended to recognize the importance of direct interactions with students in general and high-risk students in particular, given the increasing pressure of NCLB. At the same time, however, our finding adds another plausible explanation that the less hierarchically defined culture in the United States may be another reason why U.S. principals tend to spend more time interacting with individual students. Conversely, it is reasonable to believe that principals in more hierarchical societies (i.e., higher PDI societies) focus more on the traditional role of school principals such administrators or managers. Indeed, prior studies conducted in East Asian countries with higher PDIs (e.gChung & Miskel, 1989; Walker & Dimmock, 2000) have documented that principals tended to spend more time on paperwork rather than (un)scheduled meetings to deal with teachers and students.

We also found that principals working in more structured education systems spend less of their time interacting with individual students. In other words, greater standardization of education systems in terms of curriculum, textbooks, and examinations appears to divert principals' attention away from spending time with individual students. One plausible explanation for this is that principals may believe that interacting with individual students is not a major system requirement. This may well flow from their experiences when dealing with the central bureaucracy. Alternatively, principals in more tightly standardized systems may not have enough flexibility to spend more time interacting with individual students. While we propose some plausible explanations for this finding, we await further investigations.

Principals' time for interacting with individual students varies within each society

Our study also identified substantial within-society variance in principals' time use for direct interaction with individual students. Unlike previous studies, however, we note that most of the organizational variables that have been found previously to predict principal leadership behaviors or time use turned out to be insignificant. We think that this is mainly because the dependent variable of the analytical model is different from previous research which targets more traditional domains of principals' leadership responsibilities (e.g., curriculum, instruction, and administration) whereas the dependent variable in this study is principal time use for interaction with individual students. Indeed, Lee and Hallinger's (2012) study using the PIRLS data reported that school climate, school safety, school size, and location are significantly associated with principal leadership behaviors in the domain of instructional leadership, administration, and parent-community relations. In our study, principals' time use for interacting with individual students was significantly associated with the level of school resources only. Given the nature of the PIRLS data, although it is difficult to pinpoint the specific reason for this finding, existing studies suggest that ease of accessibility and utilization of school resources for leading schools impacts the leadership behavior of principals (Arikewuyo, 2007; Spillane et al., 2001). School principals in the PIRLS 2006 data may have had less time to spend with students as they focused on managing the conflicting demands for access to scarce resources. Studies of the "micro-politics" of schools posit that there is a direct relationship between the scarcity of school resources and micro-political behavior in school as individuals and groups compete for scarce resources (Iannaccone, 1991).This finding, in general, supports the observation that principals' deprioritize particular domains of leadership behaviors (e.g., interaction with individual students) as a consequence of certain organizational factors (e.g., lack of school resources).

Limitations

We note several limitations of the current study with the hope that future research advances the field of school leadership by addressing the limitations of the current study. First, the study focused on *quantity* of time use only, given the data structure of the PIRLS. We acknowledge that it is also important to consider not only *how many hours* principals spend interacting with students, but also *the way* principals interact with individual students.

Second, while we analyzed the amount of principals' time used interacting with individual students, the PIRLS data do not provide information about the underlying purpose or intention of principals' time use. Drawing upon the literature (e.g., Astor et al., 2009; Lortie, 2009; Nettles & Herrington, 2007; Robinson & Aronica, 2015), although we can speculate that one of the main reasons for principals to interact with individual students would be to address issues related to discipline and safe learning environments, we admit that PIRLS does not confirm exactly why such interactions occur. Similarly, we still do not have information about the kinds of students (e.g., immigrant students, low SES students) with who principals interact.

Third, even though our HLM analysis took into account major organizational conditions in line with previous studies, there may well be other important organizational contexts that are not considered. For example, policy environments conditioning schools' organizational capacity, such as local district policy or practice, may have an impact on school performance by influencing principals' leadership styles or behaviors (Lee, Louis, & Anderson, 2012). Therefore, research equipped with more comprehensive organizational contexts is needed.

Fourth, as mentioned earlier, there was more than one participating unit in some countries. Therefore, using each unit's PDI would have been more appropriate rather than using country-level information. However, due to the absence of information at the sub-unit level, this study relied solely on country-level PDIs. All cross-national studies using Hofstede's data face this limitation.

Finally, in terms of analysis, we expected to identify cross-level interaction between macro-societal settings and organizational settings in relation to principals' time use as it can be reasonably assumed that the impact of broad societal culture as a higher level effect could be widely permeated in individual school cultures. Our data suggest that there was no statistically significant cross-level interaction, however, future studies are needed in order to unravel how interaction between macro and organizational settings can influence principal time use.

Implications

A need for exploring principals' direct effects on student outcomes

Our study adds new knowledge to the field of school leadership. By identifying principals' time use for interacting with individual students across 34 education systems, our study contributes to building a solid foundation for future research with a focus on principals' direct effects on student outcomes, which can complement the existing indirect model of principals' effects on student outcomes. As mentioned earlier, a vast majority of research on principal leadership has focused solely or heavily on principals' indirect effects mediated mainly through teachers' practices. However, given that principals' daily interactions appear to be related predominantly to disciplinary and school safety matters (Astor et al., 2009; Lortie, 2009; Robinson & Aronica, 2015), it is reasonable to assume that principals' direct involvement in students' school life may affect students' well-being, and their sense of belonging and safety. Indeed, we recently tested the emerging narratives of principals' direct effect on student outcomes (e.g., Astor et al., 2009; Gentilucci & Muta, 2007; Nettles & Herrington, 2007; Robinson, 2015; Silva et al., 2011; Waters et al., 2004) on a large scale using PIRLS 2006. Building on our current work, we have found that school principals' time use for interacting with individual students was not directly associated with academic achievement, but it was significantly associated with student safety at school (see Lee, Ryoo, & Walker, 2021). Specifically, for non-academic outcomes such as school safety, our recent study reveals that there are "direct" effects of principals' time use on students. Principals tended to spend significantly more time interacting with individual students especially when they work at schools with more bullying or violent incidents. This brings an important implication for the current accountability policy, given that excellent principals who improve the relational dimensions of students' school life such as school safety should be recognized by policy conversations beyond current narrow accountability metrics. Drawing from Robinson et al.'s (2008) meta-analysis, we know that certain leadership styles have significant associations with student academic outcomes, but we do not know much about how and whether principal leadership can make a difference in non-academic student outcomes "directly." Based on our work, we call for more empirical studies on principals' direct effects on non-academic outcomes. We also believe that our study provides an empirical base upon which future investigations into educational leadership as enacted in a global era can be built, for example, through linking the identified patterns of principals' time use and various student non-academic outcomes (e.g., well-being, safety, sense of belonging) internationally. This line of research will enable us to further revisit and complement the major theoretical model of principals' leadership effects (i.e., indirect effects model) in existing school leadership research.

Toward researching comparative school leadership

Our study also contributes to developing the field of comparative school leadership. Even though there is ample literature, cross-national comparative research in the field of principal leadership behaviors in general and time use in particular is limited. The vast majority of studies have involved a small number of principals from single countries. One of the earliest comparative studies was conducted by Chung and Miskel (1989) who compared how South Korea and U.S. principals spend their time. In recent years, using large international data (e.g., PIRLS, TALIS, and TIMSS), a range of cross-national comparative studies on principal leadership have surfaced (e.g., Lee & Hallinger, 2012; Lee et al., 2021; Park & Ham, 2016; Shin & Slater, 2010; Ten Bruggencate & Luyten, 2010). Results from our study contribute to this emerging line of research, which has the potential to develop the field of comparative school leadership. To develop comparative school leadership research, we call for future research that identifies common and/or particular patterns, causes, and effects of principal time use across countries and develops a framework of data collection and related analytical tools of principal time use that can be widely applied to contexts of different countries (see also chapters in Part I in this book).

Acknowledgment

As noted in the chapter, our recent work (Lee et al, 2021) has substantially extended this chapter in terms of theoretical underpinnings, methodological approaches, and analytical scopes. This chapter was supported by the Ministry of Education and the National Research Foundation of Korea: [Grant Number NRF-2017S1A3A2065967]. Correspondence concerning this chapter should be addressed to Moosung Lee, University of Canberra and Yonsei University. Email: leemoosung@gmail.com

Note

1. Extreme outlying values of work hours per week reported by principals were top-coded (80 hours or more as 80) or bottom-coded (5 hours or less as 5).

References

Allison, P. (2002). *Missing Data*. Thousand Oaks, CA: Sage.

Anderson, C.S. (1982). The search for school climate. *Review of Educational Research*, 52(3), 368–420.

Arikewuyo, M. O. (2007). "Teachers' Perception of Principals' Leadership Capacities in Nigeria." *Academic Leadership Journal*, 5(3). http://www.academicleadership.org/pdf/ALJ_ISSN1533-7812_5_3_187.pdf.

Astor, R.A., Benbenishty, R., & Estrada, J. (2009). School violence and theoretically atypical schools: The principal's centrality in orchestrating safe schools. *American Educational Research Journal*, 46(2), 423–61

Bryk, A. S., Sebring, P. B., Allensworth, E., Luppescu, S., & Easton, J. Q. (2010). *Organizing Schools for Improvement: Lessons from Chicago*. Chicago, IL: University of Chicago Press.

Chung, A. K., & Miskel, C. G. (1989). "A comparative Study of Principals' Administrative Behavior." *Journal of Educational Administration*, 27(1), 45–57.

Dwyer, D., Lee, G., Rowan, B., & Bossert, S., 1983. *Five Principals in Action: Perspectives on Instructional Management*. San Francisco, CA: Far West Laboratory for Educational Research.

Gentilucci, J., & Muta, C. (2007). "Principals' Influence on Academic Achievement: The Student Perspective." *National Association of Secondary School Principals Bulletin*, 91, 219–236.

Goldring, E., Huff J., May, H., & Camburn, E. (2008). "School Context and Individual Characteristics: What Influences Principal Practice?" *Journal of Educational Administration*, 46(3), 332–352.

Hallinger, P., & Heck, R. H. (1996). "Reassessing the Principal's Role in School Effectiveness: A Review of the Empirical Research, 1980–1995." *Educational Administration Quarterly*, 32(1), 5–44.

Hallinger, P., & Murphy, J. (1985). "Assessing the Instructional Management Behavior of Principals." *The Elementary School Journal*, 86(2), 217–247.

Heck, R. H., & Hallinger, P. (2009). "Assessing the Contribution of Distributed Leadership to School Improvement and Growth in Math Achievement." *American Educational Research Journal*, 46(3), 659–689.

Hofstede, G. (1997). *Culture and Organizations: Software of the Mind*. New York, NY: McGraw Hill.

Hofstede, G. (2001). *Culture's Consequences: International Differences in Work-Related Values*. Thousand Oaks, CA: Sage.

Iannaccone, L. (1991). "Micro-politics of Education: What and Why." *Education and Urban Society*, 23(4), 465–471.

Lee, M., & Hallinger, P. (2012). "National Contexts Influencing Principals' Time Use and Allocation: Economic Development, Societal Culture, and Educational System." *School Effectiveness and School Improvement*, 23(4), 461–482.

Lee, M., Louis, K. S., & Anderson, S. (2012). "Local Education Authorities and Student Learning: The Effects of Policies and Practices." *School Effectiveness and School Improvement*, 23(2), 133–158.

Lee, M., Ryoo, J.-H., & Walker, A. (2021). "School Principals' Time Use for Interaction with Individual Students: Macro Contexts, Organizational Conditions, and Student Outcomes." *American Journal of Education, 127*(2)

Leithwood, K., & Louis, K. S. (2012). *Linking Leadership to Student Learning*. San Francisco, CA: Jossey-Bass.

Lortie, D. C. (2009). *School Principal*. Chicago, IL: University of Chicago Press.

Martin, M. O., Mullis, I. V. S., & Kennedy, A. M. (2007). *PIRLS 2006 Technical Report*. Boston, MA: TIMSS & PIRLS International Study Center, Lynch School of Education, Boston College.

Nettles, S. M. (2005). *The relationship between principal implementation behaviors and student achievement in reading* (Unpublished doctoral dissertation). Florida State University, Tallahassee, FL.

Nettles, S., & Herrington, C. (2007). "Revisiting the Importance of the Direct Effects of School Leadership on Student Achievement: The Implications for School Improvement Policy." *Peabody Journal of Education, 82*, 724–736.

Park, J.-H., & Ham, S.-H. (2016). "Whose Perception of Principal Instructional Leadership? Principal-teacher Perceptual (Dis)agreement and Its Influence on Teacher Collaboration." *Asia Pacific Journal of Education, 36*, 450–469.

Raudenbush, S. W., & Bryk, A. S. (2002). *Hierarchical Linear Models: Applications and Data Analysis Methods*. Thousand Oaks, CA: Sage.

Robinson, K., & Aronica, L. (2015). *Creative Schools: Revolutionizing Education from the Ground Up*. London, UK: Penguin-Random House.

Robinson, V., Lloyd, C., & Rowe, K. (2008). "The Impact of Leadership on Student Outcomes: An Analysis of the Differential Effects of Leadership Types." *Educational Administration Quarterly, 44*(5), 564–588.

Scott, R. W., & Meyer, J. W. (1994). *Institutional Environments and Organizations: Structural Complexity and Individualism*. Thousand Oaks, CA: Sage.

Scheernes, J. (Ed.) (2012). *School Leadership Effects Revisited: Review and Meta-Analysis of Empirical Studies*. The Netherlands: Springer.

Shin, S.-H., & Slater, C. L. (2010). "Principal Leadership and Mathematics Achievement: An International Comparative Study." *School Leadership and Management, 30*(4), 317–334.

Silva, J. P., White, G. P., & Yoshida, K. R. (2011). "The Direct Effects of Principal–Student Discussions on Eighth Grade Students' Gains in Reading Achievement: An Experimental Study." *Educational Administration Quarterly, 47*(5), 772–793.

Spillane, J. P., Diamond, J. B., Walker, L., Halverson, R., & Jita, L. (2001). "Urban School Leadership and Elementary Science Instruction: Identifying, Mobilizing, and Activating Resources in a Devalued Subject Area." *Journal of Research in Science Teaching, 38*(8), 918–940.

Ten Bruggencate, G., & Luyten, H. (2010). From School Leadership to Student Achievement: Analyses Based on TIMSS, 2007. In G. Ten Bruggencate, H. Luyten, & J. Scheerens (Eds.), *Quantitative Analyses of International Data: Exploring Indirect Effect Models of School Leadership* (pp. 29–46). The Netherlands: University of Twente.

Walker, A., & Dimmock, C. (2000). "One Size Fits All? Teacher Appraisal in a Chinese Culture." *Journal of Personnel Evaluation in Education, 14*(2), 155–178.

Waters, T., Marzano, R., & McNulty, B. (2004). *Balanced Leadership: What 30 Years of Research Tells us about the Effect of Leadership on Student Achievement*. Aurora, CO: Mid-continent Research for Education and Learning.

Part II
Principal time use in Western contexts

6 How principals use their time in Ontario, Canada

Katina Pollock and Fei Wang

Inquiry into how managers and leaders use their time has a long history. The drive to understand time use has many origins, from the quest to know how to run organizations more efficiently, to labor negotiations, to determining the monetary worth of work (Thompson, 1967). Leading and managing public education has also been investigated through the lens of time use. Drawing on Mintzberg's (1973) seminal time-on-task studies, many scholars in educational administration have investigated administrators' time use in public education over several decades (Bezzina, Paletta, & Alimehmeti, 2017; Eacott, 2013; Gaziel, 1995; Horng, Klasik, & Loeb, 2009; Kmetz & Willower, 1982; Martin & Willower, 1981; Martinko & Gardner, 1990; Sayles, 1964). Specifically, scholars in the past decade considered the managerial imperative (Cuban, 1988) in principals' work and found that, in terms of time use, school principals spend most of their days on administrative activities and organizational management tasks and little time on instructional leadership (Horng, Klasik, & Leob, 2010).

In this chapter, we consider some of the fundamental misalignments in principals' time use: between what they want to spend time on versus what they actually do spend time on and between what is expected in policy and what they are able to do in reality. The findings and analysis reported in this chapter are based on a 2013 study of Ontario principals who worked in English-language secular public education system—one of four publicly funded education systems in Ontario. The principals were all members of the Ontario Principals' Council, one of the main professional associations for school leaders in the province. In this study, we explored the changing nature of principals' work. We wanted to provide a more accurate picture of what principals do on a daily basis and the challenges and possibilities inherent in their work. The data and findings reported in this chapter are based on traditional clock time or *time-on-task*.

We adopted the concept of *work* in this study to explore principals' worlds. Work was defined as labor or effort expended to achieve a particular set of goals (Pollock, Wang, & Hauseman, 2014). This study included employment-related paid and unpaid work that was expended both within and outside principals' position-related roles. We excluded other kinds of unpaid work such as volunteerism or family responsibilities (Drago, 2007). It is difficult in this day and age to erect clear boundaries around work efforts, just as it is to define organizational boundaries (Ryan, 1996). For our research team, work was understood to take place on and off the school site, and it potentially occurred after the official opening and closing of the school day.

Methodology

One way to determine what it is that principals do at work is to gather information about the tasks they engage in on a daily basis. We employed a mixed-methods design to provide a complete picture of the nature of principals' work and to overcome the weakness and biases of single approaches (Denscombe, 2008). The mixed methods included focus groups and an online survey and provided a substantial amount of information on principals' work. The findings reported in this chapter are from our analysis of online survey data and will only focus on how the participating principals spent their time at work.

Online survey

This study was supported by the Ontario Principals' Council (OPC), a professional association representing practicing principals and vice-principals (VPs) in Ontario's publicly funded schools. The OPC provides professional services and supports to its 6,000 members representing elementary and secondary school leaders from across Ontario, Canada. The survey was developed based on the review of literature and refined and tested through focus groups with school principals. The survey contained 60 questions in 12 sections that covered how principals spend their time, their duties and responsibilities, their roles and tasks, their challenges, their work–life balance, and about themselves and their schools. The survey provided a snapshot of the nature of the principals' work across the English-speaking, publicly funded schools in Ontario.

Sampling

The sample consisted of OPC members who were working as Ontario school principals at the time the survey was online. The OPC provided our team with 2,701 email addresses, which we used to send each principal individualized URL to the survey. In addition to having direct access to the respondents, our team used a number of strategies to encourage principals to share their opinions and make their voices heard. We sent weekly email reminders to principals who had not yet completed the survey. The OPC staff also helped to generate a sense of excitement about the survey by providing updates on the OPC website and sending out tweets from the official OPC Twitter account when the survey was live. These strategies are likely the reason the survey was able to achieve such a high response rate (52.68%). A total of 1,821 responses were collected during the 26 days the survey was live. Unfortunately, 398 responses were disqualified due to missing data or because they were completed by OPC members who were not principals. Of the usable survey responses, 77.3% were from elementary principals, 16.4% from secondary principals, and 2.9% from principals of both elementary and secondary schools.

Description of sample

In our study, the vast majority of principals who responded to the online survey were between the ages of 45 and 54; 28.9% of participating principals were between the ages of 45 and 49, while 28.2% of respondents were between 50 and 54 years old. An additional 17.7% of principals who completed the survey were between 40 and 44 years of age, with those aged between 55 and 59 years old accounting for 14.2% of responses. Further, 6.3% of principals indicated that they were over the age of 60, and only 3.9% of respondents were under 40 years old.

Data analysis

Our team first conducted descriptive statistics analysis to provide a summary of the data and identify patterns. We conducted correlations, t tests, exploratory factor analysis in the second stage to explore relationships, compare group differences, and identify latent variables in the data. The analysis allowed us to deduce properties of an underlying distribution and make inferences about the population of principals (Cohen, Manion, & Morrison, 2011).

Findings

School principals play a critical role in school success (Institute for Educational Leadership, 2012). How, when, how much, with whom, and where principals spend their time at work is one way to gather information about how principals go about doing their work to create effective schools. In this section, we present our findings on how principals use their time: Specifically, on the tasks, locations, modes of communication, and interactions principals do and have in their work.

Time principals spent at work

Our 2013 survey results show that principals are working long hours. On average, Ontario principals spent approximately 58 hours per week at their work. This appears to be on par with other recent Canadian reports that indicate principals work 58 hours per week (Canadian Association of Principals & The Alberta Teachers' Association, 2014). Principals in Ontario appear to be working generally the same number of hours weekly as their colleagues across the rest of the country. When we compare principals' current weekly work hours to past data, according to Lee and Hallinger's (2012) analysis of the PIRLS 2007 data, Ontario principals (and also principals across Canada) were working 4 hours more than they did in the late 2000s. Lee and Hallinger (2012) concluded in their analysis that principals in Ontario, in 2007, *already worked 4 hours more* than their school leadership colleagues who reported the least number of hours worked per week. It could be suggested that in 2013 principals were working another *additional* 4 hours per week at their role. When comparing principals' hours of work to other managerial positions within the Canadian public sector (Pollock, Hauseman, & Wang, 2014), we found that principals work 14 more hours than Canadian occupational managers (Statistics Canada, 2013).

Differences among the principals who participated according to gender, years of work, and age

Because we were fortunate to have such a high response rate, we were curious to see if there were any differences in time use based on factors such as gender and years of work. For various reasons, public, tertiary education has a long history—that many argue still continues to some degree today—of feminization both in social practices and organizational structure evidenced by the sheer numbers of women educators and the inequities women teachers experienced gaining access to school leadership positions and maintaining successful leadership roles (Apple, 1986; Wallace, 2007). For this reason, we did an independent-sample *t* test to evaluate if there was a difference between male and female principals in terms of their use of time at work. The *t* test was significant, $t(1411) = -3.36, p = 0$. The results show that, on average, male principals ($M = 57.2$, $SD = 9.1$) spent less time at work than their female colleagues ($M = 59.0$, $SD = 10.3$). The only study that we could find that explored differences based on gender was Bristow, Ireson, and Coleman (2007), who compared male and female colleagues in time on task; in their study, the authors determined that men (50.3 hours) spent less time at work than women (55.4 hours).

The amount of time principals spent at work each week was also significantly correlated with the years of experience they had as a school principal ($r = -.10$). The more experienced principals were, the less time they would spend per week at work. Although the survey data alone was not able to account for this, possibilities could include principals becoming more proficient at their work tasks or for work–life balance, realizing that there is always work to be done and that if they did not set boundaries on the amount of time they spent at work they may experience negative well-being consequences (Pollock & Wang, 2020), or becoming able to prioritize their work in a manner that requires less work time (Grissom, Loeb, & Master, 2015; Horng, Klasik, & Loeb, 2009).

How principals spend their time

An exploratory factor analysis further indicated (see Table 6.1) that principals spent their time in four major areas: *school management* (29.2%), *instructional leadership* (9.5%), *student affairs* (8.0%), and *professional development* (PD) (6.8%). In total, these four areas accounted for 53.4% of the variance.

Table 6.1 Rotated component matrix

How principals spent their time	Factor 1 School management	Factor 2 Instructional leadership	Factor 3 Student affairs	Factor 4 PD
Budget	.705	.241	.175	.094
Personnel	.679	.042	.156	.119
Occupational health and safety	.657	.281	.147	−.188
Internal school management	.607	.103	−.085	.086
Building maintenance	.600	.540	.164	.017
District school board office committees	.538	−.206	.097	.493
Classroom walkthroughs	.104	**.834**	.129	.153
Walking hallways, playground, lunchroom, etc.	.099	**.603**	.282	−.033
Curriculum and instructional leadership	.217	**.588**	−.039	.493
Community	.266	.358	.205	.074
Student discipline/attendance	−.114	−.024	**.807**	.031
Student-related activities	.091	.212	**.590**	.193
Working with parents	.342	.256	**.569**	.067
Student transportation	.207	.171	**.441**	−.090
Principals' professional development	.011	.208	.101	**.817**

Our findings highlight that contemporary principals have difficulty when trying to balance instructional leadership with management responsibilities. On average, the task on which principals spent the greatest amount of time (7.6 hours) was dealing with student discipline concerns. On average, the participating principals indicated spending 7.5 hours per week on other internal management-related tasks. The majority of the sample (55%) indicated that they would like to spend less time on these internal school management issues. Similarly, the principals indicated that, on average, they spent 5.6 hours per week on personnel issues, while 29% of the sample would like to spend less time on these activities. The principals surveyed spend over 5 hours per week at the school district office, while 48% indicated that they would like to spend less time at the board office.

Principals indicated a desire to spend less time on management-related activities, and more time being instructional leaders. On average, principals in the sample spend 5 hours per week on curriculum and instruction, a number that 82% would like to see increase. Almost half of the principals who participated in the survey would like to devote more time to walking the hallways, playground, and lunchroom than the current 6 hour per week average. Similarly, only an average of 3 hours each week is spent on classroom walkthroughs, a practice with which 83% of the sample would like to become more engaged.

Principals also indicated that they spend an average of only 2 hours every week on professional development. Nearly three quarters of the sample (74%)

mentioned they would like to be able to spend more time engaging in professional development opportunities. Similarly, principals spent more time on classroom walkthroughs (factor loading = .834) as part of their instructional leadership. We found no significant difference in how male and female principals spent their time on classroom walkthroughs, t (1387) = −.64, p = .52. Student discipline/attendance (factor loading = .807) is substantially loaded on the factor of student affairs. On average, principals spent 8 hours per week on student discipline/attendance, which was the highest among all the work tasks on which principals spent their time. Approximately, 39% principals reported that ideally they would spend less time on student discipline/attendance and 51% of principals indicated they should spend the same amount of time in the area. An independent sample t test showed that there was a significant difference between male and female principals in terms of the time they spent on student discipline/attendance, t (1403) = −2.7, p = 0. Male principals (M = 7.5, SD = 5.5) spent less time on student discipline/attendance than female principals (M = 8.3, SD = 5.9).

Modes of communication

The different modes of communication that principals employ with stakeholders, such as formal and informal meetings, email, and phone, also affect their use of time at work. Figure 6.1 shows that email is not only a major communication tool in principals' work—it is also the most time-consuming mode of communication. On average, principals spent substantial amounts of time on email (11.5 hours/week). There was a great concern among principals that they spent too much time on emails. Of the surveyed principals, 83% indicated that ideally they would spend less time on emails. The other communicative modes that principals spent the most time using were informal (9.3 hours/week) and formal (6.3 hours/week) meetings and the phone (4.3 hours/week).

Principals' use of time is also conveyed in their daily interactions with different stakeholders. An exploratory factor analysis, shown in Table 6.2, demonstrates that the stakeholders with whom principals interact are clustered in three groups. The first group includes classroom teachers, students, custodians, educational assistants, and parents/guardians. In the first group (factor 1), the amount of interaction principals had with classroom teachers (factor loading = .786) and students (factor loading = .744) is fairly high, but lower with parents/guardians (factor loading = .480). It is possible that principals' interactions with this group are more instructionally oriented, but it is interesting to see that custodians also fall into this group. Additionally, there was a significant correlation between the factor *instructional leadership* and the extent of the interactions principals had with classroom teachers (r = .20) and students (r = .24). In the second group (factor 2), principals had a higher level of interaction with their VPs (factor loading = .686) and union stewards (factor loading = .606), and a lower level with the specialist teaching staff (factor loading = .492). The extent of interaction principals had with administrative assistants is cross-loaded on all groups. The cross-loading indicated that administrative assistants were more likely involved

How principals use their time in Ontario 101

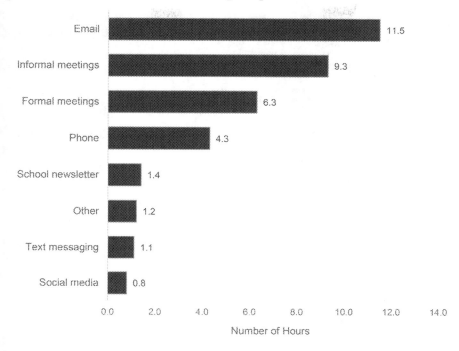

Figure 6.1 Time spent on school communication

in principals' interactions with different interest groups, especially in their interaction with the first group.

Where principals spend their time is also critical in understanding how principals use their time. Figure 6.2 shows that principals spent nearly half of their average day in their office or their VP's office. The factor *school management* is significantly correlated to the percentage of the day principals spent in

Table 6.2 The extent of interactions principals have with people

Interactions with	Factor 1	Factor 2	Factor 3
Classroom teachers	**.786**	.059	.028
Students	**.744**	−.137	.006
Custodian	**.684**	.270	.009
Educational assistants	**.643**	.058	.233
Parents/guardians	**.480**	.209	.234
Administrative assistant	.368	.127	.005
VPs	−.229	**.686**	−.220
Union steward	.266	**.606**	.092
Other school staff	.142	**.584**	.368
Specialist teaching staff	.327	**.492**	−.004
Other	−.096	.191	**.775**
ECE personnel	.320	−.241	**.709**

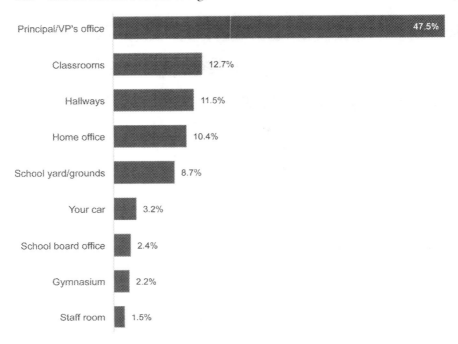

Figure 6.2 Percentage of an average day principals spend time in different locations

their/VP's office ($r = .17$), which indicates that the more time they spent in their office or their VP's office, the more likely they were to spend time on school management. However, such correlation is relatively small.

How principals spend their time according to policies that influence their work

Initiatives and policies imposed on schools intensify principals' work. Among 13 major provincial policies, eight of them are significantly correlated on the number of hours principals spent on work on a weekly basis (see Table 6.3). Such correlations indicate that the greater impact these policies have on principals' work, the longer hours principals tend to spend every week. In particular, the impact of the Parents in Partnership: Parent Engagement Policy on principals' work seems to be relatively stronger ($r = .12$) compared to that of the other policies. Further correlation analysis shows that the amount of time principals spent on student discipline/attendance is significantly correlated to the impact of Bill 13 Anti-Bullying ($r = .13$) and Bill 212 Safe Schools Act ($r = .12$) on school principals' work. Principals who spent more time on student discipline/attendance are likely to report that these bills have a greater impact on their work. Similarly, the amount of time principals spent on personnel is significantly correlated with the impact of Regulation 274/12 Hiring Practice ($r = .09$), though such correlation is fairly small.

Table 6.3 Hours spent per week and provincial policy

	Hours/week	Aboriginal Ed	Bill 115	Bill 13	Equity and inclusive	ICT	OHSA	Parent engagement	Urban priority
Hours/week	1	.077**	.083**	.086**	.055*	.073**	.052*	.106**	.073**
Aboriginal Ed	.077**	1	.159**	.163**	.189**	.056*	.108**	.104**	.062**
Bill 115	.083**	.159**	1	.385**	.231**	.102**	.200**	.175**	.017
Bill 13	.086**	.163**	.385**	1	.402**	.103**	.291**	.266**	.043
Equity and inclusive	.055*	.189**	.231**	.402**	1	.143**	.214**	.289**	.097**
ICT	.073**	.056*	.102**	.103**	.143**	1	.162**	.219**	.050
OHSA	.052*	.108**	.200**	.291**	.214**	.162**	1	.324**	.083**
PP	.106**	.104**	.175**	.266**	.289**	.219**	.324**	1	.077**
Urban priority	.073**	.062**	.017	.043	.097**	.050	.083**	.077**	1

Note: * indicates significance at 0.5 and ** indicates significance at 0.1.

Note: Bill 115 is the *Putting Students First Act*; Bill 13 refers to *Anti-Bullying*; ICT stands for *Information and Communication Technologies* in education and management; OHSA stands for *Occupational Health and Safety Act* (including Bill 168 changes—workplace harassment and violence). PP refers to the *Parents in Partnership: Parent Engagement Policy*.

How principals spend their time is also reflected in their perceptions of their work. Principals who reported working long hours every week are more likely to indicate that they never seem to have enough time to get their work done ($r = .20$), they feel pressured to work long hours ($r = .24$), and the pace of their work is too fast ($r = .14$). A significant correlation was also found between the time they spent at work and their perception of life and work balance ($r = -.30$). Principals are less likely to report having an appropriate balance between their work and life outside of work when they work longer hours each week.

Discussion

What do our findings tell us about principals' time use? Overall, principals in the Ontario English-language public school system work long hours and are a part of the long-hours work culture (Burke & Cooper, 2008). We know that principals' work is influenced by many provincial policies, especially those associated with increasing parent engagement, creating safe and accepting schools, and applying more equitable hiring practices. They also spend much of their time engaged in managerial tasks through email, meetings (formal and informal), and phone calls. This work appears to occur half of the time in their office or the office of their VP, and seems to be clustered around three groups of stakeholders.

Ultimately, these findings reflect fundamental misalignments in principals' time use. In this section, we discuss these misalignments in terms of leading versus managing and differing conceptualizations of instructional leadership.

Leading and managing

Relevant to the long work hours is the tension between leading and managing. Many principals in our study are spending a substantial amount of their time in managing the school, dealing with budget, personnel, and school safety. Meanwhile, they are also expected to demonstrate leadership to meet the expectations of school performance. This tension between leading and managing is certainly not new (Martin & Willower, 1981; Martinko & Gardner, 1990), and our findings demonstrate that the Ontario principals in this study also wrestle with this tension.

Ever since the one-room schoolhouse expanded to a school building with a grade system based on age, head teachers—now mainly referred to as school principals—have been tasked with administering, managing, and leading that school site. The tension between these roles has a long history (Cuban, 1988) and is connected to allocation of time to tasks. Generally, management can be considered the tasks and activities—such as planning, budgeting, hiring, scheduling, and so forth—associated with maintaining organizational functionality (Spillane & Hunt, 2010). Although leading can be generally understood as influencing others in various kinds of relationships focused on specific outcomes (Ryan, 2005), leadership in public education is nuanced to concentrate on improving curriculum delivery and student learning. These notions of leadership have often been referred to as instructional leadership, curriculum leadership, or pedagogical leadership (Day et al., 2009; Jenkins & Pfeifer, 2012; Robinson, Lloyd, & Rowe, 2008; Seiser, 2019). The concept of instructional leadership is most well known to Ontario principals because the Ontario Leadership Framework (Institute for Educational Leadership, 2012) prioritizes leadership instruction. Simultaneously, just as the past few decades have seen an emphasis on school leadership to improve student outcomes, so too have school systems been subjected to increased and varied accountability approaches to improve schools (Dulude & Milley, 2020; Firestone & Shipps, 2007; Pollock & Winton, 2016). It can be argued that these concurrent efforts to improve public education have had the consequence of exacerbating tension between managing and leading: Both approaches compete for priority and presence in practice, with managerial and administrative procedures often winning out over instructional priorities (Pollock, Wang, & Hauseman, 2015; Swapp, 2012). For this reason, it is not surprising that participants in this study indicated that they engage in long work weeks (58 hours per week) and feel they engage in substantial amounts of managerial work rather than less. Work intensification has exacerbated the tension between managing and leading. Another way of interpreting these findings is examining the tension that exists around instructional leadership for Ontario principals.

Conflicting understandings of instructional leadership

Just as Leithwood, Jantzi, and Steinbach described an office with more 213 books about leadership in their 1999 book, there continues to be no shortage of research on different ways to lead. To name a few: "moral leadership, participative leadership, managerial leadership, democratic leadership, transactional leadership, leadership for the differently-abled, student leadership, parent/community leadership, emancipatory leadership, shared leadership, distributed leadership, instructional leadership, transformational leadership, and teacher leadership" (Ryan, 2005, p. 22). From a policy perspective, Ontario school leaders are specifically expected to be *instructional leaders* (Institute for Educational Leadership, 2012). How principals understand this leadership role might influence the way they work and explain some of the work habits and patterns and expectations that they reported in this study.

There is no one definitive definition of instructional leadership (Powell, 2017). For example, as we have argued elsewhere (Pollock, Wang, & Hauseman, 2017), the traditional conceptualization of instructional leadership is "hands-on." Leaders who lead instructionally typically are focused on curriculum, have a strong pedagogical background, and work directly with teachers in professional learning opportunities as well as the classroom. According to the research, instructional leaders use mentoring strategies and model best practices for instruction with teachers (Horng & Loeb, 2010). Another way of understanding instructional leadership is through the lens of organizational management: Hiring practices, class assignments, scheduling, budgeting, designing professional learning opportunities that concentrate on curriculum and instruction, promoting a positive work/learning environment, and supporting overall instruction in the school are all other potential ways to enact instructional leadership (Fullan, 2014; Grissom, Loeb, & Master, 2013).

How a principal conceptualizes their instructional leadership role may influence how they use their time. If a school principal views instructional leadership from a more narrowly defined traditional, hands-on role, then they would most likely perceive that only a few set tasks and activities that they currently engage in fall within their notion of instructional leadership such as walk-throughs, co-facilitating professional learning, and evaluating teaching and learning. For example, we determined through a factor analysis that principals spent a large amount of time in four areas: school management, instructional leadership, student affairs, and professional development. Of the four areas, principals seem to be spending much of their time "managing," which they described as dealing with budgets and personnel, issues around occupational health and safety, internal school management, building maintenance, and district school board office meetings—all work tasks that those who perceive the concept narrowly would not consider instructional leadership activities. Principals who narrowly conceptualize instructional leadership may find the increased accountability pressures encroaching on what they perceive to be more purposeful work—in other words, work that is directly related to curriculum delivery, teaching, and learning.

Principals who understand instructional leadership from a more holistic, organizational management perspective might inherently believe that the majority of their work can be aligned with instructional leadership. They might not find it surprising that most of their work concentrates on budgets and personnel, issues around occupational health and safety, internal school management, building maintenance, and district school board office meetings because they may see some of this work as part of their instructional role. For example, budgeting decisions may be made on the basis of how to support teachers' professional learning or for classroom support for student learning. For principals who see most of their work tied to instructional leadership, especially those who work long hours, they may find it difficult to prioritize their work because they try to assign equal importance to most of their assigned work. This, in the long run, can lead to long work hours and an increased volume of work, which has been connected to stress and burnout (Federici & Skaalvik, 2012; Pollock, Wang, & Mahfouz, 2020).

Conclusion

Ultimately, our findings indicate that Ontario principals' time use is characterized by fundamental misalignments and reflect a global trend: Principals are not spending their time at work the way they want to, and their time at work is influenced by how they conceptualize instructional leadership. These misalignments are occurring within a context of work intensification and point toward larger issues the principalship is facing in the 21st century: The role is less appealing and there are higher rates of burnout. Next to teachers, principals have the greatest indirect impact on students (Leithwood, Jantzi, & Steinbach, 1999); if these issues are not addressed in a meaningful way, they could pose great problems for public education in the future.

References

Apple, M. (1986). *Teachers and texts: A political economy of class & gender relations in education*. Abingdon: Routledge.

Bezzina, C., Paletta, A., & Alimehmeti, G. (2017). What are school leaders in Italy doing? An observational study. *Educational Management Administration & Leadership, 46*(5), 841–863.

Bristow, M., Ireson, G., & Coleman, A. (2007). *A life in the day of a a headteacher: A study of practice and well-being*. National College for School Leadership.

Burke, J. J., & Cooper, C. L. (Eds.). (2008). *The long work hours culture: Causes, consequences and choices*. Bingley: Emerald.

Canadian Association of Principals, & The Alberta Teachers' Association. (2014). *The future of the principalship in Canada*. Author.

Cohen, L., Manion, L., & Morrison, K. (2011). *Research methods in education* (7th ed.). Abingdon: Routledge.

Cuban, L. (1988). *The managerial imperative and the practice of leadership in schools*. Albany, NY: State University of New York Press.

Day, C., Sammons, P., Hopkins, D., Harris, A., Leithwood, K., Gu, Q., Brown, E., & Kington, A. (2009). *The impact of school leadership on pupil outcomes: Final report*. Research Report DCSF-RR108. UK Department for Children Schools and Families. https://dera.ioe.ac.uk/11329/1/DCSF-RR108.pdf.

Denscombe, M. (2008). Communities of practice: A research paradigm for the mixed methods approach. *Journal of Mixed Methods Research, 2*(3), 270–283.

Drago, R. W. (2007). *Striking a balance: Work, family, life*. Economics Affairs Bureau.

Dulude, E., & Milley, P. (2020). Institutional complexity and multiple accountability tensions: A conceptual framework for analyzing school leaders' interpretation of competing demands. *Policy Futures in Education*. Advance online publication. https://doi.org/10.1177/1478210320940134.

Eacott, S. (2013). "Leadership" and the social: time, space and the epistemic. *International Journal of Educational Management, 27*(1), 91–101. doi: 10.1108/09513541311289846.

Federici, R. A., & Skaalvik, E. M. (2012). Principal self-efficacy: Relations with burnout, job satisfaction and motivation to quit. *Social Psychology of Education, 15*(3), 295–320. https://doi.org/10.1007/s11218-012-9183-5.

Firestone, W. A., & Shipps, D. (2007). How do leaders interpret conflicting accountabilities to improve student learning? In W. A. Firestone & C. Riehl (Eds.), *A new agenda for research in educational leadership* (pp. 81–100). New York, NY: Teachers College Press.

Fullan, M. (2014). *The principals: Three keys to maximizing impact*. San Francisco, CA: Jossey-Bass.

Gaziel, H. (1995). Managerial work pattersn of principals at high and average performing Israeli elementary schools. *The Elementary School Journal, 96*, 179–194.

Grissom, J. A., Loeb, S., & Master, B. (2013). Effective instructional time use for school leaders: Longitudinal evidence from observations of principals. *Educational Researcher, 42*(8), 433–444.

Grissom, J. A., Loeb, S., & Mitani, H. (2015). Principal time management skills: Explaining patterns in principals' use, job stress, and perceived effectiveness. *Journal of Educational Administration, 53*(6), 773–793. doi: 10.1108/JEA-09-2014-0117.

Horng, E. L., Klasik, D., & Loeb, E. (2009). *Principal time-use and school effectiveness.* National Center for Analysis of Longitudinal Data in Education Research. https://www.urban.org/sites/default/files/publication/28151/1001441-Principal-Time-Use-and-School-Effectiveness.PDF.

Horng, E., & Loeb, S. (2010). New thinking about instructional leadership. *Phi Delta Kappan, 92*(3), 66–68. http://search.proquest.com/docview/845795425?accountid=15115.

Institute for Educational Leadership. (2012). *The Ontario Leadership Framework: A school and system leader's guide to putting Ontario's Leadership Framework into action.* https://www.education-leadership-ontario.ca/application/files/8814/9452/4183/Ontario_Leadership_Framework_OLF.pdf.

Jenkins, J., & Pfeifer, R. S. (2012). The principal as curriculum leader: To effectively transition to a curriculum that is based on the Common Core State Standards, principals must become curriculum leaders. *Principal Leadership, 12*(5), 30–34.

Kmetz, J. T., & Willower, D. J. (1982). Elementary school principals' work behavior. *Educational Administration Quarterly, 18*(4), 62–78.

Lee, M., & Hallinger, P. (2012). National context influencing principals' time use and allocation: Economic development, societal culture, and educational system. *School Effectiveness and School Improvement, 23*(4), 461–482.

Leithwood, K., Jantzi, D., & Steinbach, C. (1999). *Changing leadership for changing times.* Milton Park: Taylor & Francis Group.

Martin, W. J., & Willower, D. J. (1981). The managerial behavior of high school principals. *Educational Administration Quarterly, 17*(1), 69–90.

Martinko, M. J., & Gardner, W. L. (1990). Structured observation of managerial work: A replication and synthesis. *Journal of Management Studies, 27*(3), 329–357.

Mintzberg, H. (1973). *The nature of managerial work.* Harper & Row.

Pollock, K., Hauseman, C., & Wang, F. (2014, October). Efforts to be an instructional leader: The changing nature of principals' work. *OPC Register,* 22–26.

Pollock, K., & Wang, F. (2019). *Le travail des directions d'école au sein des systems d'éducation de langue française en Ontario* [Principals' work in Ontario's French-language education systems]. Report prepared for the Association des directions et directions adjointes des écoles franco-ontariennes (ADFO). https://www.edu.uwo.ca/faculty-profiles/docs/other/pollock/pollock-ADFO-Report-Revised-Final.pdf.

Pollock, K., & Wang, F. (2020). Principal well-being: Strategies and coping mechanisms in times of uncertainty. *OPC Register, 22*(3) 22–27.

Pollock, K., Wang, F., & Hauseman, D. C. (2014). *The changing nature of principals' work. Final report for the Ontario Principals' Council.* Toronto, ON: Ontario Principals' Council.

Pollock, K., Wang, F., & Hauseman, D. C. (2015). Complexity and volume: An inquiry into factors that drive principals' work. *Societies, 5*(2), 537–565. doi:10.3390/soc5020537.

Pollock, K., Wang, F., & Hauseman, D. C. (2017). *The changing nature of vice-principals' work. Final report for the Ontario Principals' Council.* Toronto, ON: Ontario Principals' Council.

Pollock, K., Wang, F., & Mahfouz, J. (2020). Guest editorial. *Journal of Educational Administration, 58*(4), 389–399. https://doi.org/10.1108/JEA-08-2020-237.

Pollock, K., & Winton, S. (2016). Juggling multiple accountability systems: How three principals manage these tensions in Ontario. Canada. *Educational Assessment, Evaluation and Accountability, 28*(4), 323–345. doi:10.1007/s11092-015-9224-7.

Powell, G. (2017). *Understanding instructional leadership: Perceptions of elementary principals* [Doctoral dissertation, University of Western Ontario]. https://ir.lib.uwo.ca/etd/5076/.

Robinson, V., Lloyd, C., & Rowe, K. (2008). The impact of leadership on student outcomes: An analysis of the differential effects of leadership types. *Educational Administration Quarterly, 44*(5), 63–674. doi: 10.1177/0013161X08321509.

Ryan, J. (1996). The new institutionalism in a postmodern world: De-differentiation and the study of institutions. In R. Crowson, W. L. Boyd, & H. Mawhinney (Eds.), *The politics of education and the new institutionalism: Reinventing the American school* (pp. 189–202). London: Falmer.

Ryan, J. (2005). What is leadership? In W. Hare & J. Portelli (Eds.), *Key questions for educators* (pp. 22–25). Edphil Books.

Sayles, L. (1964). *Managerial behavior: Administration in complex organizations.* McGraw-Hill.

Seiser, A. F. (2019). Exploring enhanced pedagogical leadership: An action research study involving Swedish principals. *Educational Action Research.* doi: 10.1080/09650792.2019.1656661.

Spillane, J. P., & Hunt, B. R. (2010). Days of their lives: A mixed-methods, descriptive analysis of the men and women at work in the principal's office. *Journal of Curriculum Studies, 42*(3), 293–331. doi: 10.1080/00220270903527623.

Statistics Canada. (2013). [Table 282-0026: labour force survey estimates (LFS), by actual hours worked, class of worker, National Occupational Classification of Statistics (NOC-S) and sex]. http://www5.statcan.gc.ca/cansim/a05?lang=eng&id=2820026&pattern=2820026&searchTypeByValue=1&p2=35.

Swapp, D. H. (2012). *Exploring the current nature of a school principal's work* [Master's thesis, University of Western Ontario]. https://ir.lib.uwo.ca/etd/845/.

Thompson, E. P. (1967, December). Time, work-discipline, and industrial capitalism. *The Past and Present Society, 38,* 56–97.

Wallace, J. (2007). Equity hierarchies and the work of female school administrators with/in the multicultural State. *Journal of Educational Administration and Foundations, 18*(1–2), 147–170.

7 Managing time? Principal supervisors' time use to support principals

Laura K. Rogers, Ellen B. Goldring, Mollie Rubin, Michael Neel, and Jason A. Grissom

In the United States, school principals are "instructional leaders" who lead their schools by carrying out tasks such as setting an ambitious instructional vision for the school, providing feedback to teachers, and facilitating school-wide professional development (Neumerski, 2013). As principals' work has become more instructionally focused, the need for public school districts to support principals in the work of school improvement has grown (Honig et al., 2010; Kimball et al., 2015). Unfortunately, many districts continue to structure their central offices in ways that privilege school monitoring over school improvement.

Prior research has shown that district administrators can play a powerful role in school support (Elmore, 1993; Honig, 2012; Johnson & Chrispeels, 2010; Marsh et al., 2005). Principal supervisors—the individuals who directly oversee principals—have emerged as the central office administrators with the most potential to help principals become stronger leaders (Goldring et al., 2018; Honig, 2012; Honig & Rainey, 2015; Thessin, 2019). Traditionally, the principal supervisor role focused on evaluating school principals and monitoring their compliance with district policies and regulations (Rogers et al., 2018; Sergiovanni & Starratt, 1998). However, principals can benefit a great deal when the principal supervisor role is reframed as one of instructional leadership support and coaching. Honig (2012) found that principal supervisors who frame their role as one of teaching rather than managing can more competently deepen principals' instructional leadership. Teaching-oriented supervisors work to improve principals' performance by engaging them in *joint work*: coconstructing learning through activities such as classroom walkthoughs, coaching and strategizing sessions, and using data and tools (Honig, 2008, 2012; Thessin, 2019). These activities require frequent one-on-one visits from the supervisor, typically at the principal's school. Principal supervisors also facilitate principal learning by leading professional learning communities in which groups of principals share, reflect, and engage in critical inquiry (Goldring et al., 2018; Honig & Rainey, 2014).

The characteristics of the new principal supervisor role—teaching, coaching, relationship-building, and coconstructed learning—represent a major departure from its former compliance orientation. To help districts in the United States facilitate the transition to the new role, the Chief Council of State School

Officers released a set of Model Principal Supervisor Professional Standards in 2015 that codified the research about principal supervisor best practices into a set of eight standards.

Revising the principal supervisor role does not come without challenges, however. As recently as 2012, principal supervisors received little training or support from their districts in how to support principal leadership (Corcoran et al., 2013). They could also expect to manage large numbers of principals at a time: A 2012 national survey of principal supervisors conducted by the Council of the Great City Schools found that the average principal supervisor span of control (i.e., the number of people each supervisor is assigned to manage) was 24 principals (Casserly et al., 2013). Because the new principal supervisor role requires principal supervisors to work intensively with each principal to observe teacher instruction, coach, and plan for improvement, a large span of control can prevent supervisors from spending adequate time with their principals. Moreover, even with a lower span of control, supervisors require district support structures to protect their time by reducing their other noninstructional responsibilities, such as directing district initiatives or programs (Honig, 2012).

Districts bear the responsibility for providing principal supervisors with adequate training, reducing their spans of control, and protecting their time to realize the goal of increasing the quantity and quality of time they spend with principals. Some districts may struggle to provide this support due to internal organizational barriers or lack of resources. Additionally, principal supervisors may find it difficult to absorb the new mindsets and skills associated with the role. Above all, principal supervisors require the time to develop new skills, to collaborate with one another, and to work with principals on a regular basis. Overcoming such barriers was an implicit goal of the Principal Supervisor Initiative (PSI), the initiative we study in this chapter.

The Principal Supervisor Initiative

The PSI, a four-year effort by The Wallace Foundation to change the quality of principal supervision in six urban districts across the United States, focused on maximizing principal supervisors' ability to support and develop principals' instructional leadership. The initiative began in the 2014–2015 school year and formally ended in the 2017–2018 school year, although districts were expected to continue the work independently after this time (Goldring et al., 2020). The PSI asked districts to implement five core components (see Goldring et al., 2018): (a) revising the principal supervisor job description to focus on instructional leadership; (b) reducing principal supervisors' span of control and changing how supervisors are assigned to principals; (c) training supervisors and developing their capacity to support principals; (d) developing systems to identify and train new supervisors (i.e., succession planning); and (e) strengthening central office structures to support and sustain changes in the principal supervisor role. The PSI's theory of action—that principal supervisors can improve the quality of principal leadership—hinged heavily on supervisors' ability to work directly with principals. Supervisors and principals reported that, prior to the initiative, they spent neither sufficient time together nor enough of their time focusing on instructional matters (Goldring et al., 2018). Thus, increasing the quantity and quality of supervisors' time with principals became a major goal for PSI districts.

Focus on supervisor time use

In this chapter, *time use* refers to how individuals allocate and focus their time during the workday. Previous studies have addressed the importance of principals' ability to manage work time and the barriers they face in managing their time effectively (Grissom et al., 2015; Horng et al., 2010). Less is known about principal supervisor time use; for example: how supervisors decide to allocate and balance their time among many responsibilities, meet with their principals, and focus their time with principals. The same national survey of principal supervisors that identified large spans of control also reported that supervisors experienced demands on their time that limited their ability to work with principals, such as the need to attend district meetings (Casserly et al., 2013), although the survey did not directly address supervisor time use.

In our study of the PSI's implementation, we collected information that specifically addressed supervisors' time use as their role evolved. In this chapter, we present a first-of-its-kind description of principal supervisors' time use in the redesigned role and in their work with principals in the six urban districts that participated in the PSI. Specially, we address the following three questions:

1 How do principal supervisors in the new role spend their time?
2 To what extent does time use vary across principal supervisors, and what accounts for this variation?
3 What lessons do the PSI districts offer regarding how districts can facilitate the quantity and quality of principal supervisors' time with principals?

Studying principal supervisors' time use provides insight into their work in three ways. First, as the notion that principal supervisors can drive principal improvement has gained traction, district central offices have grappled with how best to define and allocate supervisors' new work and time with principals. Within the bureaucratic context of the central office, these changes are potentially disruptive because they are zero sum: Principal supervisors must give up some of their prior formal responsibilities within the central office to accommodate the expectations for increased work with principals. Principal supervisors' time use therefore depends on the extent to which the central office can successfully release them from time constraints such as paperwork, meetings, ombudsman work, and other formal roles.

Second, principal supervisor time use depends on supervisors' own knowledge and skills, including their capacity to protect their own time (Honig & Rainey, 2019). Supervisors who are completely new to the new role may have little understanding of how to effectively prioritize their time, especially when they are saddled with multiple formal job responsibilities. Conversely, veteran supervisors trained in the former compliance-focused role may struggle to reconfigure their time to place greater focus on instructional leadership work with principals. In both cases, supervisors' existing capacity affects their time use.

Third, variation in principal supervisor time use can provide insight into how supervisors differentiate their work in response to the specific needs of their principals. Just as principal time use has been shown to be responsive to school contextual factors (Grissom et al., 2015; Huang et al., 2018; May et al., 2012), principal supervisor time use may be tied to specific goals they have for their work with each principal. Supervisors may differentiate the frequency of their visits to each principal as well as the content of those visits.

Data and sample

Our analyses draw upon data we collected in the second (2015–2016) and third (2016–2017) years of the PSI from the six urban PSI districts: Baltimore, Broward County, Cleveland, Des Moines, Long Beach, and Minneapolis. These large urban districts ranged in size from 30,000 to 270,000 students. Unlike small or rural districts with small central offices where principal supervisors may be more likely to occupy multiple roles within the central office, the PSI districts all employed multiple administrators whose sole focus was principal supervision.

As the independent research team that studied the implementation of the PSI, we administered surveys and visited each district multiple times during the implementation process to collect information about the progress of the initiative. We collected annual surveys from all principals and principal supervisors working in the six PSI districts. We also interviewed a subsample of key central office leaders, principal supervisors, and principals in the PSI districts during the same time period. From each district, we selected two key central office leaders, as many as six principal supervisors, and a sample of 10 principals. To ensure maximum variation, we first stratified principals according to their principal supervisor before randomly selecting. Table 7.1 details the total number of survey and interview participants across the six districts for both years.

Table 7.1 Description of PSI survey and interview participants

	2015–2016			2016–2017		
	Total surveys	*Survey response rate*	*Interviews*	*Total surveys*	*Survey response rate*	*Interviews*
Central office leader	–	–	15	–	–	13
Principal supervisor	50	100%	35	51	100%	37
Principal	635	94%	59	639	92%	60

Note: Central office leaders were not surveyed.

The surveys asked principals and principal supervisors to report on the quantity and quality of their time spent working together, such as:

- The percentage of time principal supervisors spent visiting schools, leading group meetings with principals, and participating in meetings.
- The number and duration of meetings principals had with principal supervisors at their school in a three-month period.
- The percentage of their time together that principal supervisors and principals spent on different issues, such as instructional leadership issues (e.g., observing classroom instruction together, analyzing school data together, and providing coaching and feedback to help the principal improve his or her leadership), operational issues (e.g., managing the school budget and creating class schedules), parent and community issues (e.g., resolving parent complaints about a teacher), human resource issues (e.g., hiring or dismissing teachers), and other issues (e.g., paperwork).

We further probed topics of time use in interviews, including how principal supervisors made decisions about allocating their time, the barriers principal supervisors faced when attempting to increase their time in schools, and principals' responses to spending more time with their supervisors.

How do supervisors spend their time?

Supervisor time allocation

Principal supervisors spent the greatest part of their time working with principals at their schools and in networks of principal groups. Across both years, principal supervisors in the PSI reported that they spent 48% of their total job time working one-on-one with principals in schools, and 13% of their time working with principals in group settings, such as monthly principal professional learning meetings (Figure 7.1). The remainder of principal supervisors' time was spent in meetings with central office personnel (21%), in meetings with fellow principal supervisors (14%), and working on other activities such as paperwork and email (4%).

Quantity of time with principals

Most of the PSI districts attempted to regulate principal supervisors' time with principals by setting targets for how often they should meet together one-on-one at school. Targets varied: In one district, this target was a minimum of two visits to each principal per month. In another, supervisors were expected to be in schools exclusively three days a week. In addition, all districts required principal supervisors to lead group or "network" meetings with principals, typically once a month, in which they gathered principals together to deliver professional development and information about district policies and requirements.

In interviews, supervisors universally emphasized the importance of spending the bulk of their time working with principals in schools. School visits allowed

Principal supervisors' time use 115

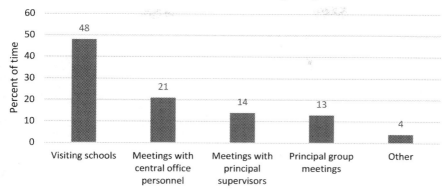

Figure 7.1 Principal supervisors' use of time at work
Note: Data from principal supervisor surveys, 2016 (N = 50) and 2017 (N = 51).

them to coach and relate with principals around their specific school needs. One supervisor explained, "I don't want to be 'the absent supervisor.' For me, it's important to have a good handle on what's taking place." When they were not in schools, principal supervisors went to great lengths to maintain a direct connection with principals, as the following supervisor described:

> I've come in this year really focused on building relationships and supporting the work of the principals ... I go out to sites at least once a month for an informal visit, and then I communicate with principals via email, phone, or any time they need something. It's [creating a] support system and service back to the principal.

In practice, some supervisors fell short of meeting district targets for spending one-on-one time with principals. We asked principals to report the number of meetings they had together at schools in the last three months (one semester). Over the two years, the median principal reported having three meetings at school with their supervisor in three months, or about one meeting per month—far fewer than any of the district minimums. Principals also reported that they met with principal supervisors at principal group meetings about three times in a three-month period. These results suggest that principal supervisors were able to meet regularly with principals in groups but still struggled to meet district expectations for one-on-one meetings with principals.

Nevertheless, principals and supervisors emphasized that although barriers to visiting schools existed, supervisors were generally spending more time with principals than they had prior to the role change. Reflecting on the old supervisor role, a veteran supervisor explained that most principals in the past could expect infrequent visits from their supervisor, typically only to put out "fires" and address crises: "If you saw your [supervisor] once a month, you were lucky."

Quality of time with principals

In addition to creating targets for the frequency of supervisors' meetings with principals, the PSI districts also focused on providing supervisors with the training and tools to focus their time on matters of instructional leadership with principals. Supervisors received ongoing training that focused on building their skills as coaches, evaluating principal performance and providing feedback, and helping principals monitor the quality of instruction in their schools. In some (but not all) districts, supervisors also developed common tools—such as inquiry cycles, rubrics, and observation forms—that were intended to allow them to organize their work more efficiently around supporting principal instructional leadership.

Principals and supervisors reported that the nature of their work together had become more focused on teaching and learning since the PSI began, as supervisors sought to improve the quality of both teachers' instruction and the principal's leadership of the school's instructional program. A common activity during one-on-one principal meetings at school was a "learning walk" during which the supervisor and principal visited one or more classrooms together to observe instruction. Supervisors then coached principals to create a plan for teacher improvement based on the findings of the observation. Another common activity was to conduct "data dives" in which principals and principal supervisors analyzed patterns in school achievement data and diagnosed changes that needed to be made to support improved achievement. On average, principals reported that the majority (58%) of their work with their supervisor centered around instructional leadership activities (Figure 7.2). The rest of the time was devoted to operational tasks (17%), human resource issues (13%), parent and community issues (11%), and other miscellaneous issues (1%) such as assisting the principal with student discipline.

Although supervisors across districts spent the greater part of their time with principals focusing on instructional leadership, they were cognizant of the need

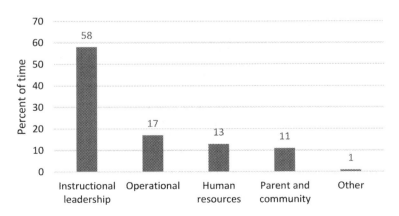

Figure 7.2 Principal supervisor focus of time with principals

Note: Data from principal surveys, 2016 (N = 635) and 2017 (N = 639).

to ensure that principals' and their schools' basic noninstructional needs were being met. A supervisor described this balance as working "two jobs":

> I don't visit a school without being in classrooms or seeing student work or asking principals information about their data ... That's the bulk of my work. But it's almost like two jobs because we [supervisors] are also doing a lot of the stuff we used to do around maintenance and facilities, because it's not going to get done if we don't.

The persistence of noninstructional responsibilities as an extra "job" was common, even three years into the initiative. Although no district revised the role to focus 100% of principal supervisor time on instructional leadership, supervisors spoke of sacrificing precious instructional leadership time with principals to help them navigate convoluted district bureaucratic processes and policies, nonresponsive central office departments, sudden budget crises, or issues of student safety and discipline. Even though many of these activities were technically no longer a part of the supervisor job description, supervisors often elected to help principals solve noninstructional problems because they believed that this was the quickest and most efficient way to help them return their focus to instruction. We discuss this problem and other barriers to supervisor time use in greater detail in the next section.

What explains variation in supervisor time use?

Although the supervisors spent most of their time working with principals, the principals indicated that the frequency and focus of their work with their supervisors varied across districts and even across supervisors within the same district. Although the median was three visits, principal-reported meetings with their supervisor at school in a three-month period ranged from zero to 20. Such wide variation existed even within individual supervisors. Figure 7.3 displays the range of school-site meetings that principals reported over a three-month period in 2017. Each bar in the figure represents the range of school meetings reported by principals with the same supervisor that year.

In our analysis of the interview data, we identified two possible sources of the variation in supervisor time use with their principals. First, variation in time use was the intentional result of policies that encouraged supervisors to differentiate their time with principals according to their assessment of each principal's needs. Second, supervisors dealt with organizational and individual barriers that impinged upon their ability to spend time with their principals.

Intentional differentiation of time with principals

In all PSI districts, supervisors categorized their principals according to support-related needs. In some districts, this process was known as "tiering" (Goldring et al., 2020): Supervisors designated principals as needing *high, medium,* or *low* intervention. The criteria for sorting principals varied by district but typically involved

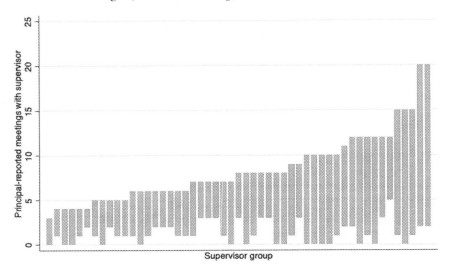

Figure 7.3 Range of principal-reported school meetings with supervisor in 3 months, by supervisor

Note: Data from principal surveys, 2017 (N = 639). The number of principals in each supervisor group ranged from 6 to 19.

both quantitative and qualitative factors. Supervisors used school achievement test scores, climate survey scores, their own evaluations of principal performance, and their holistic understanding of principals' leadership growth to sort principals.

Once grouped, principals received differing levels of support from supervisors. In one district, principals were grouped into tiers of *basic*, *essential*, or *targeted* support. Supervisors were expected to spend at least twice as much time (8–10 hours) with targeted support principals each month compared to basic support principals (3–4 hours). In other districts, the process for differentiating time and support to principals was more loosely and informally defined. A district leader in one such district framed the district's looser philosophy of differentiation as an affirmation of supervisors' street-level understanding of principals' needs:

> They definitely do have a high level of discretion of how they're using their time and how they're moving their [principals] … That's something that is really up to the [supervisory] team because they're close to the building and know the issues that are happening on the ground.

District leaders and supervisors also described differentiation as a balancing act between communicating high and consistent performance expectations to all principals and addressing the unique context of each school. In several cases, supervisors were forced to abandon predetermined criteria for differentiated support to help principals navigate sudden school crises.

Often, the principals who required additional support were new to the role, new to their school, or working in schools with academic or safety concerns. A principal in a low-achieving school described the hands-on nature of his supervisor's increased support:

> I've noticed she's been much more involved: more interaction, more discussions together, more visits, things like that ... I'm at a struggling school, so I probably see my director more than typical, even prior to her having less schools, she still came around more.

Higher performing principals were also sometimes aware that they received fewer visits from their supervisors than other principals. These principals tended to express satisfaction with this arrangement because they believed it confirmed that they were doing well and because they felt they were still receiving more support overall than they had prior to the role change and reduced span of control, as the following principal described:

> Since I was higher performing ... I wouldn't have seen him as much. I didn't need as much support, I was having success, he trusted me. But now that it's [a] lower [span of control], I'm seeing him a little more. And he did give us several things to work on.

However, not all supervisors were able to maintain regular visits to their high-performing principals. One supervisor came to believe that the isolating nature of the principal job meant that even the most high-performing principals needed more visits than she was currently providing: "[Next year] I hope to be more equally distributed, with the recognition that some people will need more, but everybody deserves a weekly check-in."

Supervisors also differentiated the focus of their work with principals. Generally, supervisors provided more comprehensive support for first-year principals, who needed help managing school schedules, facilities, and budgets as they learned to lead their new buildings. Supervisors spoke of differentiating not only the content of their visits with principals, but also their style of coaching depending on the principal's needs. For instance, a supervisor discussed taking a "support" stance with one principal and "supervisor" stance with another during conversations about data use:

> With my principal who needs a lot of support, I'm a supervisor. I'm very directive. He has a plan of improvement with dates, timelines, specific things that he needs to be working on ... And the principal who needs the least direction, he follows right behind my modelling and will run his data for his own building. The difference is I have to tell [one principal] what reports to run, whereas in the other case, he's telling me what data he needs from me in order to drive conversations with his staff.

PSI districts did not mandate how supervisors should differentiate the content of their work with principals. Some supervisors reported that they addressed content differentiation in their own supervisor trainings and meetings. Consequently, supervisor approaches to content differentiation varied a great deal across individuals.

Unintentional variation in time use: barriers

Supervisors encountered barriers that hindered their ability to spend time with principals. These barriers stemmed from (a) central office organizational conditions and systems that shaped supervisors' work and (b) individual barriers related to supervisors' own mindsets and practices around principal support.

Organizational barriers

We identified two organizational barriers that prevented supervisors from meeting their role expectations for spending time with principals: (a) large spans of control and (b) central office demands for supervisors' time.

LARGE SPANS OF CONTROL

Although all districts were able to reduce their spans of control in the first three years of the PSI—from an average of 16 to 13—these reductions were uneven across supervisors. In some districts, supervisors continued to oversee groups (sometimes called *networks*) of as many as 19 principals. Supervisors with larger spans of control relative to their peers expressed that they were not able to spend adequate time with all principals.

School context also influenced whether or not a supervisor was able to manage their span of control. Supervisors noted that schools with high academic or safety needs, special programmatic needs, or very large schools (such as comprehensive high schools) required greater effort. When these schools were grouped together, they often required more frequent or intensive support from the supervisor as well. A supervisor of a low-achieving school network described this situation:

> Even if you only have 13 schools, it depends on the 13 that you have whether one person is enough. It's about efficacy, you know? ... You can't give everybody 13 schools and give one person 13 schools that are extremely needy and expect them to be able to do the same work as their counterpart who has 13 schools that could operate really without any support.

Although there were benefits to grouping similar schools into one network, rather than spreading them out over many supervisors, the ideal size of these special networks remained an open question.

CENTRAL OFFICE DEMANDS

All districts created supports that allowed supervisors to spend more time working with principals and away from the central office, such as by shifting supervisors' managerial responsibilities to other personnel and releasing supervisors from dual roles. However, these supports did not always buffer supervisors from central office demands. Supervisors in some districts reported that mandatory central office meetings were often scheduled during hours when they were supposed to be in schools, forcing them to cancel their planned visits to principals, or even to leave midway through a visit.

Supervisors also explained that although their role had changed internally, other departments remained "siloed" or "stuck" in old structures and mindsets that were not aligned with principal supervisors' new work. In many cases, these departments were not even aware of the changes to the supervisor role. As a result, some departments continued to make requests of supervisors that were no longer part of the supervisor job description and treated them as go-betweens for the departments and the schools. A supervisor described this problem:

> I am supposed to be in schools, supporting principals. The majority of my time, I am down here [at the central office] in meetings, which is very unfortunate. I need to be out in schools. And as much as we say we need to be out in schools, we're constantly pulled. Everyone looks to us, whether they acknowledge it or not, as the funnel. So, we lead our principals, but we also lead cross functional teams from every department in the organization.

Encroachment from other central office departments extended to principal group meetings. In two districts, supervisors reported that central office departments "hijacked" principal supervisor group meetings by asking supervisors to yield time to them so that they could deliver important messages about district policies and initiatives. These demands from central office tended to intensify toward the end of the academic year.

Personnel turnover, layoffs, and department reorganizations created additional barriers that prevented supervisors from maximizing their time working with principals. Turnover and vacancies elsewhere in the central office also affected supervisors' ability to efficiently support schools. When principals could not rely on personnel in another department to support them, they often requested intervention from their supervisors. Supervisors then spent time navigating other departments so that principals' noninstructional needs could be met, resulting in both less time spent with principals and less time spent focusing on instructional leadership.

Supervisor barriers

Variation in supervisor time use also appeared to stem from supervisors' own ability to effectively support all of their principals. Some supervisors were new to the role, while others were veteran supervisors who were used to the former compliance-oriented role. Both sets of supervisors experienced challenges in using their time to provide individually tailored coaching and support. In several districts, central office leaders spoke of having to have "hard conversations" with veteran supervisors who were unable or unwilling to "rise to the occasion" and shift to the new instructionally focused role.

Some principals with newly hired supervisors reported that they received less targeted support than they would have liked because the supervisor was still learning the new role and learning about the principal. A principal who had had three different supervisors in one year described a desire for more "personal" support from their current supervisor:

> I would like for her to get to know my staff and get to know who I'm dealing with and in a more personal manner. I think it's important so that when I make certain decisions that she is understanding of that ... Just getting to know the community and the staff that I'm dealing with, that's important.

The PSI districts instituted training to help principals develop the skills they needed to effectively support all principals. Supervisors found these trainings beneficial but also noted that new skills in coaching, providing feedback, and facilitating adult learning took time to develop. Some supervisors also desired direct training in time management skills.

Lessons from the districts: supporting supervisor time use

As the principal supervisor role solidifies around coaching and teaching principals, districts are wrestling with how to prescribe supervisors' use of time so that they will be effective. The PSI has yielded several considerations for how districts could successfully improve the quantity and quality of time supervisors spend with principals.

Provide supervisors with a clear and realistic vision for how their time should be spent

All PSI districts communicated clear guidelines for how much time principal supervisors should be spending with principals. These guidelines varied from a minimum number of visits per month, to a percentage of total time, to a set number of hours. Districts also created guidelines that allowed supervisors to differentiate their support for principals in a structured way. These guidelines were most powerful when they were coupled with a clear vision for how supervisors should work with principals. Most districts trained their supervisors in models for improving principal instructional leadership, including specific coaching and feedback protocols, observation rubrics, and data cycles. In doing so, districts set a common standard of support that supervisors worked to attain.

Create conditions that support supervisors' ability to spend time with principals

Supervisors needed system-wide support to meet the new expectations for spending time with principals. This support included shifting some of supervisors' noninstructional responsibilities to other personnel, providing them with support teams with whom they could coordinate their work, and reducing their extra commitments and roles in the central office. Supervisors also benefitted when their time with principals was viewed as "sacred," meaning the central office did not schedule meetings or interrupt supervisors during times when they were supposed to be working with principals.

Build flexibility and discretion into supervisor time use

Guidelines for time use that are too rigid or one-size-fits-all can hamper supervisors' ability to make informed, context-dependent decisions about how to spend their time. Some PSI districts recognized that supervisors constantly adapted their work to meet the evolving needs of principals and schools. Supervisors needed the freedom to adjust their work in response to academic trends, policy shifts, or school crises.

Encourage the use of tools to help supervisors manage their time

Several PSI districts created common tools, such as monthly calendars and inquiry cycles, to allow supervisors to organize their use of time. Supervisors with common tools for time management were able to monitor their own time use to ensure they were on track to meet their district's expectations for time use. The tools also facilitated supervisors' discussions of time use with their colleagues.

Recognize that quantity of time is not the same as quality of time

Throughout the PSI, we asked principals to reflect on the effectiveness of their supervisor's work. Principals defined supervisor effectiveness not according to quantity of interaction but rather quality of practices, such as tailoring the work to the principal's individual needs, listening to the principal, getting to know the principal and the school context, following up with the principal, and working jointly with the principal to set goals. Even when supervisors met district expectations for spending time with principals, the content of that time seemed to matter most for principal development.

Conclusion

In this chapter, we explored how supervisors in the PSI used their time. Most PSI supervisors spent their time working with principals in groups or one-on-one, and about half of that time was spent focusing on matters of instructional leadership. Time use varied greatly across individual supervisors, however: Even principals with the same supervisor could report strikingly different experiences regarding the frequency and focus of their work together. This variation was likely a combination of both intentional differentiation by supervisors and external challenges that prevented supervisors from using their time efficiently and effectively. These findings echo those described in the interim report of the PSI (Goldring et al., 2018).

Increasing the quantity and quality of supervisors' time with principals is a necessary step for districts wishing to support principal leadership, but this change must be enacted within a coherent, system-wide model of school support. Just as supervisors face many demands on their time, principals' time is also precious. Supervisors must have the expertise and training to ensure that they are developing principals' leadership in valuable, relevant ways. Before supervisors can use their time with principals effectively, districts must determine what effective principal support looks like, how it is best delivered, and how it can be sustained in constantly evolving school and district environments.

Author note

This chapter uses data collected from the PSI, an initiative funded by The Wallace Foundation. The contents of this chapter and the views expressed are those of authors and do not necessarily reflect the views of The Wallace Foundation. We acknowledge the collaboration of Melissa Clark from Mathematica Policy Research during this project.

References

Casserly, M., Lewis, S., Simon, C., Uzzell, R., & Palacios, M. (2013). *Principal evaluations and the principal supervisor: Survey results from the Great City Schools.* Council of the Great City Schools. http://eric.ed.gov/?id=ED543309.

Corcoran, A., Casserly, M., Price-Baugh, R., Walston, D., Hall, R., & Simon, C. (2013). *Rethinking leadership: The changing role of principal supervisors.* Washington, DC: Council of Great City Schools.

Elmore, R. F. (1993). The role of local school districts in instructional improvement. In S. Fuhrman (Ed.), *Designing coherent education policy: Improving the system* (pp. 96–124). San Francisco, CA: Jossey-Bass.

Goldring, E. B., Clark, M. A., Rubin, M., Rogers, L. K., Grissom, J. A., Gill, B., Kautz, T., McCullough, M., Neel, M., & Burnett, A. (2020). *Changing the Principal Supervisor Role to Better Support Principals: Evidence from the Principal Supervisor Initiative.* New York, NY: The Wallace Foundation.

Goldring, E. B., Grissom, J. A., Rubin, M., Rogers, L. K., Neel, M., & Clark, M. A. (2018). *A new role emerges for principal supervisors: Evidence from six districts in the Principal Supervisor Initiative.* New York, NY: The Wallace Foundation.

Grissom, J. A., Loeb, S., & Mitani, H. (2015). Principal time management skills. *Journal of Educational Administration, 53*(6), 773–793.

Honig, M. I. (2008). District central offices as learning organizations: How sociocultural and organizational learning theories elaborate district central office administrators' participation in teaching and learning improvement efforts. *American Journal of Education, 114*(4), 627–664. https://doi.org/10.1086/589317.

Honig, M. I. (2012). District central office leadership as teaching: How central office administrators support principals' development as instructional leaders. *Educational Administration Quarterly, 48*(4), 733–774.

Honig, M. I., Copland, M. A., Rainey, L., Lorton, J. A., & Newton, M. (2010). *Central office transformation for district-wide teaching and learning improvement.* Washington, DC: Center for the Study of Teaching and Policy, University of Washington.

Honig, M. I., & Rainey, L. R. (2014). Central office leadership in principal professional learning communities: The practice beneath the policy. *Teachers College Record, 116*(4), 1–48.

Honig, M. I., & Rainey, L. R. (2019). Supporting principal supervisors: What really matters?. *Journal of Educational Administration, 57*(5), 445–462.

Honig, M. I., & Rainey, L. R. (2015). *How school districts can support deeper learning: The need for performance alignment.* Students at the Center: Deeper Learning Research Series. Jobs for the Future.

Horng, E. L., Klasik, D., & Loeb, S. (2010). Principal's time use and school effectiveness. *American Journal of Education, 116*(4), 491–523.

Huang, T., Hochbein, C., & Simons, J. (2018). The relationship among school contexts, principal time use, school climate, and student achievement. *Educational Management Administration & Leadership, 48*(2), 305–323.

Johnson, P. E., & Chrispeels, J. H. (2010). Linking the central office and its schools for reform. *Educational Administration Quarterly, 46*(5), 738–775.

Kimball, S. M., Arrigoni, J., Clifford, M., Yoder, M., & Milanowski, A. (2015). *District leadership for effective principal evaluation and support.* Teacher Incentive Fund, US Department of Education, Washington, DC.

Marsh, J. A., Kerr, K. A., Ikemoto, G. S., Darilek, H., Suttorp, M., Zimmer, R. W., & Barney, H. (2005). *The role of districts in fostering instructional improvement: Lessons from three urban districts partnered with the Institute for Learning.* Santa Monica, CA: RAND Corporation.

May, H., Huff, J., & Goldring, E. (2012). A longitudinal study of principals' activities and student performance. *School Effectiveness and School Improvement, 23*(4), 417–439.

Neumerski, C. M. (2013). Rethinking instructional leadership, a review: What do we know about principal, teacher, and coach instructional leadership, and where should we go from here? *Educational Administration Quarterly, 49*(2), 310–347.

Rogers, L. K., Goldring, E., Rubin, M., & Grissom, J. A. (2018). Principal supervisors and the challenge of principal support and development. In S. J. Zepeda & J. Ponticelli (Eds.), *The Wiley handbook of educational supervision* (pp. 433–457). Hoboken, NJ: Wiley-Blackwell.

Sergiovanni, T. J., & Starratt, R. J. (1998). *Supervision: A redefinition.* New York, NY: McGraw-Hill.

Thessin, R. A. (2019). Establishing productive principal/principal supervisor partnerships for instructional leadership. *Journal of Educational Administration, 57*(5), 463–483.

8 How successful school principals balance their leadership and management roles to make a difference

Lawrie Drysdale, David Gurr, and Helen Goode

Most studies on how school principals use their time are based on the clock—minutes, hours, days, and weeks. We propose an alternative view: Principals' work should be measured in terms of what is achieved in the long term rather than what is enacted in units of time. We argue that productivity should be measured rather than activities and that this measurement should focus on what key goals, priorities, and targets can be achieved over time. We explore how successful principals balance their leadership and management roles to achieve major contributions that positively impact their schools. We present a model, the *total role concept* (TRC), that distinguishes between leadership and management and draws on findings from extensive case studies from the International Successful School Principalship Project (ISSPP) to show how successful principals can achieve great things over time.

Background

Studies on how principals use their time are often based on standard units of time; in Western thought, clock time is privileged and productivity comes from efficient use of this time. This focus on the units of time and productivity can be traced back to early management thought and the advance of scientific management through Fredrick Taylor's description of the principals of scientific management (Taylor, 1911), Frank and Lillian Gilbreth's studies on time and motion (Gilbreth & Gilbreth, 1917), Henry Towne's systematic approach to organizing work (Towne, 1912), and Henry Gantt's work on measuring activities by time and the progress of items completed over time, with this work culminating in the invention of the Gantt chart (Gantt, 1919). In school education, the influence of these early approaches still echoes loudly today. In schools, the day is constructed through units of time: for example, units of instruction, schedules, timetables, and notions of student progression through year levels. It is therefore unsurprising that studies based on how principals use their time—what they do and what they focus on, measured in units of time—remain common today (Eacott, 2018).

Time-use research seeks to understand and determine how time is allocated across numerous activities. A key finding that permeates most studies of principals' time use is that they work long hours (Sebastian et al., 2018). With high accountability and responsibilities for overall leadership, management, and development of the school, principals often work 60 hours a week (Sterrett, 2019). In Australia, 60-hour work weeks have been a consistent finding (Cooperative Research Project, 1998; Victorian Department of Education and Training, 2004), with the results of The Australian Principal Occupational Health, Safety, and Well-Being Survey (Riley, 2019) indicating that 53% of principals worked more than 56 hours a week, and a quarter worked between 61 and 65 hours.

If principals spend as much as 60 plus hours a week on their work, what are they doing with this time and how effectively and efficiently are they using it? In an earlier review of principal work, Gurr (2008) made the following observation about a 60-hour work week:

> It is easy to see how this figure is obtained. If you are a principal you are likely to be at school before it starts, you will have meetings (staff, parents, community, system-based) to attend after school and some paperwork to do, meaning that you will always be working past the end of the school day. Include attending to emails before or after work, a couple of evening meetings/activities each week, a few hours of paperwork on the weekend, and maybe some time for reflection and creative thinking, and quickly you have totalled up 60 hours give or take a few; there are enough principals reporting 80–100 hour weeks for this to be a concern. (p. 3)

One advantage of time studies in this context is that they can highlight the complexity and range of tasks. This can often be confirmed by calculating the percentage of time spent on tasks: administrative tasks, curriculum tasks, student interactions, parent interactions, and other (Hoyer & Sparks, 2017). Unfortunately, there is great variation in the findings of this type of research and often it is not clear whether this is because of variation in the actual work being recorded or variation in how the work is categorized. For example, Spillane et al. (2007) found 63.4% of principals' time was spent on administration, while Bristow et al. (2007) reported 24% and Gurr (2008) reported 26.3%. Although the principals in Spillane's study reported spending 22.2% of their time in instruction and curriculum, these figures were not matched in the other studies. Fostering relationships—be it with students, parents, staff, or external bodies—was cited in all these studies: for example, 8.7% in Spillane's research, 38% in Bristow's, and 46.8% in Gurr's. Professional development varied between 3.9% (Gurr) and 9% (Bristow). Indeed, Hochbein (2018) identified 55 studies that empirically examined principals' time use and found that not only did the methods for collecting and capturing the data vary, but there were also issues of bias, miscoding, aggregating observations, and low reliability.

Although these studies show the complexity and range of work, they do not capture the effectiveness of time use; moreover, categorizing principal work may not readily correlate with school outcomes (Horng et al., 2010). For example, May et al. (2012) found that principals' time use was highly variable and that changes in leadership activities over time did not necessarily forecast changes in student outcomes. Given the complex nature of their work and the different contexts in which they work, we suggest that measuring units of time and segmenting a principal's role into numerous tasks do not provide a clear picture of a principal's effectiveness. There are other views of time that argue against using the clock as a measure for conceptualizing effective practice. Eacott (2018) explored time and space based on relational theorizing in which a person's work is viewed as part of the complex flow of activities in an organization. He argued that principals can recast their time use to go beyond the limitations of the clock and focus on temporality in which they can generate time rather than merely having time. For Eacott (2019), the clarity of purpose, coherence of activities, and generation of a narrative need to be considered to fully understand the work of a principal.

Perhaps surprisingly, we also find that some of the literature on time management suggests that principals can better use their time and have more control over events that matter. Traditionally, time management is about the process of planning and organizing tasks and events: It is an attempt to control the amount of time spent on specific activities. For example, Covey et al. (1994) argued that it is more significant to focus on what is important rather than what is urgent. They used the analogy of the compass and the clock, arguing that it is no good being efficient with activities if you are heading in the wrong direction. They argued that leaders should use a compass first and a clock second: effectiveness, then efficiency. They also use the analogy of "big rocks" to determine what is important. The big rocks represent important priorities and everything else is gravel. To be effective, leaders need to put the big rocks in place first, rather than attempt to put these down later when the space is full of events and activities that may be unimportant or wasteful (gravel).

Following Eacott and Covey, we argue that principal achievement is best considered by focusing on what is important over a longer time frame. Rather than exploring their role by the clock, we argue that it is better to see how they define, approach, and prioritize their role. We have developed a conceptual model that helps explain this approach, which we will outline in the next section.

The total role concept

The TRC is a model of leadership and management we have developed (Drysdale et al., 2016) to conceptualize how principals use their time, based on how they conceive their role, to make a difference in their schools. Since the initial research by Drysdale (1998), we have investigated and trialed this concept through observations, workshops, and case studies. We explore this approach in more detail in this chapter.

Leadership and management

The TRC is a framework that defines leadership and management as two different approaches. It proposes that principals need to balance these roles to be effective, but to make a difference they should take up the challenge of leadership.

There seems to be consensus in the noneducation literature that management and leadership are different concepts, with much of this debate occurring in the 1990s. For example, Bass (1990) noted that:

> Leaders facilitate interpersonal interaction and positive working relations; they promote structuring of the task and the work to be accomplished ... Managers plan, investigate, coordinate, evaluate, supervise, staff, negotiate, and represent. (p. 383)

Kotter (1990) defined leadership as setting direction, aligning people, and motivating and inspiring, whereas management is planning and budgeting, organizing and staffing, and controlling and problem solving. Similarly, Bennis et al. (1997) argued that leaders set direction, vision, goals, objectives, effectiveness, and purpose, while managers focus on day-to-day and short-term efficiency.

There is a similar thread among educational administration writers. In the 1960s, Lipham (1964) recognized that leadership and management were separate but entwined. Management was keeping the school running and leadership was more creative; leadership was a force that motivates people to do things they would not ordinarily do. Cuban (1988) posited that leadership is focused on change and management is about maintaining order. Starratt (1993) conceived management as concerned with maintenance and leadership with growth: Leaders write the script and managers follow the script. Bush (2003) argued that leadership is about values or purpose, while management relates to implementation or technical issues. Leithwood (1994) equated *transformational* leadership with leadership, whereas *transactional* leadership equates to management. For Leithwood (1994), leadership adds value to management. Similarly, Sergiovanni (1990) argued that leadership is perceived as a value-added dimension that can produce excellence.

Our approach to leadership and management builds on previous notions developed by the key writers we have noted above. There are four aspects that underpin our approach. First, most of the writers we mentioned argued that both leadership and management are needed (Bass, 1990; Bennis et al., 1997; Bush, 2003; Deal & Peterson, 1994; Kotter, 1990). Second, the writers often mention balance in management and leadership and how this is often tipped in favor of one over the other. For example, Kotter (1990) argued that organizations were overmanaged and underled throughout the world, whereas we believe that, today, the balance may have shifted to leadership over management. Third, leadership is a value-added concept (Leithwood, 1994; Sergiovanni, 1990): There appears to be a common view among these writers that leadership requires people to do more than is expected and to reach for something better. Burns' (1978) initial concept of transforming leadership was an attempt to define how leaders can influence followers by striving for a higher ideal and higher purpose, and we see it continuing over time with writers such as Collins (2001), Handy (1994), Heifetz et al. (2009), and Peters (1994). This is also reflected in our research on successful principals (Drysdale et al., 2016; Gurr et al., 2005, 2006;

Gurr & Drysdale, 2003). Later in the chapter, we use three examples from this research to show how these three principals have gone beyond the expectations of their role to promote school success.

The total role framework explained

The TRC framework is an adaptation of Levitt's *total product concept*, which is used in marketing to distinguish the different dimensions of a product (Levitt, 1960, 1986). Levitt argued that there were various levels to a product, ranging from the concrete or tangible aspect of a product to the abstract or intangible aspects.

Levitt argued that a product is a promise—a cluster of value expectations of which its nontangible qualities are as integral as its tangible parts. An example is the purchase of a new car: The tangible aspect (i.e., the physical qualities or characteristics) might be the type of car, the color, and the additional features. In addition, there are sets of expectations that go along with purchasing the car—for example, the car performs to its specification and is delivered as contracted. More intangible aspects of the purchase might include the servicing of the car. Finally, an even more intangible aspect might be the brand's promise: the excitement of owning the brand, the feeling and exhilaration of driving the car, and the pride in owning it. These are the meanings and perceptions buyers take from the brand traits. People buy a car based on the tangible and intangible benefits that are bundled into the entire package. We have adapted this concept and applied it to the role of the principal. Principals have numerous complex roles but we can categorize these roles into management and leadership dimensions—the tangible and intangible aspects of the role, respectively.

The TRC framework is presented as concentric circles (see Figure 8.1) in which each circle represents a level or aspect of the principal's leadership and management role. The inner circle is the *core* role, the next circle is the *expected* role, the third circle represents the *augmented* role, and the final, outer circle is the *potential* role.

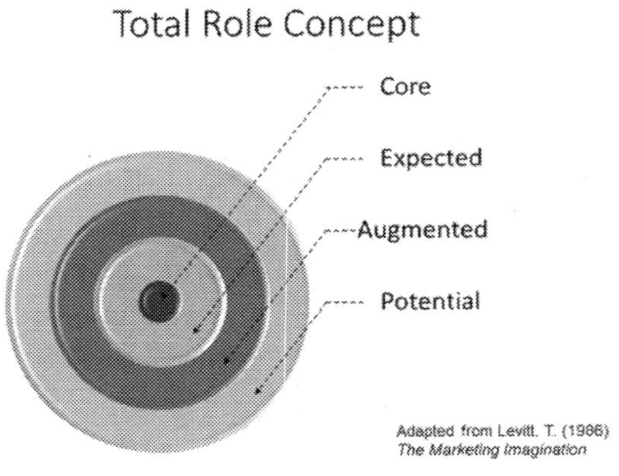

Figure 8.1 Total role concept 1

The core

The center of the diagram is the core. The core represents the formal aspects of the leader's role, which are usually written down. It comprises the duties and responsibilities that are prescribed and understood to be fundamental to the role. Functions associated with the core include planning and budgeting, organizing and staffing, and controlling and problem solving (Kotter, 1990). These functions satisfy the organizational needs for efficiency and accountability.

Expected

These represent the set of expectations that various groups have of the principal role. They may not be formalized or stated in a duty statement but they are assumed and are implicit in the role (e.g., attendance at social and sporting functions). These expectations will vary from one school community to another.

Augmented

These are the aspects of the role that principals believe encompass their responsibility but are neither implicit nor explicit. They are the things principals believe are important and would like to do (e.g., challenging the concept of literacy within the school community or challenging the school to become a learning community).

Potential

The outer circle of the role comprises initiatives, the creative, innovative, and entrepreneurial aspects of the role. These are the aspects, together with the augmented role, that can make a major difference to school direction and outcomes.

Leadership and management in the TRC

We conceive that each circle represents a level or aspect of a principal's leadership and management role. The two inner circles or levels (the core and the expected) represent management. The two outer circles (the augmented and the potential) represent leadership. What distinguishes the inner levels from the outer levels of the role? The core and expected role functions necessitate rational decision-making, tough-minded analytical skills, stabilizing and structural processes, attention to the human potential, and political maneuvering. These exemplify the skills that most management courses focus on and are the more tangible elements of the role; in other words, those that are more concrete than abstract, and are more measurable and definable. The leadership role (augmented and the potential circles)—pushing the boundaries—requires inspiration, courage, experimentation, imagination, innovation, passion, and vision. This aspect of the role is more intangible and spiritual. It is more ambiguous, abstract, symbolic, and cultural. The skills are conceptual rather than technical. The inner circles are more to do with what must be done, while the outer circles are about possibility and what could be done.

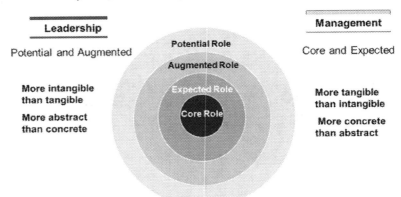

Figure 8.2 Total role concept

Figure 8.2 shows that the management roles (core and expected) are more concrete and tangible and tend to be roles created by the organization. Thus, principals are often more comfortable and secure within these roles. The leadership roles (augmented and potential) are less defined and more abstract and intangible. Principals may feel less secure in these roles because they tend to be outside their comfort zones and are more often created by the individual. The shading from dark to light emphasizes the move from management to leadership behaviors.

Conceptual ideas underpinning the model

To explain our view that leadership is more difficult and challenging because it is more intangible, we draw on the concept of *cognitive dissonance* (Festinger, 1957), the *doughnut principle* (Handy, 1994), and *self-imposed limits* (Bennis, 1989). Festinger (1957) described how two competing ideas can cause cognitive dissonance, which may then need to be resolved. In the workplace, for example, there may be a gap between what we like to do and what we have to do. This creates a tension, and, if the gap is great enough, it can lead to behavior changes that resolve the tension, such as leaving a job. To describe the work of principals, Handy (1994) employed the metaphor of a doughnut. The hole in the doughnut contained the duties and responsibilities of the principal, and the doughnut itself was what principals could do to go beyond expectations. Finally, Bennis (1989, 2009) argued that the work of leaders can be considered at three levels: what I am able to do, what I want to/should do, and what I think I can do. He argued that leaders often do not go beyond what they can do or want to do, and rarely explore what they are fully capable of—what we would refer to as the tangible and the intangible.

Methodology

In this chapter, we draw on three cases from the many case studies we have developed as part of the ISSPP. This project has operated since 2001 and is ongoing. It started with eight countries and now involves researchers from 20 countries who have investigated the characteristics and circumstances of successful school principals and how principals contribute to school success. This research has produced many publications. In his foreword to the fourth project book (Day & Gurr 2014), Caldwell (2014) described the project as "the most comprehensive and coherent international comparative study of the principalship ever undertaken" (p. xxi).

The ISSPP generally adopts a multiple-perspective interview and observational approach to conducting the case studies. This includes data collected and analyzed from individual interviews with the principal; senior staff and school board members; group interviews with teachers, parents, and students; and the collection and analysis of appropriate documents. Many cases include observation data. This chapter explores findings from research conducted with three successful principals from Victoria, Australia and how the TRC was applied in their leadership. We have worked with each of these three principals, completing extensive research, for more than a decade. The data collection on these principals included all the methods just described.

The principals

Bella Irlicht

Bella Irlicht was principal of Port Phillip Specialist School in Melbourne, Australia. Student ages at the school ranged from 2 to 18. During her 23 years as principal, she transformed this school from a small school of 20 for children with special needs located in a converted house, to a school of 150 pupils with state-of-the-art buildings, an innovative curriculum based on visual and performing arts (VPAC), and a rigorous system of reporting that recognized the progress each student made. Bella was recognized with numerous awards, including the Order of Australia Medal (OAM) and CEO of the Year for Not for Profit Organizations. Research publications about Bella's leadership include Di Natale (2005), Drysdale (2007), Drysdale et al. (2014), Drysdale et al. (2009), and Goode (2017).

Jan Shrimpton

Jan was principal of Morang South Primary School, a government primary school of about 500 students in a growth corridor in outer Melbourne for 10 years. When she was appointed, the school had a poor reputation. Student outcomes were well below standard, there was low student and teacher morale, and the parent body was disenchanted and disengaged with the school. During her 10-year tenure, Jan turned the school's performance around by improving staff morale, changing the school culture, and building good relationships with the community. Research publications on Jan's leadership include Drysdale et al. (2014), Drysdale et al. (2009, 2011), Goode (2017), and Ylimaki et al. (2011).

Rick Tudor

Rick Tudor was the headmaster of Trinity Grammar School in Melbourne, Australia for 15 years. This school, founded in 1902, is a high-fee, independent Anglican boys' school of more than 1,300 students that operates programs from preschool (age 3) to Year 12 (age 18) in a location about 7 kilometers from the central business district of Melbourne. Rick was only the seventh principal in the school's history. The school was high performing academically and enjoyed a strong reputation within the community for both its academic and broader outcomes, such as student leadership and community service. Rick was awarded an OAM for his services to education. Research publications on Rick's leadership include Doherty (2008), Doherty et al. (2014), and Goode (2017).

Exploring the principals' work using the total role concept

Core and expected

All three principals clearly understood their responsibilities as principals. The schools were well run, with efficient and effective processes. All schools operated appropriate surplus budgets, with the surpluses used to finance innovative projects and manage contingencies. Resource acquisition and allocation were targeted to support school goals and directions. Although all Australian schools receive the bulk of their money through commonwealth and state government funding based on school type and student characteristics and student fees, it is how principals use these funds that make a difference.

Augmented and potential

The three principals demonstrated that they could embrace the augmented and potential of their role through leadership which was underpinned by their values, personal qualities, sense of purpose, and skills. We have labeled their leadership as *post-heroic* (Drysdale et al., 2014). Post-heroic leaders transcend the heroic model of command and control to a model of collaboration and shared responsibility. Our post-heroic leaders showed a combination of heroic qualities such as courage, drive, and assertiveness, as well as the ability to build teams, empower others, and distribute leadership. Their leadership was also underpinned by a clear sense of purpose.

Bella operated consistently in the augmented sphere. She strove to achieve her vision for creating a world-class specialist school. She challenged the traditional curriculum replacing it with a performing arts-based curriculum, and she challenged the mindsets of her staff to refocus the school as an educational as opposed to a welfare institution. Bella introduced the concept of a full-serviced school in which families could access a range of medical and educational services such as physiotherapy, occupational therapy, speech therapy, and psychological and dental services. Her entrepreneurial skills helped build the school's facilities such as a school swimming pool, hydrotherapy pool, performing arts center, music room, a multisensory room, and a two-bedroom, fully equipped transition house for older students to help them prepare for independent living. This was done through attracting sponsors and forming partnerships with philanthropists and community agencies. Within the potential sphere, she organized an international conference, *Reimagining Special Education Through Arts Education and Therapy*, which attracted international speakers and delegates as well as sponsoring her own staff to attend. A formal reception was held at Government House in Victoria. This successful conference explored what was possible in special education.

Jan operated extensively in the augmented sphere. Jan succeeded in changing the school environment from "rules-based" to "values-based." She courageously resisted external pressure from authorities to continuously raise test scores at the expense of losing positive aspects such as an emphasis on whole child development, values-based school community, and a staff development culture. Social competency development, citizenship formation, and an emphasis on holistic education were her central planks. Jan introduced a range of distinguishing programs to extend gifted students and support more challenged students. Pet dogs were introduced to help calm some students and curb behavioral problems. All of this was done within a distributed leadership framework that empowered and developed staff capacity.

Rick challenged the established the organizational structures and many of the traditions of the school's past. For example, through careful and respectful consultation he replaced a hundred year-old house system. He left a legacy of creating innovative learning spaces and purpose built facilities, such as the *Centre for Contemporary Learning* building that has become the symbolic center of learning of the school. The curriculum was changed to focus on both academic and whole-child curricula. Boys' leadership was his top priority. Leadership programs were developed at every level to encourage boys to become global citizens, accept social responsibility at the community level and be "gentlemen." Rick established international partnerships, developing a global perspective for students. Expanded global opportunities included Kokoda track expeditions in the highlands of Papua New Guinea; language experiences in Germany, France, and Italy; European history tours; international cricket tours; reciprocal student exchange programs; and social justice programs in the Philippines. All Year 9 boys participated in an Asia Experience (China) program at Yu Xin School in Beijing. Rick was the first school principal in Australia to establish a remote indigenous school campus in the Northern Territory of Australia, which staff and students visit twice a year.

Discussion

We have outlined three examples of how principals' focus on long-term change enabled them to make a difference in their schools and for their students, while successfully balancing their roles of leadership and management. The literature

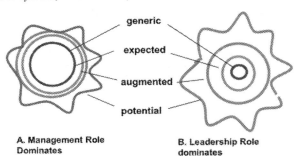

Figure 8.3 Balance between management and leadership role

underpins that the principal role is complex (Leithwood et al., 2017); unfortunately, many principals are overwhelmed by the task and degenerate into mere functionaries. In many cases, they spend too much time in administrative and operational matters to survive (Duignan, 2007). By doing so, they avoid the real challenge of leadership. The day-to-day and immediate demands of running the school take over at the expense of leadership activities like setting direction and developing, motivating, and aligning people to this direction. They are captured by the demands of the system, planning and budgeting, and developing policies and procedures. In terms of our model, many principals are limited by solely responding to the core and expected aspects of their role rather than focusing on the augmented and potential aspects of their role. Our examples show that principals need to look beyond the structural and routine and set their sights on leadership. Each of these three principals—Bella, Jan, and Rick—was prepared to tackle the augmented and potential aspects.

Figure 8.3 shows the balance between management and leadership roles. Diagram A is when someone's work is dominated by their management roles: There are many management matters that need to be accomplished effectively and efficiently, but leave little time for thinking about how their work could be more creative, visionary, and leadership-oriented. Diagram B shows appropriate attention to the management roles, but also represents going beyond these roles into leadership areas. Bella's work is best represented by Diagram B because of her focus on leadership to develop a world-class special school. Jan and Rick lie somewhere between the two diagrams given that they were not only attendant to the management side, but also created successful schools through their leadership work and their desire to make a difference to students and families.

In our description of the principals, we pointed out key personal characteristics that strengthened their capabilities to focus on leadership. In summary, we can say that each had a broad vision for their school that they successfully shared with their education community and as such were able to get buy-in from school community members. Each articulated personal, professional, and social values that underpinned their personal philosophy. Vision and philosophy functioned as their compass while allowing them to set direction. Each was what we have termed a post-heroic leader. They showed courage, commitment, and determination to do what they thought was right for their school community. Each prioritized and put "first things first" (Covey et al., 1994), which supported their leadership approach to focus on what matters most. Finally, each was aware of their context. They were not captured by their context but rather straddled, navigated, maneuvered, and sometimes changed aspects of the context. They saw opportunities within their environment and seized opportunities. We argue that the TRC can encourage principals and other leaders to think more broadly and creatively about their use of time and work toward the augmented and potential dimensions of their role.

Conclusion

There are various approaches to measuring how principals use their time. Using the clock to the measure a principal's role is a common method. Although this approach is useful for exploring how principals allocate their time between tasks and activities on a day-to-day or short-term basis, there are many challenges associated with this approach such as methodology, interpretation, and effectiveness. We offer an alternative approach that explores a principal's effectiveness over the long term and posit that a principal's overall impact on their school is determined by the time they spend leading the organization rather than managing the organization. We propose the TRC as a means of defining leadership and management: The model is based on the perspective that the core and expected roles are management-related and operational and functional aspects whereas the augmented and potential roles are leadership-related and as such represented the more intangible and abstract aspects of the role. Because it is more intangible, leadership is more challenging. Principals often focus on management to gain a sense of security and of accomplishment.

Our model challenges principals to leave the sanctuary of their core and expected roles and to focus on their augmented and potential roles. We provide three examples of principals who took up the challenge of leadership and dared to make a difference. We have argued that this approach enables principals to use their time more effectively and contribute more meaningfully to their schools' overall organizational success. The three principals in this paper demonstrated that they could move past the core and expected aspects of their role and tackle the augmented and potential aspects. As noted in the literature, management and leadership are both important, and these principals are examples of school leaders adept at both.

References

Bass, B. M. (1990). *Bass & Stogdill's handbook of leadership: Theory, research, and managerial applications* (3rd ed.). New York, NY: The Free Press.

Bennis, W. (1989). *Why leaders can't lead: The unconscious conspiracy continues.* San Francisco, CA: Jossey-Bass.

Bennis, W. (2009). *On becoming a leader.* New York, NY: Basic Books.

Bennis, W., Parikh, J., & Lessem, R. (1997). *Beyond leadership: Balancing economics, ethics and ecology*. Hoboken, NJ: Blackwell.

Bristow, M., Ireson, G., & Coleman, A. (2007) *A life in the day of a headteacher: A study of practice and well-being*. Nottingham: National College for School Leadership.

Burns, J. M. (1978). *Leadership*. Manhattan, NY: Harper & Row.

Bush, T. (2003). *Theories of educational leadership and management* (3rd ed.). Thousand Oaks, CA: SAGE Publications.

Caldwell, B. J. (2014). Forward. In C. Day & D. Gurr (Eds.), *Leading schools successfully: Stories from the field* (pp. xxi–xxii). Abingdon: Routledge.

Collins, J. C. (2001). *Good to great: Why some companies make the leap…and others don't*. Manhattan, NY: Random House Business.

Cooperative Research Project. (1998). *Assessing the impact: Report of the Cooperative Research Project on "Leading Victoria's Schools of the Future."* Department of School Education, Victorian Association of State Secondary Principals, Victorian Primary Principals' Association, The University of Melbourne, Melbourne.

Covey, S. R., Merrill, A. R., & Merrill, R. R. (1994). *First things first: To live, to love, to learn, to leave a legacy*. New York, NY: Simon and Schuster.

Cuban, L. (1988) *The management imperative and the practice of leadership in schools*. Albany, NY: SUNY Press.

Day, C., & Gurr, D. (Eds.) (2014). *Leading schools successfully: Stories from the field*. Abingdon: Routledge.

Deal, T. E., & Peterson, K.D. (1994). *The leadership paradox: Balancing logic and artistry in schools*. Jossey-Bass Education Series, San Francisco, CA.

Di Natale, E. (2005). *What are the qualities, skills and leadership styles adopted by a successful school principal in a successful Victorian Specialist School?* [Unpublished Master's thesis]. University of Melbourne, Melbourne.

Doherty, J. (2008). *Successful leadership in an independent school in Victoria* [Unpublished doctoral dissertation]. University of Melbourne, Melbourne.

Doherty, J., Gurr, D., & Drysdale L. (2014). The formation and practice of a successful principal: Rick Tudor, Headmaster of Trinity Grammar School, Melbourne, Australia. In C. Day & D. Gurr (Eds.), *Leading schools successfully: Stories from the field* (pp. 85–97). Abingdon: Routledge.

Drysdale. L. (1998). Dare to make a difference: Pushing the boundaries of your role. *Prime Focus, 4*(4), 28–29.

Drysdale, L. (2007) Making a difference. In P. Duignan & D. Gurr (Eds.), *Leading Australia's schools* (pp. 132–138). Sydney: ACEL and DEST.

Drysdale, L., Bennett, J., Murakami, E., Johansson, O., & Gurr, D. (2014). Heroic leadership in Australia, Sweden, and the United States. *International Journal of Educational Management, 28*(7), 785–797.

Drysdale, L., Goode, H., & Gurr, D. (2009). An Australian model of successful school leadership: Moving from success to sustainability. *Journal of Educational Administration, 47*(6), 697–708.

Drysdale, L., Goode, H. & Gurr, D. (2011) *Sustaining School and Leadership Success in Two Australian Schools*, in Moos, L., Johansson, O., & Day, C. (Eds) (2011) *How School Principals Sustain Success Over Time: International Perspectives* Netherlands: Springer-Kluwer), pp 25–38.

Drysdale, L., Gurr, D., & Goode, H. (2016). Dare to make a difference: Successful principals who explore the potential of their role. *International Studies in Educational Administration, 44*(3), 37–54.

Duignan, P. (2007) Educational Leadership: Key Challenges and Ethical Tensions (Cambridge: Cambridge University Press).
Eacott, S. (2018). Theoretical notes on a relational approach to principals' time use. *Journal of Educational Administration and History*, 50(4), 284–298.
Eacott, S. (2019). High impact school leadership in context. *Leading and Managing*, 25(2), 66–79.
Festinger, L. (1957). *A theory of cognitive dissonance.* Redwood City, CA: Stanford University Press.
Gantt, H. L. (1919). *Organizing for work.* San Diego, CA: Harcourt, Brace, and Howe.
Gilbreth, F. B., & Gilbreth, L. M. (1917). *Applied motion study.* New York, NY: Sturgis and Walton.
Goode, H. M. (2017). *A study of successful principal leadership: Moving from success to sustainability* [Unpublished doctoral thesis]. University of Melbourne, Melbourne.
Gurr, D. (2008). Principal leadership: What does it do, what does it look like, and how might it evolve? *Monograph*, 42. Strawberry Hills: Australian Council for Educational Leaders.
Gurr, D. (2014). Successful school leadership across contexts and cultures. *Leading and Managing*, 20(2), 75–88.
Gurr, D., & Drysdale, L. (2003). Successful school leadership: Victorian case studies. *International Journal of Learning*, 10, 945–957.
Gurr, D., Drysdale, L., & Mulford, B. (2005). Successful principal leadership: Australian case studies. *Journal of Educational Administration*, 43(6), 539–551.
Gurr, D., Drysdale, L., & Mulford, B. (2006). Models of successful principal leadership. *School Leadership and Management*, 26(4), 371–395.
Handy, C. (1994). *The empty raincoat: Making sense of the future.* Sydney: Random House Australia.
Heifetz, R., Grashow, A., & Linsky, M. (2009). *The practice of adaptive leadership: Tools and tactics for changing your organization and the world.* Boston, MA: Harvard Business Press.
Hochbein, C. (2018, April 12). Finding time to lead. *Lehigh Research Review*, 4. https://www2.lehigh.edu/news/examining-principal-time-use.
Horng, E. L., Klasik, D., & Loeb, S. (2010). Principal's time use and school effectiveness. *American Journal of Education*, 116(4), 491–524.
Hoyer, K. M., & Sparks, D. (2017). *How principals in public and private schools use their time: 2011–12.* Stats in Brief, National Centre for Educational Statistics, Institute of Education Sciences and American Institutes for Research, Arlington, VA. Australian Council for Educational Research.
Kotter, J. (1990). *A force for change: How leadership differs from management.* New York, NY: The Free Press.
Leithwood, K. (1994). Leadership for school restructuring. *Educational Administration Quarterly*, 30(4), 498–518.
Leithwood, K., Sun, J., & Pollock, K. (2017) *How school leaders contribute to student success: The four paths framework.* Cham, Switzerland: Springer International Publishing.
Levitt, T. (1960). The marketing myopia. *Harvard Business Review*, 38(4), 45–56.
Levitt, T. (1986). *The marketing imagination.* New York, NY: The Free Press.
Lipham, J. M. (1964). Leadership and administration. In D. E. Griffith (Ed.), *Behavioural science and educational administration: The sixty-third yearbook of the National Society for the Study of Education.* Chicago, IL: University of Chicago Press.
May, H., Huff, J., & Goldring, E. (2012). A longitudinal study of principals' activities and student performance. *School Effectiveness and School Improvement*, 23(4), 417–439.

Peters, T. (1994). *The pursuit of wow!: Every person's guide to topsy-turvy times*. New York, NY: Vintage Books.

Riley, P. (2019). *The Australian principal health, safety and wellbeing survey: 2018 data*. Sydney: Institute for Positive Psychology and Education, Australian Catholic University.

Sebastian, J., Camburn, E. M., & Spillane, J. P. (2018). Portraits of principal practice: Time allocation and school principal work. *Educational Administration Quarterly*, 54(1), 47–84.

Sergiovanni, T. J. (1990). *Value-added leadership*. New York, NY: Harcourt Brace Jovanovich.

Spillane, J. P., Camburn, E. M., & Pareja, A. S. (2007). Taking a distributed perspective to the school principal's workday. *Leadership and Policy in Schools*, 6(1), 103–126.

Starratt, R. (1993). *Transforming life in schools: Conversations about leadership and school renewal*. Camberwell: Australian Council for Educational Administration.

Sterrett, W. (2019, August 14). How to make the most of your time as a principal. *Education Week*. https://www.edweek.org/ew/articles/2017/11/15/how-to-make-the-most-of-your.html.

Taylor, F. W. (1911). *Principles of scientific management*. Manhattan, NY: Harper and Brothers.

Towne, H. R. (1912). The general principles of organization applied to an individual manufacturing establishment. *Transactions, Efficiency Society Incorporated*, 1, 77–83.

Victorian Department of Education and Training. (2004). *The privilege and the price: A study of principal class workload and its impact on health and wellbeing*. Victoria: Victorian Department of Education and Training.

Ylimaki, R., Gurr, D., & Drysdale, L. (2011). *Sustaining improvement in challenging, high poverty schools*. In L. Moos, O. Johansson, & C. Day (Eds.), *How school principals sustain success over time: International perspectives* (pp. 151–166). Dordrecht: Springer-Kluwer.

9 "Wasting time talking to students and parents"

Neoliberal efficiency myths about principal discretionary time use in Australia

Philip Riley

Case study: Australia

Australia is a federation of nine states and territories, each providing a tripartite education system of Government, Catholic, and Independent (fee paying) schools: 27 bespoke systems that vary considerably in funding models, ideology, and standard operating procedures despite various attempts by the federal government to harmonise national education delivery. In this case study of one government jurisdiction (N = 1539 schools), differing interpretations of the same policy settings reflect the internal philosophical and political struggles of many education systems that significantly impact school principals' time use.

Principal efficiency, time usage and neoliberalism

Time use and workload are inexorably linked; as a result, any discussion of principals' discretionary time use must be contextualised by workload requirements. Over the last 20 years, school leaders' workload has increased exponentially for two main reasons: (a) increasing complexity of the role and (b) increasing accountability requirements from the education systems who employ them (Ball, 2012; Berliner, 2012; Berliner & Biddle, 1995; Dicke et al., 2019; Pollock & Hauseman, 2019; Sellar & Lingard, 2014; Stahl, 2014; Wang, Pollock, & Hauseman, 2018). The main driver of increased workload, however, is education systems' diminishing trust in educators (Tschannen-Moran, 2014).

Although education systems dictate much of how principals use their time, they also promote the myth that principals are increasingly autonomous by transferring many complex administrative tasks—such as building audits and occupational health and safety requirements that were once carried out by central and regional office staff—to school leaders, while maintaining tight control over all significant educative functions such as curriculum content. Although this is not real autonomy, the language has been carefully chosen as autonomy is an important concept in the job demands and resources theory (JD-R) (Bakker & Demerouti, 2007, 2014), which is increasingly used in educational research (Dicke, Linninger et al., 2018; Dicke, Marsh et al., 2018). Examples of *job demands* include workload, work pace, time pressure, and accountability. *Job resources* can be extrinsic (e.g., financial rewards, job security, level of autonomy, and social support), intrinsic (e.g., feeling one is contributing to society, or carrying out meaningful work), and personal (e.g., intelligence, confidence, persistence, and creativity). Important resources for school leaders with high cognitive and emotional demands include the level of control they are able to have when dealing with job demands appropriately (autonomy) and the quality of social and institutional support they receive personally and professionally.

Promoting the myth that principals are increasingly autonomous seems to be an attempt to communicate to parents and the community that schools and therefore leaders are responsible for student results, not departments of education (DoEs). In most education systems, however, autonomy in practice has meant the transfer of accountability for student results from central systems—which set the parameters under which schools operate—to school leaders who largely must work within the confines of those parameters whether they agree with them or not. A neat trick indeed: retain control but devolve responsibility. In the case described presented in this chapter, I contrast two philosophical silos that exist within the same DoE to elucidate the tension between the varying conceptions of leader autonomy and trust, and the workload implications for principals who are concurrently accountable to both groups.

Competing silos: knowledge equals power

DoEs are large organisations in which information and communication are often siloed for internal political advantage rather than external system improvement. When knowledge equals power it is unwise to share—hence, silos emerge. The positive aspect of silos is that they afford opportunities for other key players in the system who hold different conceptions of problems and solutions to also shape and enact policy. In this case study, both silos were addressing continuous school improvement and responding to research that indicated Australian principals were suffering significant health challenges as a result of their work (Beausaert, Gallant, & Riley, 2016; Dicke, Linninger et al., 2018; Maxwell & Riley, 2016; Riley, 2016, 2017). These findings have been widely reported in the media and the DoE was subsequently under political pressure to respond (Department of Education and Training, 2017). Thus, two silos emerged within the DoE: The first silo used Command and Control (CaC) model of school improvement and the second silo developed a Service Delivery Model (SDM). In the CaC silo, the problem is always "the other" and the solution is always control. This silo claimed policymakers were education experts, and principals' work was simply to follow policy. The SDM silo regarded principals as the experts and looked to alter the system demands on them to provide more agile support.

Command and control (CaC)

The CaC silo model of school improvement was implemented in 2015, based on the new public management (NPM) contractual model assumption that uniformity equals quality (Tolofari, 2005). The CaC response to principal stress was to assume that principals' poor time use must be the cause. Although the *Principal Health and Wellbeing Studies* reports did indicate this was a factor involved in principals' occupational health—principals who self-reported better use of their time also reported slightly higher general health scores—there were many other factors contributing to the declining health of principals generally (Beausaert et al., 2016; Dicke, Marsh et al., 2018; Dicke et al., 2019; Gallant & Riley, 2017, 2018; Maxwell & Riley, 2016; Riley, 2016, 2019; Riley & See, 2020). Despite this, the CaC silo zeroed in on time use as the issue to be addressed.

Time and motion study

The CaC model of school leadership improvement assumed principals' inefficient use of time was causing them distress. They conceived this as a tame—albeit adaptive rather than technical—problem (Heifetz, Grashow, & Linsky, 2009). This silo within the DoE contracted a business consulting group to conduct a review of principal time use with the aim to reducing principal inefficiency. The consulting group described their services as "specialising in process improvement, business operating model design, and change management."[1]

It is likely the consulting group was also hired under the following explicit or tacit assumptions: First, schools are akin to businesses that produce products. In this case, school products are "student learning outcomes"—a common phrase among DoE staff whose key performance indicators (KPIs) are linked to school mean scores, rather than students' improvement scores, on national literacy and numeracy tests. The KPIs are not affected by outcomes such as whether students are happy, safe, well cared for, stimulated, creative, future focused, or engaged citizens.

The second assumption was that literacy and numeracy outcomes are a good proxy for school functioning, with higher mean scores suggesting more efficient schools. This is open to serious question and debate among scholars (for a review, see Sahlberg, 2015), although there are some signs that this may be changing in some jurisdictions, and indeed was not the operating model in the SDM silo.

The third assumption behind the appointment of a business consulting group was likely that school leaders' efficiency is key to school efficiency. Leaving aside discussions about the nature of "efficiency" across school systems that vary widely in terms of resources, student and school demographics, and geography (to name a few), this assumption is consistent with the literature (see, for example, Leithwood, Pollock, & Sun, 2017).

The consulting group conceived schools as process organisations; I deduced this from their advertising material rather than through direct engagement, as I was only afforded access to the final documents supplied to individual principals, as well as their recollections of the results the consultants verbally provided to the DoE. I triangulated these reports between all of the informants and found them to be consistent. The consulting group appeared to assume the education system functioned as a series of throughputs that could be streamlined by eliminating waste in the process—a stance that downplays or even ignores the issues of educational process at the granular level: the teacher–student, student–student, teacher–leader, and leader–student/family interactions. Unlike production industries, the quality of the relationships between individuals drives educational successes and failures. This is not to say that curricula and processes are not important, but they are also not everything. I have previously argued that relationships are the foundation of all sensible educational processes (Riley, 2011) and, even by the crude measure of literacy and numeracy outcomes, better relationships between teachers and students result in stronger "student learning outcomes" (Cornelius-White, 2007).

The consultants' proprietary model of organisational functioning aimed to eliminate what they described as *interface activity noise* (Bevington & Samson, 2012), which they argued is often mistakenly classified as essential. They took the view that all interfacing, which might equally be labelled relationship-formation and maintenance, should be directed towards the "business process"—presumably, teaching and learning as measured by national literacy and numeracy testing. They also argued that all interfacing that is "not performed to compensate for the problem associated with a particular transaction at that step in the business process, the 'stuff' cannot be processed" (Bevington & Samson, 2012). That language is significant: "Interfacing" removes the humanity from relating in schools. If one assumes that (a) interfacing means relating, (b) relating means a series of transactions, and (c) the "stuff" that needs to be processed is curriculum delivery from teacher to student, most educators would not recognise their profession.

The consultants argued that "identifying and reducing the 'noise' in the interfacing activities provides a significant cost and performance improvement opportunity" (Bevington Group, n.d.). The language is also important here in that it reveals the underlying conceptualisation of their work. The consultants appeared to assume that the process of constructing a chair, for example, is similar to constructing a "student learning outcome." The CaC silo engaged these consultants in the hope that they would identify and eliminate a great deal of "interface activity noise" from schools. The process involved a modern version of a time and motion study.

The consultants asked principals to estimate the time it took them to perform all daily tasks. The data collection was repeated annually. In 2015, the first year of the study, N = 29 principals were selected to report every day on 1,004 discrete activities, grouped under 19 headings, for a period of two weeks. The tasks were as large as reviewing school performance against the four-year strategic plan, and as small as entering appointments into the diary. The list of identified tasks runs to 31 pages.

The findings on time use are shown in Figures 9.1 and 9.2.

Translated into hours, principals spend 24.6 hours per week (41%) on administrative and accountability tasks and 31.8 hours (59%) on educative tasks.

Assuming that *self* is performing administrative tasks such as email and document work, principals spent 22.8 hours per week (38%) on administrative tasks and up to a further 8.4 hours per week on accountability tasks.

Neoliberal myths about principal time use 145

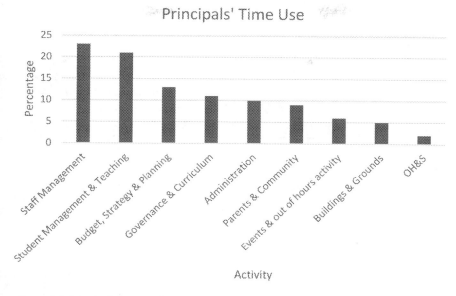

Figure 9.1 Principal time use by percentage

The average time spent at work during the week for Australian principals is approximately 60 hours during school terms and approximately 25 hours per week during holiday periods (Riley & See, 2020). This is similar to the United States (Lavigne et al., 2016) Canada (Pollock, Wang, & Hauseman, 2014; Pollock & Wang, 2019) and New Zealand (Riley, 2019), while Irish principals reported slightly lower numbers (Riley, 2014).

The consulting group reported that, on average, principals directly supervised 20 staff members. They suggested that this should be reduced to between 8 and 12, which is typical for business organisations but still thought to be

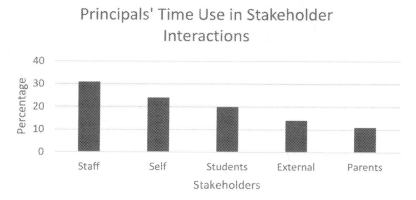

Figure 9.2 Principal time use according to the stakeholders with whom they interact

less than the ideal number, which is seven (Blenko, Rogers, & Mankins, 2010). The consulting group further suggested that the DoE develop and use differing leadership models for several typical school types, clarify the role definition, and increase "effective delegation techniques ... the time spent by principals on meetings and communication can be reduced by delegating responsibility. More effective communication and decision-making techniques can be explored to also free up their time" (Department of Education and Training, 2015).

In their verbal reports to principals, the consultants advised that principals were "wasting 30% of their time talking to students and parents." They saw this as low-level interface activity noise that could be more effectively carried out by subordinates. The informants, who provided this unsolicited information to me, considered this advice to be a very strong indication that the consultants did not understand the education process and that consequently the whole of their findings and recommendations were useless. It also diminished their perception of the DoE in general. However, the CaC silo saw value in this approach because the research has continued annually. One source told me that, in recent years, newly appointed principals are strongly advised to volunteer to participate. The problem with this approach is that new appointees are at their least competent in terms of time management simply because they are new to the role, and therefore the data they provide will be skewed towards inefficient time use.

A concurrent study for the Catholic Education Office of the same geographical area as the consultancy group included information from N = 495 schools found that on average principals worked ~60 hours per week. The distribution appears in Figure 9.3.

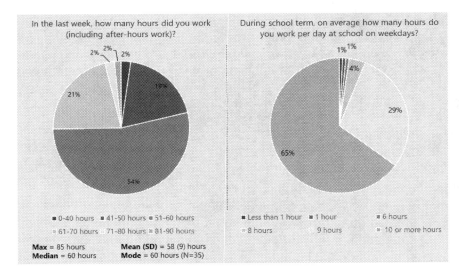

Figure 9.3 Hours at work per week for catholic primary school principals
Source: *Nous Group & Independent Education Union of Australia, 2018, p. 8.*

Neoliberal myths about principal time use 147

In the right-hand graph above, it is interesting to note that the question relates only to time at school rather than time at work which occurs both at school and offsite. The combination of the two graphs appears to indicate that a significant portion of leaders' working time is completed offsite, despite long days onsite.

This workload was reported to be a result of the following drivers:

1 Compliance, reporting, and administration
2 School leadership and governance arrangements
3 Teaching and learning expectations
4 Changing student needs and expectations
5 Parents and community
6 School size and composition
(Nous Group & Independent Education Union of Australia, 2018)

This list demonstrates that it is the system generating the workload that takes principals away from the core business of teaching and learning; it does this most powerfully through compliance requirements. In this structure, the compliance requirements are similar to government-run schools, but with the added responsibility of providing religious formation alongside the prescribed curriculum.

In presenting the comments below, I aim to put some "flesh on the bones" of the statistics reported above. They reveal a systemic failure to support principals in carrying out their work and are all drawn from *The Australian Principal Occupational Health, Safety and Wellbeing Survey: 2018 Data* (Riley, 2019). The comments are drawn from every state and territory in Australia and from all education sectors (Government, Catholic and Independent [fee paying schools]); I have grouped them by theme.

Administrative burden: sheer quantity of work

- Teaching principals' workloads are not being considered … they are still required to have a full-time teaching load, organise contractors, etc., as well as the expectations of leadership and management of a school principal.
- I love my job, but it is exhausting. The sheer volume of work is overwhelming. I felt completely demoralised by the new (Enterprise Bargaining) Agreement in which principal workload was only addressed in the most token way.
- Workload for principals—especially around compliance issues, maintenance, facilities, and surveys—is escalating to a ridiculous point.
- The workload has reached an unsustainable level and there is no one addressing this very real problem.
- The workload intensification over the past 12 months has been difficult. The last three terms have been extremely stressful and has meant working almost 'round the clock some weeks, especially the end of Term 4 last year. Term 1 and Term 2 have also been extremely busy.
- The workload has now begun to affect my health and state of mind.

Administrative burden: compliance

- There are too many system processes that have become complicated and add to the workload. What should be a simple task can take half a day or a whole day to do, at least!
- Increasing demands around governance has also impacted the growing chasm between being a manager and an educational leader.
- The workload is crazy, and expectations around compliance and knowledge beyond teaching and learning have made being a principal more like being a business manager and one who manages resources. This is not the job I love doing nor wish to continue doing for much longer.
- Levels of compliance have become over the top and timelines to be compliant are ridiculous. There seems to be a level of distrust creeping back into the system with principals bearing the brunt of some poor performance at the most senior system levels over the past years.

Administrative burden: email

- There are far too many emails and administrative work that are having a major impact on teaching and learning. It is becoming more and more difficult to get out of the office and into the classrooms.

Lack of time to devote to teaching and learning

- It is a shame as there is a lot of excellent educational material coming out of the department and principals won't have time to implement it as they should.

These comments indicated to the second silo in the department that a new focus on this information might be a better way to begin working with principals to regain their trust in the system to support them. This silo then began to formulate new ways of working that could better support principals by asking them in more detail what was needed.

Service Delivery Model (SDM)

The SDM silo's conceptual model was more nuanced. It took into account the differing contexts of schools within a broad system of education in which equity does not necessarily mean uniformity. The model assumed that a small rural school where the leader is also teaching is different from a large urban school where the leader is managing multiple stakeholders in much larger numbers and may be less close to the classroom, but still responsible for what goes in within the school. In early 2017, the SDM silo of the Australian DoE created a significantly different systematic support system for principals than had previously been in place. The process the DoE undertook to implement this system was driven by a specially selected taskforce in the department that focused on the central internal processes of engaging with principals. The SDM initiative had the benefit of a long lead time that afforded extensive consultation with all key stakeholders, including the research community; it was also driven by the findings of *The Australian Principal Occupational Health, Safety, and Well-Being Surveys* (Riley, 2015a, 2019; Riley & See, 2020). The resulting health and well-being strategy had dual foci: (a) to incorporate proactive policies and procedures to support principals; and (b) to align with the state government well-being strategy that had been launched a year previously.

The process undertaken to consult principals first involved asking a number of principals in different contexts if the SDM staff could monitor their email inboxes to gain insight into their experiences with departmental email communication. They were "shocked to discover" how many emails flooded the inboxes of principals across the state (Director, personal communication, April 7, 2018). They discovered low-level staff were able to send global emails to all principals and did so often. It was estimated that, at worst, a principal of a large secondary school was receiving more than 200 emails per day and that the department was responsible for far too many of them. They changed their email protocols and reduced the number of departmental emails by up to 90% without any loss of information going out to principals.

The second strategy was to consult widely with principals about their frustrations in dealing with the department at all levels. This led to a number of initiatives that were implemented in a staged process from late 2017. The elements of the strategy appear in Table 9.1.

The early uptake of these services is listed below.

The usage figures for the Principal Health and Well-being Services (as at end of October 2019) are listed below:

- School Policy Templates Portal (to minimise administrative workload)
  - *Usage:* 394,688 page views with 33,232 unique users
- Principal Mentor Program (to reduce isolation and build social capital)
  - Uptake: 140 mentee applications
- Proactive Well-being Supervision (to provide opportunities to debrief with experienced psychologists and new starter check-ins)
  - *Uptake:* 91 principals
- Principal Health Checks (free and confidential physical and mental health consultations)
  - *Usage:* 532 completed health checks
- Complex Matter Support Team (to minimise workload and stress associated with managing and responding to complex cases)
  - *Uptake:* 299 cases supported by the team

Table 9.1 Principal health and well-being strategy components

Services	Proactive				Responsive		Early intervention
	School policy template portal	Principal mentor program	Professional supervision	Personal health checks	Complex matter support team		
	Suite of online, relevant policy templates meeting legal, departmental policy, and school registration requirements. Easily adapted for each school and updated regularly	On demand access to experienced principal mentors, who are trained in psychological first aid	Opt-in allied health model, bi-annual debriefing sessions with and experienced psychologist	Access to physical and mental health checks	A lead professional will:		Support for illness, injury, or early warning signs of health and well-being issues
			Proactive check-ins with new principals 6–8 week post- commencement.	Detailed health assessment report	• Coordinate and connect principals with supports from a number of areas • Assist with (legal) responding to correspondence from parents and advocates		

- Early Intervention Program (to provide professional support to prevent health and wellbeing risks from escalating)
  - *Uptake:* 476 principals have accessed this service

(Department of Education Staff, personal communication, December 17, 2019)

Given that the initiative is still new, the success of the program has yet to be fully determined; however, there have been significant and almost instant reductions in principals' workload as a result of the school policy template portal. This part of the strategy had a soft launch in 2017, well before the full strategy was launched. The department recorded approximately 3,000 individual visits to the website in the first month—nearly double the number of schools in the jurisdiction. This has continued since, demonstrating that principals will strongly engage with supports that are beneficial. Since the official launch, there has also been a strong take-up of the professional supervision services as well, which although not directly related to workload should significantly impact optimal time use by principals over time. This strand of the policy acknowledges that principals' work also now involves significant understandings of psychological issues, for which they are mainly untrained. They are routinely dealing with student anxiety, depression, and other mental health issues alongside managing student cognitive development, which has been the most rapidly rising cause of stress for principals over the last decade (Riley & See, 2020). This suggests that principals should be afforded the same professional supervision as other workers in the space: psychologists, social workers, health professionals. The supervision should be run by psychologists who have completed further training in professional supervision. Supervision is not the same as mentoring or coaching; rather, it involves a skifully handled relationship that allows the supervisee to examine issues in depth in a safe, secure, and completely confidential environment. Two jurisdictions in Australia have trialled professional supervision to test its efficacy in the education sector. If take-up by principals is a success indicator, both appear very successful. The third trial starts in 2021 for teachers and will include a full evaluation to be conducted by an independent research team.

After approximately 18 months of the strategy being rolled out there have been two further iterations of *The Australian Principal Health and Wellbeing Survey* (Riley, 2019; Riley & See, 2020). The results show that the jurisdiction in question has had a significant shift from their trend results following the introduction of the strategy. Although it would be unwise to attribute cause at this early stage, the positive trend in job satisfaction indicates that early success may be real.

Discussion of principal time use

Any discussion of principal time use needs to include workload demands induced by accountability and reporting requirements. In this chapter, I have presented two examples of system-level responses to the increasing demands of the principalship; although one was more typical than the other, it did not appear to be as successful in reducing principal workload. Neoliberal conceptions of work, production, output, and employer–employee relationships remove trust from the relationship between the state (employer) and principals (actors) and replace it with accountability frameworks (Tolofari, 2005). But as Tschannen-Moran (2014) argued, trust matters. The SDM approach to principal support suggests there are better ways of conducting the business of education—schools might benefit from principals talking to parents and students *more*. If principals were trusted to act on the information they receive in those discussions, and supported with technical expertise to do so—such as School Policy Template Portal and complex matter support teams—significant gains for students might just follow. The staggering use of the policy template portal (394,688 page views with 33,232 unique users, from a pool of only N = 1,539 schools) demonstrates the usefulness of such resources: This one change has been able to reduce principals' administrative workload because they can delegate the task of school policy writing to aspirant leaders or teachers with a specific interest in a particular policy, safe in the knowledge that the necessities of any particular policy have been covered by the department legal team. In other words, using these templates frees up more of principals' time for educative tasks. Moreover, when DoEs actively support principals, their job satisfaction increases.

Neoliberal approaches have led to significant increases in contractualism between employers and employees that date back at least 15 years (Tolofari, 2005). Contracts represent implicit, obligational, or relational protocols between the parties entering into the contract, depending on how much mutual trust exists between them. Contracutalism has been increasingly adopted by education bureaucracies globally. For example, scholars have increasingly documented the rise of performance reviews for teachers and school leaders—with the associated work intensification related to compiling evidence for the review rather than doing the work itself (Blackmore, 2004; Blackmore, Thomson, & Barty, 2006; Gurl et al., 2016; Jewell, 2017). This makes education a more precarious profession than the historical norm in which job security was a significant attractor (Enrion, 2016; Reback, Rockoff, & Schwartz, 2014). Job precarity, through contractualism, has been a key lever in NPM approaches and has a significant impact on both compliance behaviours and work intensification.

There has also been a concomitant rise of a mythology promulgating around the world through the Global Educational Reform Movement (GERM) (Sahlberg, 2015). The myth is that uniformity equals quality, and the only way to improve student learning is through uniform "best" practice, regardless of contextual nuance. Education bureaucracies promote themselves as the designated expert judges of "best" practice and therefore the arbiters of all educational research. They demand that all teaching and teachers should conform to their decisions regarding "best" practice, based on the dual myths that all teaching and learning is measurable, and all teaching should be monitored otherwise teaching "standards" and student results will decline. This was the model the CaC silo adopted in the case study presented in this chapter.

The CaC/NPM world view conceptualises education as the exchange of teachers' knowledge to students for payment. Under this conception, contractualism is a management tool used to secure an outcome predetermined by the employer: continuous improvement in literacy and numeracy results. Teachers on short-term employment contracts will be more focused on achieving the employer's aims, rather than their own professional goals which may differ slightly from the employer: for example, well-informed citizens, critical thinkers, creative inventors of new technology, artists, musicians, or simply self-actualised individuals. None of these outcomes compete with an employer's aims but rather appear as surplus to requirements when the high-stakes measures, literacy and numeracy, are so narrow (Nichols & Berliner, 2007a, 2007b).

When the proxy of literacy and numeracy test results is used to determine the value of education, and by implication the staff within each school, teaching quality is reduced to test scores that are, at best, dubious (Berliner, 2012). At worst, NPM-driven policymakers remain ignorant of the wealth of complex interactions true pedagogy affords: opportunities and feedback, along with all the associated learning that educators provide (Sahlberg, 2015). NPM reduces this complexity to a market exchange—teachers, as providers of a service, become only interested in the extrinsic reward of the work (the pay) and students lack agency in the exchange as they have no control over the quality of the service they receive. NPM further assumes that a provider of a service will always offer the least possible effort to gain the reward (Tolofari, 2005). Therefore, teachers must be held to account for as many actions in the exchange as possible so that the work will be done. This was the CaC model at work.

The SDM process offers a very different conception of schools, expertise, and support. The changes resulting from a few simple supports and adjustments to departmental functioning show that positive change can be both significant and relatively quick when that starting point for bureaucrats is listening rather than telling. Perhaps the GERM movement could be put to good use by systematically learning from each other's successes to improve education across the globe.

Note

1. All quotations from the business consultants have been drawn from their public website.

References

Bakker, A. B., & Demerouti, E. (2007). The Job Demands-Resources model: State of the art. *Journal of Managerial Psychology*, 22(3), 309–328. doi:http://dx.doi.org/10.1108/02683940710733115.

Bakker, A. B., & Demerouti, E. (2014). Job demands-resources theory. In P. Y. Chen & C. L. Cooper (Eds.), *Work and wellbeing* (Vol. 3, pp. 37–64). Hoboken, NJ: Wiley-Blackwell.

Ball, S. J. (2012). *Global education inc.: New policy networks and the neo-liberal imaginary.* Abingdon: Routledge.

Ball, S. J. (2013). *Foucault, power, and education* (1st ed.). Abingdon: Routledge.

Beausaert, S., Gallant, A., & Riley, P. (2016). *What about school principals' well-being? The role of human and social capital.* Paper presented at the ECER 2016, Leading Education: The Distinct Contributions of Educational Research and Researchers, Trinity College Dublin, Ireland, August 22–25.

Berliner, D. C. (2012, December 2–6). *Confusing assessment with testing and quantification: The overzealous promotion of value-added assessment of teachers.* Paper presented at the The Joint Australian Association for Research in Education and Asia-Pacific Education Research Association Conference World Education Research Association Focal Meeting: Regional and Global Cooperation in Educational Research, University of Sydney, Sydney, Australia.

Berliner, D. C., & Biddle, B. J. (1995). *The manufactured crisis: Myths, fraud, and the attack on America's public schools.* Boston, MA: Addison-Wesley.

Bevington Group. (n.d.). *Understand interface activity noise.* Retrieved from http://www.xep3.com/interface-activity-noise.html.

Bevington, T., & Samson, D. (2012). *Implementing strategic change: Managing processes and interfaces to develop a highly productive organization.* London: KoganPage.

Blackmore, J. (2004). Leading as emotional management work in high risk times: The counterintuitive impulses of performativity and passion. *School Leadership & Management*, 24(4), 439–459. http://www.informaworld.com/10.1080/13632430410001316534.

Blackmore, J., Thomson, P., & Karin Barty. (2006). Principal selection: Homosociability, the search for security and the production of normalized principal identities. *Educational Management Administration & Leadership*, 34(3), 297–317. http://dx.doi.org/10.1177/1741143206065267.

Blenko, M. W., Rogers, P., & Mankins, M. C. (2010). *Decide and deliver: Five steps to breakthrough performance in your organization.* Brighton: Harvard Business Review.

Cornelius-White, J. (2007). Learner-centered teacher-student relationships are effective: A meta-analysis. *Review of Educational Research*, 77(1), 113–143.

Department of Education and Training. (2015). *Work and wellbeing review: Summary for participating principals.* Melbourne: People and Executives Services Group. Department of Education and Training.

Department of Education and Training. (2017). *Principal health and wellbeing strategy discussion paper.* Victoria Department of Education and Training https://www.education.vic.gov.au/hrweb/safetyhw/Pages/PrincipalHWB.aspx.

Dicke, T., Linninger, C., Kunter, M., Stebner, F., & Leutner, D. (2018). A longitudinal study of teachers' occupational well-being: Applying the job demands-resources model. *Journal of Occupational Health Psychology*, 23(2), 262–277. doi:10.1037/ocp0000070.

Dicke, T., Marsh, H. W., Parker, P. D., Guo, J., Riley, P., & Waldeyer, J. (2019). Job satisfaction of teachers and their principals in relation to climate and student achievement. *Journal of Educational Psychology*. doi:10.1037/edu000040910.1037/edu0000409.supp.

Dicke, T., Marsh, H. W., Riley, P., Parker, P. D., Guo, J., & Horwood, M. (2018). Validating the Copenhagen Psychosocial Questionnaire (COPSOQ-II) Using Set-ESEM: Identifying psychosocial risk factors in a sample of school principals. *Frontiers in Psychology*, 9, 1–17. doi:10.3389/fpsyg.2018.00584.

Enrion, E. H. (2016). We have to do better: Attacking teacher tenure is not the way to solve education inequity. *Missouri Law Review*, 81(2), 537–559.

Gallant, A., & Riley, P. (2017). Early career teacher attrition in Australia: Inconvenient truths about new public management *Teachers and Teaching: Theory and Practice*, 23(8), 896–913. doi:10.1080/13540602.2017.1358707.

Gallant, A., & Riley, P. (2018). Mentoring the problematic: Context matters. In M. Akiba & G. Le Tendrea (Eds.), *International handbook of teacher quality and policy* (pp. 304–317). Abingdon: Routledge.

Gurl, T. J., Caraballo, L., Grey, L., Gunn, J. H., Gerwin, D., & Bembenutty, H. (2016). *Policy, professionalization, privatization, and performance assessment: Affordances and constraints for teacher education programs.* New York, NY: Springer.

Heifetz, R., Grashow, A., & Linsky, M. (2009). Leadership in a (permanent) crisis. *Harvard Business Review, 87*(7/8), 62–69.

Jewell, J. W. (2017). From inspection, supervision and observation to value-added evaluation: A brief history of the U.S. teacher performance evaluations. *Drake Law Review, 65*(2), 363–419.

Lavigne, H. J., Shakman, K., Zweig, J., & Greller, S. L. (2016). *Principals' time, tasks, and professional development: An analysis of Schools and Staffing Survey data.* Institute of Education Sciences. http://ies.ed.gov/ncee/edlabs.

Leithwood, K. A., Pollock, K., & Sun, J. (2017). *How school leaders contribute to student success: The four paths framework.* New York, NY: Springer International Publishing.

Maxwell, A., & Riley, P. (2016). Emotional demands, emotional labour and occupational outcomes in school principals: Modeling the relationships. *Educational Management Administration & Leadership, 45*(3), 484–502. doi:10.1177/1741143215607878.

Nichols, S. L., & Berliner, D. C. (2007a). *Collateral damage: How high-stakes testing corrupts America's schools.* Cambridge, MA: Harvard Education Press.

Nichols, S. L., & Berliner, D. C. (2007b). The pressure to cheat in a high-stakes testing environment. In E. M. Anderman & T. B. Murdock (Eds.), *Psychology of academic cheating* (pp. 289–311). Cambridge, MA: Elsevier Academic Press.

Pollock, K., & Hauseman, D. C. (2019). The use of e-mail and principals' work: A double-edged sword. *Leadership & Policy in Schools, 18*(3), 382. https://www.tandfonline.com/doi/full/10.1080/15700763.2017.1398338.

Pollock, K., & Wang, F. (2019). *Le travail des directions d'école au sein des systems d'éducation de langue française en Ontario* [Principals' work in Ontario's French-language education systems]. Report prepared for the Association des directions et directions adjointes des écoles franco-ontariennes (ADFO), Ottawa.

Pollock, K., Wang, F., & Hauseman, C. (2014). *The changing nature of principals' work: Final report.* Ontario Ministry of Education. http://www.edu.uwo.ca/faculty_profiles/cpels/pollock_katina/OPC-Principals-Work-Report.pdf.

Reback, R., Rockoff, J., & Schwartz, H. L. (2014). Under pressure: Job security, resource allocation, and productivity in schools under No Child Left Behind. *American Economic Journal: Economy Policy, 6*(3), 207–241.

Riley, P. (2011). *Attachment theory and the teacher–student relationship: A practical guide for teachers, teacher educators and school leaders.* Abingdon: Routledge.

Riley, P. (2014). Principals' and deputy principals' health and wellbeing survey: 2014 results. *Leadership+* (83), 12–13.

Riley, P. (2015a). *The Australian principal occupational health, safety and wellbeing survey: 2015.* http://www.principalhealth.org/au/reports.

Riley, P. (2016). The complex and changing nature of school leadership: School principal as boundary rider. *The Queensland Principal, 43*(1), 9–14.

Riley, P. (2019). *The Australian principal occupational health, safety and wellbeing survey: 2018 data.* http://www.principalhealth.org/au/reports.

Riley, P., & See, S.-M. (2020). *The Australian principal occupational health, safety and wellbeing survey: 2019 data.* http://www.principalhealth.org/au/reports.

Sahlberg, P. (2015). *Finnish lessons 2.0: What can the world learn from educational change in Finland?* New York, NY: Teachers College Press.

Sellar, S., & Lingard, B. (2014). The OECD and the expansion of PISA: New global modes of governance in education. *British Educational Research Journal, 40*(6), 917–936.

Stahl, G. (2014). Politics, policies and pedagogies in education: The selected works of Bob Lingard. *British Journal of Educational Studies, 62*(3), 366–369.

Tolofari, S. (2005). New public management and education. *Policy Futures in Education, 3*(1), 75–89.

Tschannen-Moran, M. (2014). *Trust matters: Leadership for successful schools* (2nd ed.). San Francisco, CA: Jossey-Bass.

Wang, F., Pollock, K., & Hauseman, C. (2018). School principals' job satisfaction: The effects of work intensification. *Canadian Journal of Educational Administration & Policy, 185,* 73–90. https://journalhosting.ucalgary.ca/index.php/cjeap/article/view/43307.

10 School business leaders and principal time use in England

Paul Wilfred Armstrong

In this chapter, I explore school principal time use within the English context. I do so by focusing on the organizational and financial management of schools, which is a central function to the overarching responsibility of the principalship in England. I consider the emerging empirical research in this area of the field to explore the growth of a relatively new role within the educational workforce, the school business leader[1] (SBL). I then contemplate whether or not—and the extent to which—this role has influenced how school principals use their time and expertise. Principal time-use studies have tended to focus on principals as the unit of analysis (e.g., Grissom et al., 2015; Horng et al., 2010; Lee & Hallinger, 2012). In this chapter, I take a slightly different vantage point by exploring the implications and outcomes of a policy response intended to change how principals use their time.

The SBL role emerged in England in the early 2000s as a result of a deliberate policy drive to streamline (and ease) school principals' workload by changing the ways in which they use their capacity and expertise (Woods et al., 2012). In the period since, the role has evolved into a prominent position within the English system, as widespread structural reforms have necessitated schools to operate as small- to medium-sized businesses in an increasingly market-driven and competitive environment (Armstrong, 2018; Woods, 2014). The SBL role and the context within which it has developed therefore provide an interesting lens through which scholars and practitioners can think about principal time use.

Over the last two decades, structural reforms in England have resulted in large numbers of state schools being removed from local government control and handed greater autonomy for their financial and operational affairs (Jones, 2016). I argue that, as the English system has become more organizationally decentralized (Bush, 2016) and corporatized in nature (Courtney, 2015), SBLs have served a crucial purpose in alleviating workload and reconfiguring responsibility among principals. In this sense, the government-led response to issues surrounding principal time use in England has been successful. At the same time, however, the emergence of the SBL role has raised questions about the extent to which educational leaders are willing to relinquish the organizational and financial management of their settings and the—often conflicting—coexistence of education and business values within schools (Woods et al., 2013). Within this chapter, I draw on notions of leadership distribution (Copland, 2003; Spillane et al., 2000) and value conflict (Stewart, 2006) to examine this issue and its implications for how principals in England use their time.

The role of the principal within the English school system

The Educational Reform Act 1988 ushered in a new era of autonomy for schools in England, which paved the way for a series of seismic shifts across almost every aspect and phase of educational provision in the decades since (Chapman & Gunter, 2009; Jones, 2016). A key consequence of these reforms was that schools assumed more responsibility for their own management (Caldwell, 2008). Decentralization sits at the fulcrum of these changes. In the period since the 1988 Act, successive governments have systematically reduced capacity within district-level management structures—thereby progressively handing schools more responsibility for their own organizational and financial affairs (Higham & Earley, 2013). Over the last decade, structural reforms have resulted in a large percentage of state schools converting to academy status, which removes them from local authority[2] management (Eyles & Machin, 2019).

Interesting features of the English school system include a centralized and prescribed national curriculum and inspection framework within which state schools must operate, and, by contrast, a much more decentralized managerial environment in which schools typically function as independent operational units. Bush (2016) provided a neat summary of the English context: "A distinction can be made between what schools should do, which is prescribed, and how they choose to do it, which is discretionary" (p. 6). This educational environment has had profound implications for school leadership and management in England and, from an organizational management perspective, has led to a widening and diversification of the principal role (Eddy-Spicer et al., 2019).

The role of the principal in the English system is multifaceted and ultimately differs according to the socioeconomic, historical, and geographical context of the locality in which a school is situated as well as the community it serves. The wider political context shaping the national school system is also an influential factor (Day & Armstrong, 2016. The National Standards of Excellence for Headteachers (UK DfE, 2015) provide a framework within which the role of the principal in England can be broadly understood. The framework sets out four domains that broadly encompass the responsibilities of a typical school principal. These are *qualities and knowledge* (including the importance of values, behaviour, relationships, expertise, and political and financial astuteness), *pupils and staff* (including leadership of teaching and learning within their school), *systems and processes* (including areas such as safeguarding, staff professional development, curriculum-led financial planning, and distributed leadership), and *the self-improving school system* (emphasizing the importance of being outward facing, working with other schools and organizations, and entrepreneurialism). Some of these areas of responsibility are universally comparable with the principal role across different contexts. There are also features of the role in England that are more distinctive, however, such as the expectation that principals lead with an entrepreneurial and "outward facing" mindset and also the high level of responsibility they hold regarding their school budgets and finances (a consequence of the devolved organizational management of schools). In England, such conditions have shifted the nature of school leadership (Rayner, 2018) and necessitated the need for both pedagogical and business acumen for those who lead and manage schools (Crow, 2007; Woods et al., 2013).

The emergence of school business leadership as a response to principal time use

In 2001, the UK government commissioned a research team to identify the main factors that determined teachers' and school principals' workload in response to concerns from those within the teaching profession and their unions: Teachers and school leaders were working excessive hours and spending too much time on tasks that might be better undertaken by nonteaching staff. These tasks included administrative and technical support and financial management and extended to the work of classroom practitioners and school principals. The findings were largely confirmatory and revealed that teachers and principals had more burdensome workloads than comparable managers and professional leaders in other sectors. Moreover, the data suggested principals were spending a disproportionate amount of time on management and administration tasks that could be carried out by nonteaching staff, and suffering from low morale as a consequence (PricewaterhouseCoopers, 2001). The findings from this report formed part of a body of evidence that identified possible factors contributing to the increasing numbers of principals retiring early from the profession and fewer individuals aspiring to the principal role both in England (Gunter et al., 2004) and internationally (Whitaker, 2003). Largely in response to the 2001 PricewaterhouseCoopers report, policymakers in England initiated a nationwide agenda to reform the school workforce in an effort to build capacity among support staff as well as realign and reduce teacher and principal workload (Gunter & Butt, 2005). Time use among teachers and principals was at the centre of these changes.

This restructuring sat within a wider international programme of reform to privatize certain public services—such as health (Flood, 2003), criminal justice (Alistair & Smith, 2007), and education (Chitty, 2009)—as part of a shift from state to market as a means of provision and improved efficiency (Hartley et al., 2008). Such shifts facilitated a period of workforce reform within public services that increased the need for individuals with specialist expertise and knowledge in areas such as finance and administration to support the work and practice of existing professionals in sectors such as health, law enforcement, and education (Woods et al., 2013). This period of time—in which new roles and new types of professionals emerged within the public sphere—is often referred to as *modernization* or *workforce remodeling* (Beck, 2008; Butt & Gunter, 2007). In the English school system, this was actualized through a particular strand of activity that focused specifically on addressing principal time use by removing financial and administrative tasks from the school principal. This was achieved through a systematic "professionalization project" that was designed to train and accredit individuals with expertise in school business leadership (Woods, 2014).

Funded and initiated in 2002 by the New Labour government through their flagship National Centre for School Leadership (NCSL), this project involved the creation of a suite of developmental pathways and certification that was underpinned by the aim of professionalizing a previously disparate and fragmented cohort of the school workforce[3] involved in finance and administration (Woods, 2009). This project would create a cadre of modern SBLs who could assume responsibility in a number of different areas, including finance, administration, organizational and premises management, information technology, and human resources. These SBLs would be well placed to change how principals were using their time by alleviating their workload while making the principal role more manageable for existing incumbents and more attractive for aspiring school leaders (Wood & O'Sullivan, 2007).

It is important to appreciate the significance of a project which, as Southworth (2010) explained, initiated a shift in the composition of the school workforce in England:

> When Estelle Morris, the then Secretary of State for Education, pledged in 2001 to train 1,000 bursars by 2006, few people in the education sector anticipated that this would trigger the groundswell of interest that it did. Yet that announcement launched a movement across the school system which continues today and is set to go further in the future. It was the start of a quiet revolution.
> (p. 3)

Southworth's predictions about the future growth of school business leadership have proved startlingly accurate. During the two decades since school business leadership emerged, the state school system in England has undergone some of the most far reaching and fundamental changes the country has ever seen (Earley & Greany, 2017). In many respects, school business leadership has been positioned at the forefront of these shifts (Armstrong, 2018). For instance, since 2010, successive governments have embarked upon a programme of structural reform in which vast numbers of state schools have converted to academy status (Jones, 2016). Upon becoming an academy, a school is removed from local (district) authority control and management, instead receiving its funding directly from the national government. As such, academy schools automatically assume greater responsibility for their own operational and financial affairs. From an organizational management perspective, this has resulted in business acumen becoming a key facet of school leadership in England and facilitated the emergence of school business leadership as a crucial feature of the English system (Woods, 2014). There is little doubt regarding the growth of school business leadership and the sector of the school workforce that fulfills this function: The most recent school census data indicate there are now over 11,000 members of school support staff that identify as SBLs (UK DfE, 2017). Although this upsurge in SBL capacity and profile has purposefully impacted and influenced the ways principals are using their time and expertise, it has also brought about unintended consequences. In the next section, I turn to the empirical research to explore these issues in more detail.

School business leaders and principal time use: a look at the empirical evidence

In 2008, the NCSL initiated and launched the School Business Manager (SBM) Demonstration Project in response to growing evidence of workload strain among school principals in England (PricewaterhouseCoopers, 2007; Rhodes & Brundrett, 2006; Stevens et al., 2005) and to supplement the existing programme of training and professional development for SBLs. The Demonstration Project invited groups of single or mixed-phase schools to submit proposals for up to £50,000 to develop context-specific means of sharing school business leadership expertise. The rationale was that these groups would develop innovative models of collaborative school business leadership that could be applied elsewhere within the system. At the same time as the programme was launched, and in the first empirical research to focus exclusively on this cohort of the school workforce, the NCSL commissioned and funded a team of researchers from the University of Manchester to undertake an evaluation of the SBM Demonstration Project Programme. This mixed-methods evaluation included data generated via quantitative surveys, interviews with multiple stakeholders, and principal work diaries in each of the 35 clusters in which over 260 schools (of different phases and serving diverse contexts) developed shared SBM models by working in partnership with other schools and outside agencies (Woods et al., 2012).

Analysis of the diary data suggested school principals within the sample were not only working long hours (nearly 60 per week on average) but also that a considerable proportion of this heavy workload could be relinquished to a qualified SBM. Indeed, according to the data, an average of 16.75 hours of school principals' time was being spent every week on tasks not relating directly to their core purpose of leading, teaching, and learning. Moreover, the interviews with school principals revealed a shift in their focus from predominantly engaging with children and colleagues towards a greater emphasis on finance and administration. In this respect, school principals acknowledged that their own professional functions had grown but many raised doubts as to whether or not they were making the right decisions in these noneducational matters. However, the majority of principals interviewed also suggested that their involvement in the demonstration project (and access to a shared SBM) was favourably impacting their workload (91.4%) and their job satisfaction (83%). (Woods, 2012). Regarding principal time use, Southworth (2010) summarized the implications of these findings:

> Firstly, this indicates that the demands of the [principal] role may require a level of professional and personal commitment in some contexts that would seem likely to be injurious to health and wellbeing over the longer term. Second, the data suggest that there is untapped potential for addressing this

> state of affairs through the effective delegation of nonteaching responsibilities to qualified SBMs. Increased delegation of financial and administrative work to suitable SBMs would represent a more rational use of existing professional expertise. (p. 30)

A concluding argument to these findings was that downloading the work for which principals were less qualified (e.g., finance or health and safety) to SBMs would provide principals with more energy and space to dedicate to the educational agenda. Indeed, additional testimonies from participating school leaders suggested that access to an SBL could prove to be a purposeful strategy for retention and succession planning among hard-pressed principals (Woods et al., 2012).

Early indications were therefore encouraging and implied that the development and growth of the SBL role would start to reconfigure principal time use and workload and, in doing so, make the principal role more attractive and one to which middle and senior leaders could aspire. This was certainly the case across many schools in England where the SBL role was assimilated into the senior leadership structure and given full support by principals who understood the value and potential of its purpose and function (Wood, 2017). However, the role was not universally accepted across the system, with some principals reluctant to relinquish power and decision-making responsibility to nonteaching members of staff (Woods, 2009). Other research into SBLs and professional identity has suggested that, in a school system traditionally led, managed, and directed by trained educationalists, many SBLs have found it challenging to establish their position and build a credible and professional profile (Armstrong, 2018). Similarly, research undertaken with over 300 SBLs in England suggested professional confidence among members of the SBL community has been "tempered with apprehension regarding the uncertain and changing nature of the profession in the wake of policy reforms, in addition to the outlook of school colleagues regarding the contribution and value of input from school business professionals" (Creaby, 2019, p. 3).

The empirical evidence suggests that although the SBL position has made a difference to how principals are using their time, there remains work to be done to ensure the role is fully realized across the system. At a time when schools in England are becoming more autonomous organizations with a growing portfolio of responsibility within increasingly stringent accountability structures (Greany, 2018), the SBL role has never been so crucial. Positioned at the fulcrum of the organizational management of schools, the SBL community has arguably been impacted more by the structural reforms of the last decade than other educational stakeholders (Armstrong, 2018). In terms of principal time use, this policy context is important because it directly and fundamentally influences the services schools are expected to provide—often filling the gaps left by the reduction in state provision—and therefore the work of those responsible for school leadership and management. England's education system is a marketized arena in which schools operate as independent business units, many with multimillion pound budgets, competing for pupils and resources (both human and financial) (Armstrong & Ainscow, 2018). In addition to the pressures of school improvement (through student attainment) and the national inspectorate, schools are also expected to provide a range of services, often in partnership with other agencies, to support the holistic care and development of the young people and communities they serve (Day & Armstrong, 2016). The challenge for principals is how to respond to and deal with the growing demands of the noneducational management and leadership of their schools (Woods et al., 2012). This function is ultimately the responsibility of the school principal but one that many feel underqualified to fulfill without the support of a suitably qualified SBL (Mertkan, 2011; Moorcroft & Summerson, 2006; Woods, 2009). However, the extent to which responsibility for the educational, organizational, and financial leadership of schools is fulfilled and dispersed remains determined by individual principals and their approach to leadership. In the final section of this chapter, I consider this issue and its bearing on principal time use through notions of hierarchical and expert authority and values conflict.

School business leadership and the reconfiguration of the principal role

When a school system becomes more decentralized, the principal can typically be expected to assume more administrative control (Leithwood & Menzies, 1998) and assume greater school- and community-level authority with broadened responsibilities (Pont et al., 2008). Decentralization can emerge and develop in a myriad of ways according to the motives behind the adoption of such an approach and the context of the country/state/region in which a school system is located (Somantri, 2018). In England, a system with a tight and centralized curriculum and inspection structure, the primary manifestation of decentralization has been through the devolved site-based management of schools (Bush, 2016). For some commentators, this has been underpinned by a long established efficiency drive to reduce bureaucracy and afford schools—and those who lead and manage them—more autonomy (Chapman & Gunter, 2009; Earley & Greany, 2017). For others, there is a more deep-rooted ideological rationale to disinvest in and reorganize public services (such as health and education) so as to align with practices and structures more commonly adopted by the corporate sector (see Ball, 2008; Courtney, 2015).

From a practical perspective, this has fundamentally changed the nature and scope of school leadership and management in England and broadened the practice of the school principal, including what they are responsible for and what they are expected to do on a daily, weekly, monthly, and annual basis. As schools have adapted to a system of site-based management coupled with a reduction in services and support from the district authority, school principals have had little choice but to adopt business practices as they juggle their educational, operational, and financial priorities. As Wood (2017) explained:

> Over time, a flexible approach to school leadership, management and administration was required in order to operate within the changing world of new public management where site-based decision-making operated

alongside increasing accountability within a quality, child-focused environment. (p. 163)

As the SBL role has grown in prominence to support and fulfill this management function, questions surrounding the extent to which this responsibility is fully relinquished have also arisen. Although a great many school principals have willingly accepted and supported the SBL role and its assimilation into the senior school leadership structure, others have been reluctant. Possible reasons for this are varied. In their research with SBLs, Woods et al. (2012) suggested that school principals who traditionally inhabited the dual position of lead practitioner and chief executive may be disinclined to cede some of the responsibilities associated with the latter position to their SBLs because (a) they desire to retain control of an organization for which they remain ultimately accountable and (b) they view SBLs as a possible threat to their authority. In other words, some principals are uncomfortable with the reconfiguration of how they use their time, an issue that can be understood through notions of leadership distribution and what might be interpreted as a perceived loss of control and authority (Woods et al., 2013). Regarding financial and organizational management, the changes to the school system in England have required principals to draw on capacity from outside their pool of expertise to fulfill their professional and contractual obligations.[4] This, as Copland (2003) explained, necessitates "a view of leadership requiring the redistribution of power and authority towards those who hold expertise, and not necessarily privileging *those with formal titles*" (p. 378). For school principals trained in top-down approaches to leadership, such relinquishment can be a challenging process. Furthermore, some principals relish the organizational and business aspects of school leadership and find this work rejuvenating (Oplatka, 2004). As Mertkan (2011) suggested, despite the additional workload, "This complicates the general view that business management is a diversion, or a negative aspect of [the principal role]" (p. 159). Spillane et al. (2000) posited that the practice of school leadership is an inherently distributed one, involving actors in different roles whose work is often overlapping rather than neatly divided. In this sense, leadership is a dynamic interaction between individuals, circumstances, and contexts. Research has shown that SBLs and the function they serve within a school are more likely to be fulfilled to its potential with (a) the full support and advocacy of the school principal (Armstrong, 2018; Woods et al., 2012, 2013) and (b) the principal and SBL operating interdependently with a mutual understanding of their respective areas of expertise (Woods, 2014).

Values conflict and principal time use

In considering the growing influence of the SBL role in England, Woods et al. (2012) drew attention to the potential conflict between educational and business practices. This issue is noteworthy as, for many educational stakeholders, the idea of business and educational practices coexisting is unpalatable and represents a fundamental values conflict (Thatcher & Rein, 2004). Although business thinking and practices within education are ubiquitous (Gunter & Forrester, 2009; Hatcher, 2006), individual assumptions about the legitimacy of these practices differ within education, as do ideas about the best strategy for managing conflicting business and educational values. While suggesting such conflicts are inevitable in public policy development and enactment, Stewart (2006) put forward a number of strategies that individuals and organizations can employ to manage and resolve such conflicts. These include *structural separation*, which allows for competing priorities to be handled within a single entity, and *hybridization*, which allows for "joined-up thinking" and involves the coexistence and integration of policies and practices underpinned by different values. Drawing on research with SBLs (Woods et al., 2010), Woods and Armstrong (2012) applied these two strategies/concepts to thinking about how, and in what circumstances, the roles and practices of the SBL and the school principal might—and might not—coexist harmoniously. For instance, across some of the school groups within their research, a lead school (typically the employer of the SBL) was paid by other schools in the network to deliver business and financial services and support. In other examples, SBLs and colleagues in support roles led business leadership activities in specialist areas according to their individual skill sets and expertise (e.g., human resources, finances, site management, IT, etc.) across the network. Both these models of shared SBL expertise can be understood as enabling structural separation as a strategy for dealing with potential conflicts between business and education values. In both examples, SBLs and their support colleagues worked with other support colleagues across the school network in the operational management of the noneducational aspects of their schools, leaving principals and their leadership teams time and space (through separation) to focus on routine decision-making from an educational perspective. In an alternative model of shared business leadership, some schools decided to collectively appoint an SBL to work across the network. In these examples, the SBL typically had a good grasp of the peculiarities of managing in a school context, while the educational leaders involved were keen to learn from the SBLs' expertise as a way of improving strategic and business management in their schools. This assimilation of educational and business practice is more aligned to hybridization and seemed to smooth over potential conflicts between these two different ways of working.

The notion of values conflict and the strategies employed to address this issue (Stewart, 2006; Thatcher & Rein, 2004) can provide a useful lens through which to interpret the reconfiguration of the principal role and the simultaneous emergence of the SBL within the English school system. According to Stewart (2006), "Structural separation works well enough when there are clearly defined jobs to be done, and stable professional paradigms to accompany them" (p. 188). Hybridization is a more complex proposition, as it requires a layering of new values over existing ones:

> A good example of hybridization is the values mixture that constitutes new public management, as a result of which public servants are meant simultaneously to be professional, efficient, neutral, and responsive. The

market-oriented values have been overlaid on top of the more traditional public service ethos to form a hybridized result. (Stewart, 2006, p. 188)

An important factor in achieving harmony between the educational and noneducational aspects of school leadership and management could lie in the synergy that exists between the tacit assumptions of different actors about how best to handle conflicts between business and educational values. These are important issues to consider with respect to how principals strike a balance between using their time effectively and relinquishing responsibility to members of their leadership team, such as SBLs, who are likely to be better placed to fulfill certain tasks and duties.

Conclusion

The English case provides an insightful example of how decisions made by policymakers surrounding the function and organization of schools (and other public services) can have fundamental implications for the roles and responsibilities of those who work within the education sector—including how principals use their time. The composition of the school principal role has developed considerably over the last three decades; this development has been in line with broader shifts in which practices and structures synonymous with the business sector have become key features of schools and the wider school system in England (Courtney, 2015). In an increasingly corporatized school system, this process raises questions surrounding the level of responsibility placed upon school principals, the kind of practices they are expected to engage in, the primary focus of their professional duties (education or business), and the type of individual suitable for the principal role. The introduction and professionalization of the site-based SBL role in England has proved a bold—and, in many ways, successful—response to some of these issues. This success is evidenced in the significant growth of this cohort, whose members have individually and collectively changed how principals use their time use across the system (Armstrong, 2018; Moorcroft & Summerson, 2006; Woods et al., 2012). As schools in England continue to move towards structural and cultural alignment with the private sector, organizational and financial management will be an increasingly central function. Consequently, in England at least, the SBL role has never been a more important pillar in the school leadership structure: SBLs support principals to ensure the latter can focus more of their time and efforts on leading education.

As with other jurisdictions internationally, the principal must retain overall stewardship of the school as an organization to ensure its effective function as an educational institution (Horng et al., 2010). In organizationally devolved systems, however, there is greater pressure on school principals and how they use their time due to the wider range of responsibility they must assume. England provides an example of one such system that has attempted to address this issue through capacity-building in the area of school business leadership. Although SBLs have helped change how principals use their time in this case, barriers relating to values conflicts and workload distribution remain. Going forward, if such models are to be effective and realized more fully, then broader conceptualizations of school leadership are required that extend beyond the traditional realm of trained educators.

Notes

1. In this chapter, I use *school business leader* (SBL) when referring to the individuals who work within this sector of the school workforce in England. This is a contemporary term used to reflect the growing professionalization and widening responsibility of incumbents in this role. It is increasingly used in place of *school business manager* (SBM), the preceding label that was originally given to members of this cohort. Both terms are common within the academic and policy discourse when describing this role.
2. Local authorities, similar to district authorities in other contexts, are local and regional government structures with responsibility for a range of services across the geographical area they represent. Such services include health, social care, and education. There are 152 local authorities in England. Traditionally, they have been responsible for managing the schools in their areas; however, the significant increase in academy schools across the English system has coincided with a reduction in the capacity and resource of this tier of government in some areas of the country. One of the key features of academy schools is that they are not maintained by, and therefore operate independently of, the local authority.
3. Prior to the introduction of the SBL role, the cohort of the school workforce responsible for organizational and financial management was made up of a range of different roles, including clerical and administrative assistants, school secretaries, and bursars. The latter title was traditionally the most common and typically described the individual who managed the school finances and budget although with much less responsibility (and often less qualified) than the modern day SBL.
4. It is worth noting that principals in England are legally responsible (and ultimately accountable) for the all aspects of their school provision, including those areas that fall within the remit of the SBL, such as financial and organizational affairs.

References

Alistair H and Smith DJ (2007) *Transformations of Policing*. Aldershot: Ashgate

Armstrong, P. W. (2018). School business managers in England: Negotiating identity. *International Journal of Educational Management*, 32(7), 1266–1277.

Armstrong, P. W., & Ainscow, M. (2018). School-to-school support within a competitive education system: Views from the inside. *School Effectiveness and School Improvement*, 29(4), 614–633.

Ball, S. J. (2008). New philanthropy, new networks and new governance in education. *Political Studies*, 56(4), 747–765.

Beck, J. (2008). Governmental professionalism: Re-professionalizing or de-professionalizing teachers in England? *British Journal of Educational Studies*, 56(2), 119–143.

Bush, T. (2016). School leadership and management in England: The paradox of simultaneous centralisation and decentralisation. *Research in Educational Administration & Leadership*, 1(1), 1–23.

Butt, G., & Gunter, H. M. (Eds.) (2007). *Modernizing schools: People, learning and organizations*. London: Continuum.

Caldwell, B. J. (2008). Re-conceptualizing the self-managing school. *Educational Management, Administration and Leadership*, 36(2), 235–252.

Chapman, C., & Gunter, H. (2009). *Radical reforms: Perspectives on an era of educational change*. Abingdon: Routledge.

Chitty C (2009). Education Policy in Britain. Basingstoke: Palgrave MacMillan.

Copland, M. A. (2003). Leadership of inquiry: Building and sustaining capacity for school improvement. *Educational Evaluation and Policy Analysis*, 25(4), 375–395.

Courtney, S. J. (2015). Corporatised leadership in English schools. *Journal of Educational Administration and History*, 47(3), 214–231.

Creaby, F. (2019). *Leading school business: Professional growth and confidence in changing times*. Coventry: Institute for School Business Leadership (ISBL).

Crow, M. G. (2007). The professional and organizational socialization of new English headteachers in school reform contexts. *Educational Management Administration & Leadership*, 35(1), 51–71.

Day, C., & Armstrong, P. (2016). School leadership research in England. In H. Arlestig, C. Day, & O. Johansson (Eds.), *A decade of research on school principals: Cases from 24 countries* (Vol. 21, pp. 245–268). New York, NY: Springer.

Earley, P., & Greany, T. (Eds.). (2017). *School leadership and education system reform*. London: Bloomsbury.

Eddy-Spicer, D., Bubb, S., Earley, P., Crawford, M., & James, C. (2019). Headteacher performance management in England: Balancing internal and external accountability through performance leadership. *Educational Management Administration & Leadership*, 47(2), 170–188.

Eyles, A., & Machin, S. (2019). The introduction of academy schools to England's education. *Journal of the European Economic Association*, 17(4), 1107–1146.

Flood CM (2003) International Health Care Reform. London: Routledge.

Greany, T. (2018). Innovation is possible, it's just not easy: Improvement, innovation and legitimacy in England's autonomous and accountable school system. *Educational Management Administration & Leadership*, 46(1), 65–85.

Grissom, J. A., Loeb, S., & Mitani, H. (2015). Principal time management skills: Explaining patterns in principals' time use, job stress, and perceived effectiveness. *Journal of Educational Administration*, 53(6), 773–793.

Gunter, H. M., & Butt, G. (2005). Challenging modernization: Remodelling the education workforce. *Educational Review*, 57(2), 131–137.

Gunter, H. M., & Forrester, G. (2009). School leadership and education policy-making in England. *Policy Studies*, 30(5), 495–511.

Gunter, H., Rayner, S., Thomas, H., Fielding, A., Butt, G., & Lance, A. (2004). Remodelling the school workforce: Developing perspectives on headteacher workload. *Management in Education*, 18(3), 6–11.

Hartley J, Donaldson C, Skelcher C and Wallace M (eds) (2008). Managing to Improve Public Services. Cambridge: Cambridge University Press

Hatcher, R. (2006). Privatization and sponsorship: The re-agenting of the school system in England. *Journal of Education Policy*, 21(5), 599–619.

Higham, R., & Earley, P. (2013). School autonomy and government control: School leaders' views on a changing policy landscape in England. *Educational Management Administration & Leadership*, 41(6), 701–717.

Horng, E. L., Klasik, D., & Loeb, S. (2010) Principal's time use and school effectiveness. *American Journal of Education*, 116(4), 491–523.

Jones, K. (2016). *Education in Britain: 1944 to the present* (2nd ed.). Cambridge: Polity Press.

Lee, M., & Hallinger, P. (2012). National contexts influencing principals' time use and allocation: Economic development, societal culture, and educational system. *School Effectiveness and School Improvement*, 23(4), 461–482.

Leithwood, K., & Menzies, T. (1998). A review of research concerning the implementation of site-based management. *School Effectiveness and School Improvement*, 9(3), 233–285.

Mertkan, S. (2011). Leadership support through public-private partnerships: Views of school leaders. *Educational Management, Administration and Leadership*, 39(2), 156–171.

Moorcroft, R., & Summerson. T. (2006). Leaders backing leaders: A programme of school business management. *Journal of In-Service Education*, 32(2), 255–274.

Oplatka, I. (2004). The principal's career stage: An absent element in leadership practices. *International Journal of Leadership in Education*, 7(1), 43–55.

Pont, B., Nusche, D., & Moorman, H. (2008). *Improving school leadership: Policy and practice*. OECD. https://www.oecd.org/edu/school/44374889.pdf.

PricewaterhouseCoopers. (2001). *Teacher workload study*. London: UK Department for Education and Skills (DfES).

PricewaterhouseCoopers. (2007). *Independent study into school leadership*. London: UK Department for Education and Skills (DfES).

Rayner, S. M. (2018). Leaders and leadership in a climate of uncertainty: A case study of structural change in England. *Educational Management Administration & Leadership*, 46(5), 749–763.

Rhodes, C., & Brundrett, M. (2006). The identification, development, succession and retention of leadership talent in contextually different primary schools: A case study located within the English West Midlands. *School Leadership & Management*, 26(3), 269–287.

Somantri, C. (2018). Decentralization and effective educational leadership: Expectation versus reality. *Indonesian Research Journal in Education*, 2(2), 19–36.

Southworth, G. (2010). *School business management: A quiet revolution*. Nottingham: National College for School Leadership (NCSL).

Spillane, J., Halverson, R., & Diamond, J. B. (2000). Investigating school leadership practice: A distributed perspective. *Educational Researcher*, 30(3), 23–27.

Stevens, J., Brown, J., Knibbs, S., & Smith J. (2005). *Follow-up research into the state of school leadership in England*. London: UK Department for Education and Skills (DfES).

Stewart, J. (2006). Value conflict and policy change. *Review of Policy Research*, 23(1), 183–195.

Thatcher, D., & Rein, R. (2004). Managing value conflict in public policy. *Governance*, 17(4), 457–486.

UK Department for Education. (2015). *National standards of excellence for headteachers*. https://assets.publishing.service.gov.uk/government/uploads/system/uploads/attachment_data/file/396247/National_Standards_of_Excellence_for_Headteachers.pdf.

UK Department for Education (2017). *School workforce in England: November 2017.* https://www.gov.uk/government/statistics/school-workforce-in-england-november-2017.

Whitaker, K. S. (2003). Principal role changes and influence on principal recruitment and selection. *Journal of Educational Administration*, 41(1), 37–54.

Wood, E. (2017). The role of school business leaders. In P. Earley & T. Greany (Eds.), *School leadership and education system reform* (pp. 158–171). London: Bloomsbury.

Wood, E., & O'Sullivan, F. (2007) *School business managers' baseline study: Interim report* [Unpublished report]. National College for School Leadership, Nottingham.

Woods, C. (2009). Remodelling and distributed leadership: The case of the school business manager. In C. Chapman & H. Gunter (Eds.), *Radical reforms: Perspectives on an era of educational change* (pp. 80–90). Abingdon: Routledge.

Woods, C. (2014). *Anatomy of a professionalization project: The making of a modern school business manager*. London: Bloomsbury.

Woods, C., & Armstrong, P. (2012, July 20–22). *Let's talk business: Can sharing non educational leadership offer a viable route to effective inter-school collaboration?* [Paper presentation]. British Educational Leadership, Administration and Management Society (BELMAS) Annual Conference, Manchester, UK.

Woods, C., Gunter, H., Armstrong, P., Pearson, D., Collins, A., & Muijs, D. (2010). *School Business Directors Demonstration Project Programme evaluation and impact study: Final report*. Nottingham: National College for School Leadership (NCSL).

Woods, C., Armstrong, P., & Pearson, D. (2012). Facilitating primary headteacher succession in England: The role of the school business manager. *School Leadership and Management, 32*(2), 141–157.

Woods, C., Armstrong, P., Bragg, J., & Pearson, D. (2013). Perfect partners or uneasy bedfellows? Competing understandings of the place of business management within contemporary education partnerships. *Educational Management Administration Leadership, 41*(6), 751–766.

11 Out-of-time managers? Educational leaders' use of time in Switzerland

Pierre Tulowitzki and Laetitia Progin

School leadership is a relatively young topic in the Swiss context. Nevertheless, there has been a rapid development towards conceptualizing principalship as its own profession. Swiss school principals have their own dedicated qualification, their own professional status, and their own professional association that has some political leverage. They are expected to not only administer and manage but also to lead; furthermore, they come from a tradition in which pedagogical and administrative matters were considered central elements of school management. Finally, there are indications that the contemporary principalship in Switzerland is marked by urgency and a multitude of responsibilities, resulting in a considerable amount of work-related stress. In this chapter, we will show how the current demands of the job might limit the capacity of Swiss principals to lead effectively. We argue that principals' efficient and proficient use of time is related to professional development that explicitly deals with time management and creating favorable conditions for and a culture of shared leadership within schools. In conjunction with low-barrier opportunities for exchange across schools, encouraging a culture of shared leadership and supporting the development of time management strategies could strengthen the young profession of principalship.

In this chapter, we first establish the context by delving into the Swiss educational system, educational leadership in practice, and research on the principalship in Switzerland. Next, we present the background and results from a secondary study on principals in French-speaking Switzerland. Our secondary analysis revolved around understanding how principals managed their time at work and how in-service training might support their time management capabilities. Finally, we discuss these results vis-à-vis their implications for professional development as well as future research.

Educational leadership and the Swiss educational context

The Swiss education system is characterized by its federal nature on the one hand and by its efforts to harmonize the systems between cantons (federal states) on the other. The 26 cantons of Switzerland vary according to the predominant language: German, French, Italian, and Romansh are official languages of

Switzerland, as well as education. Cantons and their municipalities finance 90% of public expenditure on education (European Commission, 2017). For matters requiring joint action, the cantons coordinate through the Swiss Conference of Cantonal Ministers of Education (EDK) (State Secretariat for Education, Research and Innovation, 2020), which sometimes results in intercantonal agreements called *concordats*.

Although the cantons are usually responsible for school curricula, teacher training, and school governance (among other things), the Swiss constitution requires states to coordinate on educational matters of overarching relevance (State Secretariat for Education, Research and Innovation, 2020). Additionally, various intercantonal treaties exert a certain influence on the cantons to "harmonize" or align. For example, although teacher trainings and school leader qualifications differ slightly between cantons, all cantons have ratified agreements of mutual recognition for teacher training and school leader qualification. Additionally, all German-speaking cantons, all French-speaking cantons, and the Italian-speaking canton of Ticino have developed joint curricula for the primary level and the lower secondary level. Children fall under compulsory education from the age of four (kindergarten, which is considered part of the educational system in Switzerland) to age 15–16, with primary school going until and including Grade 6. Lower secondary education, where teaching is realized at different performance levels, takes three years. At the age of 15–16, students' compulsory education comes to an end (European Commission, 2017). Most children (about 95%) in Switzerland attend public schools that are free of charge (EDK General Secretariat, 2017). According to PISA data, Switzerland is one of the few school systems in which students from public schools perform better than students from private schools (OECD, 2011).

The cantons have systems in place to monitor the quality of education, including various forms of evaluation with key findings being published about every four years in a national education report (Wolter et al., 2018). Data from PISA indicates that Swiss students in lower secondary education perform around or higher than the OECD average, with a higher percentage of students performing at the highest levels (Level 5 or 6) in at least one subject assessed by PISA. Compared to the results of PISA 2006, 2009, and 2012, however, the recent data showed a decline in performance (OECD, 2019).

The introduction of the principalship in Switzerland

For much of the 20th century, Swiss schools were without principals. Instead, certain administrative tasks were handled by specially designated teachers. School boards as a form of communal self-governance played an important role: They were tasked with providing strategic leadership but also handling matters of budgeting and control for schools under their supervision (Quesel et al., 2017, p. 587). These school boards were run by democratically elected volunteers. Discourses on "New Public Management" (NPM), which began as political debates in the early 1990s and continued through the implementation of pilot projects, were manifested in the 2000s as significant changes in school leadership for the majority of cantons (Hangartner & Svaton, 2013, p. 364).

With increasing school autonomy at the end of the 1990s, the first cantons began to establish school principals in compulsory schools. With the introduction of school principals, a new level of hierarchy was created. These dedicated principals were no longer simply colleagues who took over administrative tasks in the school for a certain period of time—they now had supervisory functions, which some practitioners and scholars viewed as having potential for role conflict between teachers and school principals (Huber & Huber, 2011; Maag Merki, 2011). Now, it is expected that contemporary principals no longer "simply" manage the school, but that they also develop and improve it (Barrère, 2008).

The newly created principal role not only fundamentally changed the established multilevel governance relationships, but also subverted the impact of democratically elected school boards, which were responsible for managing the schools. Currently, almost all schools—especially in the upper secondary level—have a school administration, which is responsible for staffing, educational, organizational, and administrative tasks. Some cantons still have school boards while others have established professional (in the sense of fully paid and hired, not elected) bodies of school supervision (Wilkins et al., 2019, p. 154). These bodies set out the legal and strategic framework for school administrations with the schools usually being responsible for their implementation and also having areas of autonomy (European Commission, 2017). As in other countries, the range of principals' responsibilities has widened over time, with some cantons even giving principals full autonomy over financial and or HR matters. Although these developments have usually been accompanied by extended accountability mechanisms linked to the performance of schools in internal and external evaluations, the Swiss educational accountability system overall can be considered quite "low-stakes" (Hangartner, 2019). For example, issues related to school performance mostly trigger responses of additional oversight and in some cases additional support; there are no punitive mechanisms in place (Yerly, 2017).

Hiring and professional responsibilities

The municipal authorities are often responsible for hiring school principals at the primary and lower secondary levels while cantonal authorities are responsible for hiring at the upper secondary level (with some variation across cantons). Vacant positions are publicly advertised and candidates are in most cantons required to hold a teaching degree, have several years of experience, and, usually, an additional qualification in matters of principalship recognized by the EDK. In some cases, this qualification can also be acquired after being hired as a principal. Of the 8,808 school principals (2,878 full-time equivalents) in public schools in Switzerland in the 2015–2016 academic year, slightly over 50% were female, with significantly more female than male principals on the primary school level and more male than female principals on the lower secondary school level (Wolter et al., 2018, p. 45). Being a part-time principal is a common occurrence in Switzerland.

In terms of actual responsibilities, broadly speaking, principals are responsible for the pedagogical and organizational/administrative management tasks in local schools in all cantons. They are usually in charge of:

- Managing the teaching staff
- The pedagogical management of the school
- The organization of school operations
- Quality development
- Informing parents and the public
- Ensuring the link between school authority and the school

Additionally, they are present at meetings of the school boards (or their professional counterparts) in an advisory capacity (Hangartner & Heinzer, 2016, pp. 50–51).

The EDK has specified the following areas of management and leadership for school principals in its requirements for professional development courses for school principals:

1 Developing and implementing longer term goals and strategies for their schools
2 Leading and managing staff in schools, ensuring favorable conditions for learning and teaching
3 Managing organizational aspects of a school like administration, finances, and infrastructure in a responsible manner
4 To shape and support the collaboration and communication with staff, students, as well as with entities outside of the school
5 To create and sustain an adequate system of quality management
(Swiss Conference of Cantonal Ministers of Education, 2009)

Research on school leadership in Switzerland

Although school leadership so far has seldom been the focus of research in Switzerland (for an English-speaking overview, see Huber, 2016), there is some research available on school principals' roles and time use. In a comprehensive qualitative study, Gather Thurler et al. (2011) studied the working lives of school principals and directors of health services in the cantons of Geneva and Vaud. Drawing on a sample of 60 participants, they sought to better understand the way these leaders worked, the contextual factors that shaped the structure of their work, their conceptions of their role and work, and any possible personal and institutional dynamics that might help or hinder their ability to deal with work-related challenges. Among other things, the study revealed an average daily working time of just over 10 hours. This time was mostly spent across two domains: (a) working individually on preplanned or routine matters or on matters of communication (about 40% of the working time) and (b) working collectively through meetings, one-on-one talks, and other interpersonal interactions (about 41% of the working time) (Gather Thurler et al., 2011, pp. 7–9).

About 17% of their time was spent on unconventional matters outside of the usual working routine that were nonetheless linked to work such as visiting other schools, their own professional development, or informal networking gatherings, but also unforeseen incidents (Gather Thurler et al., 2011, p. 10). Echoing the work of the French sociologist Anne Barrèrre (2006), Gather Thurler et al. found that leaders operate in different "temporalities," with short-term and long-term matters regularly creating conflicting demands in terms of what to prioritize.

In a qualitative study, Stemmer Obrist (2014) analyzed the professional self-concepts of school principals in the canton of Aargau when mandatory school principals were introduced. The school principals Stemmer studied were able to change their professional self-concepts from teaching to leading. However, they tended to prioritize matters of administration and communication over matters of leading staff. Generally speaking, they tended to favor a cooperative and participatory leadership style. A study on school leadership by Huber et al. drew on data collected in 2011 and 2012—interviews, questionnaires, and diary entries—to investigate the preferences and burdens of school leaders in Germany, Austria, and the German-speaking part of Switzerland to gain empirical insights into the work and work contexts of principals. Compared to the German and Austrian principals who participated in the studies, Swiss principals exhibited a higher level of job satisfaction and lower levels of occupational stress and emotional exhaustion (Huber et al., 2016, p. 175). Principals were found to spend about a third of their time on administrative tasks with matters of staff management and matters of education and guidance also occupying a significant amount of time (Huber et al., 2016, p. 176).

In 2012–2013, Windlinger et al. investigated school leadership actions and their influence in schools in the German-speaking part of the canton of Bern. The researchers collected data through a quantitative survey with a sample of 181 schools (Teachers n = 3,137; principals n = 241). Results indicated that more than half of the surveyed principals worked only part-time as principals with many working additionally part-time as teachers. Within the context of their work as principals, many principals indicated working longer hours than specified in their contract. The largest proportion of working time was spent on tasks in the area of organization and administration.

Estimates regarding the subjective experience of stress indicated that strenuous working hours were a burden for school principals. More than 40% of the participating school principals reported often feeling tired and exhausted because of the professional strain and they wished for more breaks (Windlinger et al., 2014, pp. 60–61). In terms of their roles, each school principal hit upon three roles to varying degrees: *leadership, primus inter pares* (i.e., "first among equals"), and *administration*. A stronger self-identification by a principal as an *administrator* was linked to a higher experience of stress. A stronger assessment of their own role as *primus inter pares*, meaning more of a colleague with additional responsibilities, was mainly connected with having less than a full-time position and/or being a principal at a rather small school (Windlinger et al., 2014, p. 78). The vast majority of the surveyed principals reported that from their point of view, two of their tasks were to create a relaxed working situation based on mutual trust and to exemplify principles of action to guide collaborative work (Windlinger et al., 2014, p. 75).

In a qualitative study, Progin (2017) explored how novice principals coped with the challenges of their new role with a special interest in how the work-related trials they faced shaped their professional identities. She identified balancing wanting to react swiftly to arising matters and being mindful that a slower approach might be more prudent as one of the key challenges for the principals in the study (Progin, 2017). In 2017, a workplace analysis study conducted by Huber et al. examined the expectations and working conditions for school principals in the canton of Aargau using a mix of online questionnaires, online work diaries, shadowing observations, and interviews. Among other things, the study highlighted the predominance of administrative work, followed by work in the realm of HR and work around educational issues, with fragmented work-days being a frequent occurrence. In addition, principals occasionally took on tasks that were outside of the scope of their official job profiles (Huber et al., 2017).

In terms of autonomy, results from a quantitative survey-study (n = 219) in the French-speaking cantons indicated that principals wanted more decision-making power, especially concerning matters of managing the school building and infrastructure and financial administration (Soguel et al., 2015). At the same time, the surveyed principals did not want absolute autonomy in any of their working domains. The researchers interpreted this finding as an indication that many principals might conceive of their function as more administrative or as executive bodies of the supervisory authority rather than as autonomous but also accountable leaders.

Some common themes can be observed across these studies. First, school principals have to deal with a multitude of activities in parallel, often involving a broad range of interactions with agents within and outside their school. Second, their duties relate in particular to administration, human resource management, communication, guidance, and, more broadly, education. Unlike countries with a long tradition of the principalship and systems marked by high accountability and high autonomy, Swiss principals seem to conceptualize their work less in terms of exerting some type of leadership and more in terms of pedagogical and administrative work. Similar to findings from the United States (for example, Spillane & Hunt, 2010), the image of the principal as "lone wolf" acting alone can be considered a thing of the past. School principals are (increasingly) emphasizing participatory processes within their schools that encourage a redistribution of power. In sum, principalship in Switzerland can be viewed as a young profession with a strong emphasis on aspects of collaboration and shared responsibility.

Background of the study

This study is based on a reanalysis of data from two studies on principals' work and time use and the in-service training they received in the French-speaking cantons of Switzerland from 2009 to 2013 and 2015 to 2017 (Perrenoud &

Progin, 2017; Progin, 2013). A consortium of four tertiary-level institutions has been offering certified in-service training and professional development for school leaders in French-speaking Switzerland since 2008. The original objective of these two studies was to understand how such training might help prepare school leaders for the challenges they face in their daily work—a context marked by perpetual urgency. More specifically, the researchers' aim was to question the ways in which the training and actual work of school leaders in French-speaking Switzerland is influenced by the contemporary process of social acceleration (Rosa, 2010), considered to be one of the major driving forces at work in the professional world today. Simply put, social acceleration describes a process in which time becomes more and more scarce as the amount of activities within a certain span of time increases. Technical innovations, the pace of social change, and (an accelerated) pace of life can feed into each other, resulting in an overall social acceleration (Rosa, 2010).

The researchers collected data from principals using a combination of methods: A significant quantity of data was collected through participant observation during various training situations and seminars, which provided structures and opportunities for them to reflect and for the researchers to analyze their experiences and practices. As many seminars focused on the analysis of practice, the (verbalized) reflection of challenges, strategies, and emotions of the participants provided especially rich source material for gaining insight into their reality as school leaders. Observational data was collected over six days for each year between 2008 and 2017 with the exception of 2014 and 2015. The approach to collecting observational data can be characterized as "less structured and continuous" (Pollock & Hauseman, 2017, p. 92f).

In addition, Progin (2013) and Perrenoud and Progin (2017) conducted semistructured interviews with 10 principals from the pool of observed principals. They did so to complement the data around practices gathered from the observations with some insights into motives behind them (Pollock & Hauseman, 2017; Tulowitzki, 2019). The interviews focused on principals' relationship to training, the cost it generated in their working life and, more generally, their relationship to time and time use.

For the secondary analysis, we reanalyzed the data with the aim to answer the following research questions:

1 How do principals manage their work time?
2 How—if at all—does in-service training influence their ability to manage their time?

Our methodological approach can be described as qualitative, inductive, and ethnographic (Miles & Huberman, 1999) and based on principles of the grounded theory methodology (Glaser & Strauss, 2010). The material was coded in iterative passes with the aim to progressively become more familiarized with participants' reality and how they construct it throughout the process of reanalyzing the data.

There are important limitations to the study. Data was collected in the French-speaking part of Switzerland. There might be different traditions or cultural norms in other Swiss cantons that shape principals' practices there. Additionally, the observational data was collected in specific training situations as well as during reflections and interactions between principals. Although the training situations were designed to mimic and encapsulate the regular working context of school principals, they nevertheless can, at most, only represent an approximation. The downsides of this simulacrum may, however, be mitigated by the fact that these settings provided ample opportunities for reflection—something often lacking in an everyday work environment. Also, although this work is underpinned by a distributed perspective on leadership—meaning that leadership is realized in the interaction between individuals (Spillane, 2006)—the persons observed and interviewed and thus the focus of attention were, in fact, principals. Thus, the perspective on matters involving others like shared leadership is restricted in the sense that only their actions and points of view were captured.

Results

Although principals are involved in all domains of work described earlier in this chapter, administrative and managerial work were often put front and center; moreover, the "hunt for information" can take up a significant amount of time. Additional areas of work include dealing with parents' concerns or matters of staff. This goes against the expectations some of the principals had: They initially expected their work to be less managerial and more pedagogical in nature.

Limited capacity for leadership

By their own accord, as well as in official profiles of the responsibilities, articulating and implementing a vision for the school or how it could be developed is part of principals' work. However, several participants reported feeling overburdened and limited in their capacity to pay attention to such matters. Participants characterized balancing the day-to-day demands around professional development and successfully maintaining a work–life balance as very challenging. One principal explained that the overall workload actually acted as a barrier to the joint efforts of school development as there was no time to coordinate with everyone and align expectations and visions.

An additional constraint can be described as the pull from leading toward managing: In the case of unforeseen incidents, some principals shift their attention to the matters immediately in front of them, diminishing their capability to work on longer term matters. As one principal put it:

> When I am in my office [at school], I am a tool in the toolbox of that school. You get disturbed. You receive phone calls, emails, notifications. More and more, fellow principals and school authorities use WhatsApp. You really

jump from one thing to another. I think it is not possible to get anywhere. Except on Saturday morning or late in bed where you can take a moment to really take a step back.

Coping strategies

One common coping strategy seems to consist of shifting work-related tasks to the free time principals usually have available—for example, on the weekend, in the evening hours, or during the holidays. This often follows a justification logic centered around the urgency and importance of the task. Another strategy involves multitasking: for example attending a meeting or professional development activity while—at least during some of that time—(discretely) answering emails on the laptop. Another coping strategy lies in changing patterns of communication. One principal reported how, in the beginning, he used to drop whatever he was doing when a teacher came to see him with a problem. This resulted in him often losing track of whatever he was originally doing as the new problem absorbed his attention. After several months of frustration, he changed his approach to such situations and started requiring all teachers to send him a short note via email instead of dropping in, which enabled him to document the issues and exert more control over when he would respond. Although this was seen as something that could be learned (and should be taught) by some, others viewed this as personality-dependent:

> For me, the flexibility regarding the use of time is first of all influenced by the personality of the principal. You need to be structured and firm sometimes. You cannot always accept the scheduling restraints imposed by other actors. Personality makes a difference in whether you actually manage to distance yourself [from such demands] or not.

Principals have the possibility to freely schedule their working hours and decide what they do and when they do it. The principals who participated in this study largely took advantage of these possibilities by employing various ways of organizing their work time. One common goal was to find an optimal balance, or as one principal put it: "I'm trying to have a well balanced time-table over the week ... to avoid having three days overbooked and two empty days." Another goal principals often strived for was to ensure that there was time for reflection—in other words, to develop "strategies to get away from it all." Some of the participants explicitly mentioned that they considered making time for reflection as an important part of their job. As to how this could be realized, one principal explained:

> This [following type of] time is not always fixed: the reflection time. I have a vision of my days. I look a bit at my upcoming week, what the schedule looks like and I try to space everything out. By that I mean that for every day, I try to have times without appointment where I can get some reading

done. For the meeting times with my secretary, I also pay attention that they contain gaps. I organize my meetings and tasks in such a way that there is spare time available where I can potentially get some reading done.

Another principal mentioned the *urgent important matrix* as another useful approach to time management:

> I work a lot through shared calendars, with time-slots reserved for certain issues. For urgent and important things that come up, I check whether I can fit them in or move around another activity; it's a kind of negotiation. I have my vision of the day, of the week, and of the month and I negotiate the unexpected according to the "urgent important" matrix. There comes a moment where I have only very few criteria to classify the activities and stay the course.

Nevertheless, several participants explained that their working days tend to become fragmented due to the nature of the job, and they underlined the importance of preparing (and factoring in time) for the unexpected. They also described balancing out their weekly agenda to avoid high-intensity versus low-intensity days as a strategy to not only use their time efficiently but also guard themselves against unwanted interruptions. By creating balanced weekly agendas—sometimes several weeks in advance—some participants sought to "counteract" the unforeseen. Finding and maintaining protected time for reflection was characterized as a "struggle" or "walking a tightrope."

The participating principals viewed delegating and sharing responsibilities as elements of effective leadership. Several principals describe how trust fuels their approaches to shared leadership. As one explained:

> I think I don't want to control everything. A principal who wants to do everything himself, puts himself in more stressful situations and in situations where he bites off more than he can chew. I have a certain degree of control over things but I mostly trust people. This capacity to trust people also allows me to have time for myself, to do what I need to do. I have often talked to other principals who said that they just couldn't manage and that they needed to be in the know, to be informed of everything all the time and that can hinder them in making headway with their own work. [You need] to be able to delegate.

Or, according to another participant:

> For me, shared leadership is being able to work with the trust in the competencies of my colleagues.

For this principal, trustful shared leadership also added the benefit of empowering staff with them being able to do more than in an environment focused on control and with them getting a chance to grow professionally as well.

The role of training and professional development

Some participants viewed professional development courses as a double-edged sword. Some reported that they helped them "come up for air" and provided a space for reflection:

> The professional development courses have always been refreshing for me. This has to do with the persons involved and the reflections brought about by the courses. This has prompted questions, readings, and I was able to find some moments of reflection and study.

Others highlighted the value of being able to discuss matters with peers:

> There are moments of exchange which allow you to leave behind your problems with your superiors, your students, or authorities. A professional development course day is a kind of day off that takes the pressure off a bit.

However, several principals also explained that any professional development added further strain to their already full schedules:

> You are in this situation the whole time and professional development is only something that comes on top. You always have your objectives. School continues to operate. It just comes with the territory. A principal must be able to jump from one activity to the next. To get results, you must be able to juggle multiple issues. Obviously, I had to set up 'battle plans' in order to be able to manage professional development and professional demands.

Besides the time commitment, some principals also expressed concern regarding mounting stress, as professional development was viewed as one more thing upon which principals needed to stay on top:

> Honestly, attending a professional development course is rather stressful. It creates added stress. You are scrambling, you are scrambling to manage your school. It is only during the holidays that you will be able to take a step back and work on your professional development activities.

Discussion and conclusion

Our analysis gives insight into how principals use their time and navigate multiple demands and responsibilities. The results show that issues of time pressure are very present in the working lives of the Swiss principals who participated in these studies. We were able to identify different time management strategies for said pressures; however, despite such efforts, several principals reported having to work during weekends and holidays. There are indications that time management strategies are learned on the job and are not necessarily shared between the principals. In line with this conclusion, time management does not appear explicitly in the curriculum of the in-service training programs. A number of principals reported having bought management books dedicated to this subject and it was not uncommon for these books to be found among their reading materials, which seems to indicate their strong interest in the subject. The strong link between time use and the sharing of responsibilities is also highlighted through this study: It was a recurring theme when it came to effective and efficient management strategies. However, important preconditions like identifying suitable colleagues and being able to "let go" and allow others the space and autonomy to take on responsibilities pose a challenge for some.

The analyses also provide some perspectives for the training and professional development of school leaders. Knowing that exchanges with peers constitute an essential resource for school leaders in training, some of these exchanges could more specifically focus on the way they manage their time. Indeed, there are clear indications that principals in Switzerland use their initial training to create networks and exchange opinions and experiences (Progin, 2013). Therefore, providing impulses for the reflection of time management strategies could prove beneficial. Additionally, offering guidance and resources around shared leadership in school could help ensure that principals are not just willing but also able to work in shared leadership settings. Finally, creating opportunities for principals to exchange and expand their networks all along their career can serve as important impulses for lifelong learning.

As far as research perspectives are concerned, this study can only constitute a very limited first step in the Swiss context. Designing studies with multiple points of data collection that encompass the French-, Italian-, and German-speaking parts of Switzerland would provide useful insights into how these various regions, with their individual cultural identities, might shape the work of principals. Taking into account the contexts in which the principals work, looking at variations across principals but also within an individual principal's work pattern—for example, across a school year—would enrich our understanding of how school principals' work might be shaped by other factors (see also Sebastian et al., 2018). A more immediate next step could consist of carrying out shadowing-type observations within schools to more precisely identify time management strategies that school leaders use and how these strategies affect their actual work. A focus on the way in which leadership is implemented and distributed and how it is conceptualized by principals and teachers could be of particular use. As the principalship continues to evolve in Switzerland and as demands and expectations continue to rise, there is an increasing need for empirically based knowledge of the work of principals. Better understanding what principals do can help us devise valid ways to assess their impact and develop fitting forms of preparation and support.

References

Barrère, A. (2006). *Sociologie des chefs d'établissement: Les managers de la République.* Rennes: Presses Universitaires de France.

Barrère, A. (2008). Les chefs d'établissement au travail: Hétérogénéité des tâches et logiques d'action. *Travail et formation en éducation, 2,* 1–14.

EDK General secretariat. (2017). *Portrait Education in Switzerland.* http://www.edk.ch/dyn/11560.php

European Commission. (2017, October 10). *Switzerland national education System.* Eurydice: European Commission. https://eacea.ec.europa.eu/national-policies/eurydice/content/switzerland_en.

Gather Thurler, M., Kolly Ottiger, I., Losego, P., Maulini, O., Denecker, C., Aurélien, J., Meyer, A., Progin, L., & Tchouala, C. (2011). *Le travail réel des directeurs d'institutions scolaires et socio-sanitaires. Une recherche conduite en Suisse romande par trois hautes écoles partenaires.* HEP Lausanne, HETS Geneva, University of Geneva. https://archive-ouverte.unige.ch/unige:38471.

Glaser, B. G., & Strauss, A. L. (2010). *Grounded theory.* Cambridge: Huber.

Hangartner, J. (2019). Control of teachers under conditions of low-stakes accountability. *On Education: Journal for Research and Debate.* https://doi.org/10.17899/ON_ED.2019.5.4.

Hangartner, J., & Heinzer, M. (Eds.). (2016). *Gemeinden in der Schul-Governance der Schweiz.* New York, NY: Springer.

Hangartner, J., & Svaton, C. J. (2013). From autonomy to quality management: NPM impacts on school governance in Switzerland. *Journal of Educational Administration and History, 45*(4), 354–369. https://doi.org/10.1080/00220620.2013.822352.

Huber, S. G. (2016). Germany: The school leadership research base in Germany. In H. Ärlestig, C. Day, & O. Johansson (Eds.), *A decade of research on school principals* (pp. 375–401). New York, NY: Springer International Publishing.

Huber, S. G., & Huber, S. G. (2011). School governance in Switzerland: Tensions between new roles and old traditions. *Educational Management Administration & Leadership, 39*(4), 469–485. https://doi.org/10.1177/1741143211405349.

Huber, S. G., Gördel, B.-M., Kilic, S., & Tulowitzki, P. (2016). Accountability in the German school system. In J. Easley II & P. Tulowitzki (Eds.), *Educational accountability: International perspectives on challenges and possibilities for school leadership* (pp. 165–183). Abingdon: Routledge.

Huber, S. G., Kruse, C., Tulowitzki, P., Schwander, M., & Heimler, M. (2017). *Arbeitsplatzanalyse Schulleitung Volksschule Kanton Aargau – Executive Summary.* PH Zug, Institut für Bildungsmanagement und Bildungsökonomie. https://www.ag.ch/media/kanton_aargau/bks/dokumente_1/01_ueber_uns/publikationen_1/BKS_2017_IBB_Arbeitsplatzanalyse_SL_ExecutiveSummary.pdf.

Maag Merki, K. (2011). Die Leitung einer Schule. In L. Criblez & J. Oelkers (Eds.), *Die Volksschule: Zwischen Innovationsdruck und Reformkritik* (pp. 58–67). Zürich: Neue Zürcher Zeitung.

Miles, M. B., & Huberman, A. M. (1999). *Qualitative data analysis.* Thousand Oaks, CA: SAGE Publications.

OECD. (2011). *Private schools: Who benefits?* https://www.oecd.org/pisa/pisaproducts/pisainfocus/48482894.pdf.

OECD. (2019). *Programme for international student assessment (PISA) results from PISA 2018.* http://www.oecd.org/pisa/publications/PISA2018_CN_CHE.pdf.

Perrenoud, O., & Progin, L. (2017). Dites-moi tout, mais soyez brefs! Comment l'accélération sociale influence-t-elle la formation et le travail des chefs d'établissement? In J. Desjardins, J. Beckers, P. Guibert, & O. Maulini (Eds.), *Comment changent les formations d'enseignants?* (pp. 43–54). Paris: De Boeck Superieur.

Pollock, K., & Hauseman, D. C. (2017). Observational research on the work of school principals: To time or not to time. In L. Ling & P. Ling (Eds.), *Methods and paradigms in education research* (pp. 88–107). Hershey, PA: IGI Global.

Progin, L. (2013). Le rapport des chefs d'établissement à leur formation: Des étudiants (pas) comme les autres? In M. Altet, J. Desjardins, R. Etienne, L. Paquay, & P. Perrenoud (Eds.), *Former des enseignants réflexifs obstacles et résistances* (pp. 157–170). Paris: De Boeck Superieur.

Progin, L. (2017). *Devenir chef d'établissement: Le désir de leadership à l'épreuve de la réalité. Enquête sur l'entrée dans un métier émergent.* Berlin: Peter Lang.

Quesel, C., Näpfli, J., & Buser, P. A. (2017). Principals' views on civic and parental participation in school governance in Switzerland. *Educational Administration Quarterly*, 53(4), 585–615. https://doi.org/10.1177/0013161X17698016.

Rosa, H. (2010). *Alienation and acceleration: Towards a critical theory of late-modern temporality.* Aarhus: Aarhus University Press.

Sebastian, J., Camburn, E. M., & Spillane, J. P. (2018). Portraits of principal practice: Time allocation and school principal work. *Educational Administration Quarterly*, 54(1), 47–84.

Soguel, N., Huguenin, J.-M., & Ecabert, C. (2015). Autonomie souhaitée et perçue par les cadres scolaires en Suisse romande. In Y. Dutercq, M. Gather Thurler, & G. Pelletier (Eds.), *Le leadership éducatif: Entre défi et fiction* (pp. 51–70). Paris: De Boeck.

Spillane, J. P. (2006). *Distributed leadership*. San Francisco, CA: Jossey Bass.

Spillane, J. P., & Hunt, B. (2010). Days of their lives: A mixed-methods, descriptive analysis of the men and women at work in the principal's office. *Journal of Curriculum Studies*, 42(3), 293–331. https://doi.org/10.1080/00220270903527623.

State Secretariat for Education, Research and Innovation. (2020). *Swiss education area.* https://www.sbfi.admin.ch/sbfi/en/home/education/swiss-education-area.html.

Stemmer Obrist, Gabriele. (2014). *Schule führen—Wie Schulleiterinnen und Schulleiter erfolgreich sein und woran sie scheitern können.* Bern: Haupt Verlag AG.

Swiss Conference of Cantonal Ministers of Education. (2009). *Profil für Zusatzausbildungen Schulleitung [Profile for further qualifications for principalship].* http://edudoc.ch/record/35587/files/Prof_Zus_Schulleitung_d.pdf.

Tulowitzki, P. (2019). Shadowing school principals: What do we learn? *Educational Management Administration & Leadership*, 47(1), 91–109. https://doi.org/10.1177/1741143217725325.

Wilkins, A., Collet-Sabé, J., Gobby, B., & Hangartner, J. (2019). Translations of new public management: A decentred approach to school governance in four OECD countries. *Globalisation, Societies and Education*, 17(2), 147–160. https://doi.org/10.1080/14767724.2019.1588102.

Windlinger, R., Hostettler, U., & Kirchhofer, R. (2014). *Schulleitungshandeln, Schulkontext und Schulqualität: Eine quantitative Untersuchung der komplexen Beziehungen am Beispiel des deutschsprachigen Teils des Kantons Bern.* University of Teacher Education Berne. http://edudoc.ch/record/111772/files/Schlussbericht_DORE_140305_Layout_definitiv.pdf.

Wolter, S. C., Cattaneo, M. A., Denzler, S., Diem, A., Hof, S., Meier, R., & Oggenfuss, C. (2018). *Swiss education report 2018.* Swiss Coordination Centre for Research in Education. https://www.skbf-csre.ch/en/education-report/education-report/.

Yerly, G. (2017). Quel impact des politiques de responsabilisation douce sur les pratiques enseignantes? In Y. Dutercq & C. Maroy (Eds.), *Professionnalisme enseignant et politiques de responsabilisation* (pp. 121–141). Paris: De Boeck Superieur.

Part III
Principal time use in Africa and the Middle East

12 South African school principals' use of time
Learning from a qualitative study

Vitallis Chikoko and Pinkie Mthembu

Introduction

According to Taylor (2012), no resource is more poorly utilised in South African schools than time. But "time on task" is an important ingredient of success (Christie & Potterton, 1997) with Drucker (2006, p. 51) pointing out: "Time is the scarcest resource, and unless it is managed, nothing else can be managed." In this chapter, we discuss evidence from six South African school principals regarding how they use time at work.

In 1994, the apartheid system ended. The new democratic government had to rebuild the education system, a system that had hitherto been fraught with inequalities between races, between rural and urban, between the haves and have not and many more. South Africa experienced apartheid rule for over four decades. During that long period, society was racially divided. The black majority suffered severe oppression, segregation and socio-politico-economic and cultural deprivation. Transforming that education system entailed, among others, huge government expenditures. The government devised landmark strategies including decentralising school governance and management, and dividing schools into quintiles for funding purposes. A school is nowadays categorised into a quintile according to the economic status of the community where it is situated. Schools in quintiles 4 and 5 (fee-paying) comprise the richest and those in quintiles 1–3 (non-fee paying) the poorest. The latter group of schools receives larger amounts of government funding than the former, on a pro-rata basis. Every public school now has a School Governing Body (SGB) that includes representatives of parents and staff. Every school also has a School Management Team (SMT) comprising of the principal, the deputy or multiple deputies and the Departmental Heads (DHs).

While efforts to transform the education system have had significant achievements, many schools, particularly those in quintiles 1–3, have continued to underperform in many respects including learner performance. In our view, leadership is a major missing link (Chikoko, 2018) and in a school, the principal constitutes the backbone of such leadership. By leadership, we mean "... influencing others' actions in achieving desirable ends" (Cuban, 1988, p. 20). Grissom, Loeb, and Master (2013) suggest that time management skills may help principals meet job demands, reduce job stress and improve their performance. School principals often work under severe time constraints. Thus, this motivated us to examine one crucial aspect of such leadership, namely, how principals use time. The research question was: How do school principals understand and experience their use of time?

This contribution starts out by presenting the policy framework guiding the work of South African school principals. From there, we examine relevant literature, followed by a short section on the methodology. Thereafter, we present the findings, discuss them, followed by a conclusion to the chapter.

The policy framework guiding the work of a school principal

According to the Policy on the South African Standards for Principalship (Government Gazette, No. 39827), eight interdependent key areas constitute the core purpose of the school principal of any South African public school (Republic of South Africa, 2016). Table 12.1 gives a summary of these areas.

We find this policy framework to be quite detailed and exhaustive in terms of what South Africa expects of its school principals. The areas in which they should spend time appear to be laid out quite clearly. Against this backdrop, we resolve to adopt this policy framework as our theoretical "lens" in seeking to understand practice.

"Listening" to the literature

Through a case study in selected schools in South Africa, Botha (2013) studied time management abilities of school principals according to gender. He found that male principals had less effective time management than females. It therefore seems that gender may be important, but the context is likely to be even more crucial, hence our focus on both genders but all in similar contexts.

Victor (2017) studied time management strategies of 291 secondary school principals in Enugu State, Nigeria. Therein, principals did not adopt delegation strategies to involve their deputies and teachers. The absence of delegation suggests a monopoly of decision-making and the downstream effect is likely a risk of burnout on the part of the principal.

Through a review of research, Duncheon and Tiernery (2013) found that school leaders wrestle with how best to allocate their time given both instructional and administrative demands. Teachers' work is fundamentally defined by and interpreted through how time is used. As we indicated earlier, how people spend their time will largely determine what may and may not be achieved.

Against widespread emphasis on increased accountability, Weick (1996) underscores the spontaneous and unplanned nature of principals' work while emphasising the urgency thereof. Weick (1996, p. 565) likens principals' work with that of firefighters:

> If you listen to educational administrators describe a typical day at work, they talk about taking the heat, putting out brush fires, getting burned by

Table 12.1 Summary of the core purpose of the South African school principal

Key purpose	Description of requirements
1. Leading Teaching and Learning in the School	Five main kinds of leadership:

Strategic Leadership

- Develop in staff, an understanding of the need to support every learner
- Create a challenging climate of inquiry
- Set the school on a continuous improvement path
- Keep up to date with national and international education policy trends
- Support teamwork and promote cohesion
- Promote stakeholder wellness
- Inspire self-awareness and reflection

Executive Leadership

- Create a common school identity
- Create a climate of transparency
- Create an environment of discipline and trust
- Be visible in and outside the school

Instructional Leadership

- Make the school a professional learning community
- Lead continuous curriculum improvement
- Lead the school into the future
- Foster the success of all learners
- Empower staff to become instructional leaders

Cultural Leadership

- Embrace cultural diversity
- Ensure there is tolerance

Organisational Leadership

- Carefully manage the school's operational budget
- Ensure the recruitment and retention of quality staff
- Manage conflict
- Communicate with stakeholders regularly and efficiently
- Comply with policies and directives
- Establish implementable management systems
- Promote the interests of all learners and staff

2. Shaping the Direction and Development of the School

- Work with the SGB, SMT and parents to create and implement school vision and mission
- Take into account community and national values
- Establish and maintain effective quality assurance systems
- Account to the Department of Education, SGB, parents, staff, learners and community
- Have knowledge of South African legislation, strategic thinking and acting, leading and conflict management

(*Continued*)

Table 12.1 (Continued)

Key purpose	Description of requirements
3. Managing the School as an Organisation	• Continuously strive for improved organisational structures and functions • Equitably deploy resources and maximise their use • Oversee curriculum implementation, human resources, data, discipline, inclusion, application of knowledge and learner assessment • Know organisational models, financial management, legal frameworks and technology
4. Managing Quality Teaching and Learning and Securing Accountability	• Ensure there is quality teaching and learning • Maintain effective quality assurance systems • Know accountability systems, regulatory frameworks, quality assurance systems and mechanisms of data collection and use
5. Managing Human Resources in the School	• Understand the school's requirements • Ensure all vacancies are filled • Ensure equitable workloads • Guide staff on labour issues • Report all cases of misconduct • Facilitate regular parent-teacher meetings
6. Managing and Advocating Extramural Activities	• Enable the offering of extramural activities • Know: diverse sports codes; physical education and movement; occupational health and safety; parental involvement; and relevant policies
7. Developing and Empowering Self and Others	• Embrace the philosophy of Ubuntu (Humanness) • Cultivate effective interpersonal relationships • Practice participatory decision-making • Build personal capacity • Encourage continuous professional development (CPD) • Know: methods of participatory decision-making, importance of *Ubuntu*, performance management approaches and approaches to CPD
8. Working with and for the Community	• Build collaborative relationships • Ensure that school improvement and community development complement • Know: current affairs, the socio-politico-economic context of the school and ways of harnessing stakeholders

decisions, stopping rumours that spread like wildfire, looking for fire where they spot smoke, facing explosive situations, and watching the fireworks on board meetings.

School principals seem to spend a relatively large portion of their time on activities associated with student affairs and other administrative activities (Camburn, Spillane, & Sebastian, 2010; Horng, Klasik, & Loeb, 2010) and less time on instructional leadership (Camburn et al., 2010; Van Vooren, 2018).

Grissom et al. (2013) found that principals spent an average of 12.7% of their time on instruction-related activities. Similarly, a study in Canada found that principals work an average of 58.7 hours per week, preoccupied with operational tasks, with only five hours spent on curriculum and instruction (Pollock, Wang, & Hauseman, 2014). Horng et al. (2010) found that principals spent about half of their time on administrative tasks and another one-fifth on internal and external relations. Instructional tasks only accounted for between 13% (Grissom et al., 2013; Horng et al., 2010) and 19% (Camburn et al., 2010; May, Huff, & Goldring, 2012) of principals' time use per day.

To discover principals' time use scholars of the most recent decades have used descriptive methods such as direct observations (Grissom et al., 2013; Horng et al., 2010), daily logs (Goldring, Huff, May, & Camburn, 2008; May et al., 2012; Sebastian, Camburn, & Spillane, 2018), experience sampling (Spillane & Hunt, 2010) and surveys (Lee & Hallinger, 2012; Smith, 2013). These scholars sought answers to questions such as what percentage of time principals spend on various leadership functions (administration, instruction, professional growth and fostering relationships) (Spillane & Diamond, 2007); how much time principals spend on leading instruction (e.g. coaching teachers, evaluating teachers, classroom walkthroughs, developing the educational programme) (Grissom et al., 2013); how much time principals spend alone or with others (Sebastian et al., 2018); where principals spend their time (Horng et al., 2010); and whether the principals lead or co-lead activities (Spillane & Diamond, 2007).

The key findings were as follows: (1) The contexts and experiences varied. (2) All principals prioritised students by ensuring that they were visible around the school and by doing class visits. (3) Principals perceived themselves as working around the clock and unable to accomplish their planned work. (4) Principals indicated that district initiatives were not streamlined and felt that there were too many meetings. (5) Principals also felt that they required more support.

Ghamrawi and Al-Jammal (2013) cite Hager (2006) who listed five key mistakes principals made around time use. These were (1) spending time on non-priorities, (2) under-estimating the time tasks actually take, (3) allowing too many interruptions, (4) saying yes too often and (5) not getting help. Ghamrawi and Al-Jammal found that principals largely lacked work management skills. They also did not delegate effectively.

Goldring et al. (2008) sought factors that influence principal time use in relation to the school context and individual characteristics. They used 46 principals' daily logs and a survey of principals and teachers across one district. Findings showed that principals were not as fragmented across numerous realms of responsibility as previous research suggested. Some principals spent considerable time on instructional leadership. The researchers were able to distinguish three groups: "Eclectic" Leaders (activities are distributed evenly across different activities); Instructional Leaders (focused most on Instructional Leadership); and Student Leaders (emphasised student affairs).

Through time logs, interviews and observations, Spillane and Hunt (2010) examined patterns of time use of 38 principals in the United States. They identified three patterns of practice: administration centred, solo practitioners and people-centred. Administrative activities dominated principals' practices with limited time on curriculum issues. Only 22% of principals' time was spent on curriculum and teaching-learning matters. Instead of proactive and self-initiated activities, principals were largely reactive and firefighting with their work consumed by ever-changing, unplanned and unscheduled encounters. Similarly, Huang, Hochbein, and Simons (2018) found that the nature of a principal's job involved long hours as well as spontaneous and unplanned activities. The pace of work was hectic and unrelenting, and many workday activities were reactive.

White, Brown, Hunt, and Klostermann (2011) surveyed Illinois principals on how they understood their work, their preferences and priorities. They found that principals inevitably juggled multiple roles, including instructional leadership, organisational management, internal and external relations, day-to-day administrative demands, all leading to long, highly stressful hours.

We find that literature is rich in both methodological approaches to studying school principals' time use and findings thereof. Methodologically, approaches including time logs, observations, interviews, surveys and systematic reviews are evident. We take comfort in that our own approach-interviews with the principals, features prominently therein.

Methodology

We conducted the study in one district of the KwaZulu-Natal province of South Africa. Through a qualitative research approach, we studied the experiences and understandings of six purposively selected (Creswell, 2007; Merriam, 2009) primary and secondary school principals (three of each). The schools were in quintiles 1–3 and rural contexts. The participants were experienced school principals, with more than five years' experience each in that role.

We conducted semi-structured individual interviews (one each) with each of the six principals. Interviews lasted between one and a half to two hours each. We deliberately left it open to the participants to tell us how they spent time. We audio-recorded the proceedings with participants' permission. In analysing the data, we adopted a model of thematic analysis by Braun and Clarke (2006) and supported by Miles and Huberman (1994) that can be characterised as follows:

Familiarising self with data: We listened to the recordings, transcribed all interviews, read and re-read transcriptions. This is a process of data reduction (Miles & Huberman, 1994).

Generating initial themes: Having familiarised with the data, we identified preliminary codes, drawing excerpts from participants' full texts.

Searching for themes: Thirdly we collated the codes and organised the data into more stable themes.

Reviewing themes: We re-examined the data, seeking to decide whether to combine, refine, separate or discard initial themes. We ensured data coherence within themes and identifiable distinctions between them. This was a process of evaluating the themes (Miles & Huberman, 1994).

Defining and naming themes: At this stage, we named the themes and gave them clear definitions. This is a process of data display (Miles & Huberman, 1994).

Producing the report: Finally, we adopted the themes to present and discuss the data in response to the research question.

In seeking to ensure trustworthiness of the findings, we had all participants verify the interview transcripts. Additionally, we present verbatim quotations of participants' responses in the findings section (Creswell, 2007; Miles & Huberman, 1994). Regarding ethical considerations, we obtained permission from the relevant authorities and informed consent of the participants.

Findings

We categorise the time use of the interviewed principals into two categories. One is "The Perspiring Principal." These are the reactive, overwhelmed, fire-fighting principals who are constantly experiencing stress. The other group can be categorised as "The Inspiring Principal." They are largely in charge of their time. They create a vision for the school and help it work towards it. Although it was not our original intention to quantify the responses, it is noteworthy to report that five of the participants came across as "perspiring" principals while only one was "inspiring."

The "perspiring" principal

The "perspiring" principals were in a constant state of anxiety and often experienced a lack of time. Five domains could be identified as being quite time-intensive:

Scheduled and unscheduled meetings and workshops

Meetings, scheduled and unscheduled, consumed a lot of these principals' time. One of them said:

> What is taking most of one's time is meetings. The Department has got many sections. There is governance, examinations, teacher development etc. When they plan their activities, sometimes the right-hand does not know what the left hand is doing. You receive an invitation; then somebody else

phones you from another section, they also want the principal on that same day. They only know about the other meeting when you tell them. ... and so meetings take a lot of our time.

Some meetings were reportedly announced on very short notice:

It happens that you are just going to school, you thinking that it will be a normal day, then during the course of the day they call, please come for this and that ... such things happen more often than not. You cannot do the work that you planned to do that day.

Principals found it discouraging and disarming that their plans were severely interfered with:

There is nothing more discouraging than interference with your day's plan ... Like a circular or message that directs you to stop this and attend to that... meeting or workshop. Some of these sessions are not even useful.

Attending to parents

Principals detailed various instances in which a parent wanted to see the principal in person and how this was a responsibility that—in many cases—only they could fulfil:

Parents seek to see the principal for various reasons. Sometimes you are able to delegate, but many times parents just want to see the principal and they insist, so you try not to disappoint them.

The notion of urgency echoed across several interviews:

Sometimes you come to school, and you are going to meet with a certain department, a parent comes, something happened to their child. The child was bullied but did not report that to their teacher. At that time, the parent is agitated. So, you suspend whatever you wanted to do at that particular time.

At this time of the year, the beginning of the first term, there are so many interferences, parents wanting to have their children admitted without birth certificates ....

Nevertheless, some principals noted that not all meetings could be held as intended:

Parents' meetings, the general one is the one we hold towards the end of the year for the school budget. We call parents quarterly to look at their children's work. But I must be honest with you; we cannot do this for all grades.

Being visible

Being visible was another domain that was described as time-consuming. This entailed walking around the school building to show presence and as a monitoring approach:

> Sometimes I don't go round the classrooms; I just stand, you see, in a strategic point where I am going to make sure I see all the classes.

Some interviewees also framed this as a way to ensure that classes take place as planned:

> When it is time to teach, I ensure that everybody, including all teachers, go to class timeously, that there is no delay and they have got to stay for the duration of the period.
>
> What you want to see is all staff and learners at school. You need to monitor from time to time because if you don't, you will be surprised to find things not going on well. If you sit in the office all the time, you will never know what is happening. From time to time, you must be visible.

Teaching and learning

While several principals expressed that in their opinion, teaching and learning should take the bulk of their time, they conceded that this was not actually happening. Additionally, principals also expressed trouble finding the time to teach themselves:

> I love teaching, but because we are very busy I do not get enough time to teach to such a point that I do not have classes.

Idling in the office

In some cases, the firefighting mentality seemed to take up a lot of space with one principal seemingly using his time to wait for new "fires" or problems to tackle:

> But if I am not in class, I will be in the office waiting for anybody, perhaps who would like to see me so that we talk you see, as individuals and deal with the problem.

The inspiring principal

While this principal still experienced stress and was occasionally pressed for time, the overall impression is that he was more proactive and more in control when it came to managing time. This principal can be characterised across several domains or issues.

Looking after oneself and others

The notion of self-care was mentioned as a precursor to being able to support others:

> My daily programme, in the morning, I exercise. After one hour, I come back, bath, pray, eat and come to school. I have a clear-cut programme of life for myself because life is not easy. I have to be fit and ready spiritually, physically, mentally and otherwise. If you are a kind of educator who is a mess, for sure that mess will come to the school.

Closely linked to this was the ability to reflect on one's role and actions:

> At the end of the day, I have got to reflect upon my day. How was my day, where did I go wrong, where did I go right? How can I improve? That, to me is a fundamental principle.

Additionally, this principal evoked spirituality as relevant for his time management:

> Things happen by the Grace of God. My individual plans must be aligned to the master plan of God. As a result, my work has become very easy. I am now managing the school far better than when I was using corporal punishment.
>
> I have committed to guiding these young, up and coming educators. We now have got a programme whereby educators, led by me, participate in athletics. We run, participate in marathons, talk about Mandela Marathon, about Maritzburg, we have been there as a team. I am trying to impact and influence the private lives of those young educators. In the mornings, we pray as a staff, as a team.

Opening up to staff and colleagues was seen as a way to connect and to care for oneself and others:

> I try to influence the private life of an educator in a good way. I am not ashamed to tell educators about my private life. I am very clear about who I am, where I come from, and what it is that I want from every educator and learner.

Vision crafting

While short-term tasks and pressing responsibilities might try to draw away the focus of the principal, he believed that a longer-term vision that touches on deep-seated issues about the purpose of a school, was key in managing time successfully:

> Learners dropping out is a major challenge at many black schools. But I want to tell you about our Vision 2021. We have 400 Grade 9 learners this

year [2018]. It is our vision to have a Grade 12 (final year) of more than 300 learners from this group. Our vision says all of them shall get Bachelor passes. There will be many learners getting distinctions. This is meant to try and eliminate this tendency whereby learners somehow just throw in the towel and disappear at Grade 10.

We have a clear vision and mission because this must be clear. What do I want from a school? I want results. The school must be a centre of academic excellence. It must be a beacon of hope.

Managing time

While the work of a principal can entail unforeseen events, the interviewee pointed out that a certain amount of structure provided a foundation for being in charge of his time:

At 0645, I am here. I am the last person to leave the school. I have my daily programme diarised; time for financial matters, monitoring classes, resolving conflict, this and that.

Curriculum management

The interviewee mentioned effective curriculum management as another way to ensure an effective time management, not just for himself but overall. In order for this to be possible, he needed detailed knowledge of what happened in their schools all the way to the classroom level:

The key responsibility of a principal is curriculum management. As I sit here, I must know what is happening in Grade 8A, who is teaching, how far are they, what challenges do they face? Yes, I make use of the Deputy and DHs, but I still need to have those one-on-one sessions with the deputy, DH and educator.

Now teaching is over; I shall be supervising a revision programme. I need to know what shall be happening in every grade, what is being revised. I guide the learners even on study skills: how to study, how to look after your body, study groups: what size, how does it work, how does your memory work, what is forgetting. So we have a clear programme of revision. You don't experiment with these things, you have to know.

Creating a dynamic culture and leading by example

Part of an effective time management was understood to be a modelling behaviour that—ideally—inspired others to do the same. The interviewed principal sought to create a culture of teamwork and commitment. Thus, punctuality was seen as an important component in the sense that it was an aspect of time management that was immediately visible to staff. After investing time in modelling behaviour and nurturing a culture of ambition and support, the principal believed that his staff became more self-driven:

> We have built a team of dynamic, highly committed and passionate educators here. They are here on Saturdays and Sundays, over holidays, early in the morning at 6 O'clock and the whole day until late in the evening.

Discussion

The "perspiring" principals were—by their own account—perennially caught in meetings, attending to parents' concerns, and policing teachers and learners. While some of them taught some classes (which is expected of them), others did not find the time in their busy schedules. Findings from the interviews suggest that they struggled to perform the various tasks as prescribed in the policy framework. From our perspective, to exercise all of these leadership-related activities, one must be able to manage time. Some of the principals' responses indicated that the way they currently used time was not ideal as they could not recall any ideal day when talking about their experiences. We can conclude that these principals' time use can be characterised as firefighting.

A common feature we found between the two types of time users was that the job of a principal was very demanding. The policy framework itself testifies to that through the vast array of areas listed in it. Before looking at data from the inspiring principal, one may be tempted to conclude that the job of a school principal is simply impossible to fulfil. However, the data from the interview with the inspiring principal offers us clues as to how such a feat might be accomplished. The inspiring principal spent time seeking to know and manage himself. He sought to manage affairs from inside going out. Reaching out to other people such as the staff, the approach was holistic involving the physical, mental, social and spiritual. In looking at the entire school as an organisation, the inspiring principal spent time crafting the vision and mission, then building the requisite culture, "the way things are done around here." In doing so, every stakeholder, the teacher, the learner and the parent, knew and appreciated the main purpose of the school: teaching and learning for high performance.

Conclusion

Our study's findings are consistent with many previous studies that school principals tend to be strapped for time. The findings are also consistent with studies that characterise some principals as mere firefighters in the way they spend time. What we think is unique in that even where many principals seem not to find any other way but to firefight, even in poor school contexts such as the ones we studied, at least one principal can fruitfully manage time. This can serve as a jumping-off point to understanding ties between the effective-time use of principals and successful schools.

References

Botha, R. J. (2013). Time management abilities of school principals according to gender: A case study in selected Gauteng schools. *Africa Education Review*, *10*(2), 364–380.

Braun, V., & Clarke, V. (2006). Using thematic analysis in psychology. *Qualitative Research in Psychology*, *3*(2), 77–101.

Camburn, E. M., Spillane, J. P., & Sebastian, J. (2010). Assessing the utility of a daily log for measuring principal leadership practice. *Educational Administration Quarterly*, *46*(5), 707–737.

Chikoko, V. (2018). The Nature of the deprived school context. In V. Chikoko (Ed.), *Leadership that works in deprived school contexts of South Africa (1–9)*. New York, NY: Nova Publishers.

Christie, P., & Potterton, M. (1997). *School development in South Africa: a research project to investigate strategic interventions for quality improvement in South African schools*. Johannesburg: Education Department; University of the Witwatersrand.

Creswell, J. W. (2007). *Qualitative inquiry and research design: Choosing among five approaches* (2nd ed.). Thousand Oaks, CA: SAGE.

Cuban, L. (1988). *The managerial imperative and the practice of leadership in schools*. Albany, NY: State University of New York Press.

Drucker, P. (2006). *The effective executive*. New York, NY: Harper Collins.

Duncheon, J. C., & Tierney, W. G. (2013). Changing conceptions of time: Implications for educational research and practice. *Review of Educational Research*, *83*(2), 236–272

Ghamrawi, N., & Al-Jammal, K. (2013). Time flies—A statement that best applies to school principals. *British Journal of Education*, *1*(1), 52–66.

Goldring, E., Huff, J., May, H., & Camburn, E. (2008). School context and individual characteristics: what influences principals' practices? *Journal of Educational Administration*, *46*(3), 332–352.

Grissom, J. A., Loeb, S., & Master, B. (2013). Effective instructional time use for school leaders: Longitudinal evidence from observations of principals. *Educational Researcher*, *42*(8), 433–444.

Horng, E. L., Klasik, D., & Loeb, S. (2010). Principal's time use and school effectiveness. *American Journal of Education*, *116*(4), 491–523.

Huang, T., Hochbein, C., & Simons, J. (2018). The relationship among school contexts, principal time use, school climate, and student achievement. *Educational Management Administration & Leadership*, 1–19

Lee, M., & Hallinger, P. (2012). National contexts influencing principals' time use and allocation: Economic development, societal culture, and educational system. *School Effectiveness and School Improvement*, *23*, 461–482.

May, H., Huff, J., & Goldring, E. (2012). A longitudinal study of principals' activities and student performance. *School Effectiveness and School Improvement*, *23*(4), 417–437.

Merriam, S. B. (2009). *Qualitative research: A guide to design and implementation* (3rd ed.). San Francisco, CA: Jossey-Bass.

Miles, M. B., & Huberman, A. M. (1994). *Qualitative data analysis: an expanded sourcebook*. London: Sage.

Pollock, K., Wang, F., & Hauseman, D. (2014). *The changing nature of principals' work*. Final Report for the Ontario Principals' Council, Toronto, ON, Canada.

Republic of South Africa (2016). *Policy on the South African Standard for Principalship: Enhancing the Professional Image and Competencies of School Principals* (Government Gazette No. 39827). Retrieved from www.gpwonline.co.za.

Sebastian, J., Camburn, E. M., & Spillane, J. P. (2018). Portraits of principal practice: Time allocation and school principal work. *Education Administration Quarterly, 54*(1), 47–84

Smith, P. A. (2013). The relationship between principal time allocation and work effectiveness: evidence across city, suburban, town and rural school districts. *National Teacher Education Journal, 6*(2).

Spillane, J. P., & Diamond, J. B. (2007). *Distributed leadership in practice*. New York, NY: Teachers College Press.

Spillane, J. P., & Hunt, B. R. (2010). Days of their lives: A mixed methods, descriptive analysis of the men and women at work in the principal's office. *Journal of curriculum Studies, 42*(3), 293–331.

Taylor, S. (2012). Modelling educational achievement. In N. Taylor, S. van der Berg, & T. Mabogoane (Eds.), *What makes schools effective? Report of South Africa's national school effectiveness study*. Cape Town: Pearson Education.

Van Vooren, C. (2018). An examination of K-5 principal time and tasks to improve leadership practice. *Educational Leadership Administration: Teaching and Program Development, 29*(1), 45–63.

Victor, A. A. (2017). Time management strategies as a panacea for principals' administrative effectiveness in secondary schools in Enugu State, Nigeria. *Journal for Studies in Management and Planning, 3*(9), 22–31.

Weick, K. E. (1996). Fighting fires in educational administration. *Educational Administration Quarterly, 32*(4), 565–578.

White, B. R., Brown, K. S., Hunt, E., & Klostermann, B. K. (2011). The View from the Principal's Office: Results from the IERC Principals Survey. Policy Research: IERC 2011-2. *Illinois Education Research Council*.

13 Policy context and time use of primary school head teachers in Kenya

Evidence from the Snapshot of School Management Effectiveness (SSME) survey

Peter Moyi

Introduction

From the early 1970s, the government of Kenya enacted policies to increase access to quality education with limited success (Amutabi, 2003; Mugo, Moyi, & Kiminza, 2016; Nkinyangi, 1982; Sifuna, 1980). Research indicates that the quality of education can be improved if there are capable educational leaders on the ground (Bruns, Filmer, & Patrinos, 2011; De Grauwe, 2001; Fuller, 1987; Hallinger & Heck, 1998; Horng, Klasik, & Loeb, 2010; Leithwood, 1994; Waters, Marzano, & McNulty, 2003; UNESCO, 2005; Vespoor, 2008). With a growing emphasis on decentralization of decision-making and greater accountability, capable head teachers are critical (Glassman & Sullivan, 2008; Vespoor, 2008).

Despite the fundamental role head teachers play, there has been limited attention from policymakers and researchers in non-Western countries. Available educational leadership studies indicate that head teachers in these countries operate under different role expectations than those in Western countries (Brown & Conrad, 2007; Harber & Davies, 1997; Oplatka, 2004). Therefore, an understanding of the impact of the national context can provide important insights into head teachers' time use and practices. Furthermore, if training is to be provided to aspiring and practicing head teachers, it is important to establish what needs stem from their work (Harber & Davies, 1997).

This study seeks to answer the following questions. What role does the government expect head teachers to play? What skills or competencies are implied by government policy documents? Key documents will be analyzed to determine the skills that are needed by primary school head teachers. Second, within this policy environment, how do primary school head teachers spend their time?

Primary school leadership in Kenya

Head teachers are a key component of systemic educational reform (Bruns et al., 2011; Chapman & Burchfield, 1994; De Grauwe, 2001; Vespoor, 2008), yet there is no systematic leadership development policy in Kenya (Asuga, Eacott,

& Scevak, 2015). This neglect can be traced, in part, to colonial times when early British school leaders with a liberal arts education and colonial government administration field experience successfully ran schools (Lungu, 1983). Lungu (1983) found that these early school leaders were successful because the "educational systems were relatively small, their clients few, and technology simple" (p. 85). However, after gaining independence, the government positioned the education system to be one of the drivers of socioeconomic development, equality, and racial/tribal cohesion (Republic of Kenya, 1964; Sifuna, 1990). As the role of education changed, so did the need for competent education leaders especially head teachers (Republic of Kenya, 2005b, 2008b).

Plank (1987) partly blames the failure of education reform initiatives on the disregard of the role of school leaders. In Kenya, there is no pre-service training for head teachers and they are typically chosen from the ranks of teachers based on years of experience and seniority (Asuga et al., 2015; Bush & Oduro, 2006; Kitavi & van der Westhuizen, 1997; Republic of Kenya, 2005b). In the past, the government has taken steps to address some of the educational system's leadership deficiencies. For example, in 1988, the government established the Kenya Education Staff Institute (KESI), intending to provide in-service courses for school leaders. However, KESI, renamed Kenya Education Management Institute (KEMI), has not received adequate financial resources to carry out its mandate to develop the management capacity of all leaders in the education sector (Republic of Kenya, 2005b).

Research methods: data sources and analysis

The study uses two methods to answer the research questions. First, document analysis was conducted to examine key government policies to establish primary school head teachers' roles and the skills/competencies they require. Second, a descriptive analysis was conducted using data from the Kenya 2012 Snapshot of School Management Effectiveness (SSME) collected by the Ministry of Education and RTI International. The data is designed to let school leaders learn what is currently going on in their schools. Management data collected by the SSME include pedagogical approaches used; time on task; interactions among students, teachers, administrators, district officials, and parents; record keeping; discipline; availability and condition of school infrastructure; availability of pedagogical materials; and safety (RTI, 2012).

The process of document analysis involved the following steps: (a) development of inclusion criteria, (b) document collection, (c) document coding and analysis, and (d) reporting (Altheide & Schneider, 2013). Included in the sample for analysis were commission reports, sessional papers, and the 2010 constitution. During the first round of coding, the researchers examined all the government commission reports, sessional papers, and acts of parliament using open coding to inductively code for preliminary themes. The government commission reports reviewed included the 1964 Ominde Report, independent Kenya's first education commission (Republic of Kenya, 1964), the 1976 Gachathi Report

(Republic of Kenya, 1976), the 1981 Mackay Report (Republic of Kenya, 1981), the 1988 Kamunge Report (Republic of Kenya, 1988), 2000 Koech Report (Republic of Kenya, 1999), Sessional Paper No. 1 of 2005, Sessional Paper No. 14 of 2012, Teachers Service Commission (TSC) Act 2012, Basic Education Act 2013, and National Education Sector Plan 2013–2018.

The second round of coding focused only on the policy documents that were directly relevant to primary school leadership roles and responsibilities. The following government documents were analyzed to better understand the role and responsibilities of primary school head teachers: Sessional Paper No. 1 of 2005, Sessional Paper No. 14 of 2012, TSC Act 2012, Basic Education Act 2013, and National Education Sector Plan 2013–2018. All these government documents are available in the public domain.

Data analysis: Government policy documents on the role of primary school head teachers

Sessional Paper No. 1 of 2005

The Sessional Paper No. 1 of 2005 was based on recommendations from the 2003 National Conference on Education and Training. To improve the quality of education, the authors of the paper highlighted the need to "(s)trengthen the management of school administration and School Management Committees (SMCs)" (Republic of Kenya, 2005a, p. 34). On efficiency, the authors recommended the education sector be decentralized. They found that "provincial and district education officers act as transmittal agents from the field to the headquarters, but do not make any binding decisions as they lack the power and authority to make conclusive managerial and administrative decisions" (Republic of Kenya, 2005a, p. 61).

There was an attempt to clarify the roles of the various actors within the sector: "Issues relating to day-to-day operations, local supervision and resource mobilization to support education and training as well as counselling of students and staff will be left to local stakeholders [emphasis added] but with backstopping services from the Ministry and other national level actors" (Republic of Kenya, 2005a, p. 57). In the paper, head teachers are considered managers with limited authority to make major decisions. It is significant to note that there is no direct mention of instructional supervision as a role for head teachers. However, supervision and resource mobilization may be instructional supervision.

The Basic Education Act (2013)

To address the unequal distribution of national resources, the 2010 Constitution of Kenya adopted a devolved form of government. The key rationale for devolution was that county governments would more efficiently allocate resources because of their better knowledge of local needs. Under the new constitution, local government structures were consolidated into 47 counties. The counties are responsible for four key sectors: agriculture, health, transport, and water. The education sector was partly devolved; counties were to provide youth polytechnics and pre-primary education, including infrastructure development.

The 2010 constitution was groundbreaking for two reasons. For the first time in Kenya, education was made a basic human right, and the other, affirmative action programs were developed to address inequality issues. Parliament passed the 2013 Basic Education Act to give effect to Article 53 of the constitution. The Act, with 21 guiding principles, seeks to ensure access to quality education for all children while promoting national cohesion. It is essential to highlight that the Act promotes "accountability and democratic decision-making within the institutions of basic education" (p. 225).

For decentralized decision-making, the Act established a 13-member County Board of Education. Members of the County Board of Education must include representatives from the TSC, the county executive, religious groups, teacher unions, Parent Teacher Associations, persons with disabilities, and association of private schools. The country Board will ensure that all primary schools establish a Board of Management. The head teacher is the Secretary to the Board of Management. The Board has a wide range of functions, including school quality, procurement, finance, academic standards, discipline, student, and staff welfare. These functions encompass all aspects of a school; ideally, this should free up time for head teachers to concentrate on pedagogical/instructional leadership. However, since the Board is only required to meet once every four months, it is unclear how much it assists head teachers in their work.

The Act also established the Education Standards and Quality Assurance Council (ESQAC) to replace the Directorate of Quality Assurance. Unlike the Directorate of Quality Assurance which was under a department in the Ministry of Education, the ESQAC was established to be an autonomous body whose primary role is to ensure quality education. Section 70 of Part IX expects quality assurance to be a collaborative process between schools and Standards and Quality Assurance (SQA) Officers (Republic of Kenya, 2013). The expectation is those head teachers will work as instructional leaders in collaboration with the SQA officers.

Sessional Paper No. 14 of 2012

The Sessional Paper No. 14 of 2012 was based on the findings of the Taskforce on the Alignment of the Education Sector to the Constitution of Kenya (Republic of Kenya, 2014). The taskforce found two broad challenges. First, ESQAC is severely constrained by heavy bureaucratic structures and limited human and financial resources. Most SQA officers lack the required skills, and the lack of financial resources makes it difficult for SQA officers to visit schools (Republic of Kenya, 2012a). Second, there is a disconnect between head teachers and the SQA officers. Head teachers were excluded from the standards and quality of curriculum delivery; the head teachers and SQA officers' relations were often strained (Republic of Kenya, 2012a). Despite the Education Act requiring

ESQAC and head teachers to work collaboratively to ensure quality education, this disconnect exists. A study found that head teachers viewed SQA officers as fault-finding and dictatorial (Njogu, 2003).

The taskforce concluded that "The current management structure within the MoE is top-heavy and centralised, hierarchical and bureaucratic. Decision-making is inefficient with field officers preferring to refer matters up the chain of command rather than take action which could result in censure from the Ministry" (Republic of Kenya, 2012a, p.177). The Sessional Paper spells out six responsibilities for head teachers. They include, curriculum and policy implementation, resource allocation, instructional supervision, promoting positive school climate, community relations, and teaching. These responsibilities are a departure from Sessional Paper No. 1 of 2005 that excluded head teachers from curriculum development and instructional supervision.

National Education Sector Plan 2013–2018

In 2014, the government released the National Education Sector Plan (NESP), a sector wide reform program to implement the 2013 Basic Education Act. The plan had six priority areas: sector governance and accountability, access, quality, relevance and assessment, equity, and social competencies and values. On quality assurance, the NESP found minimal participation by some school heads (Republic of Kenya, 2014). The plan recognized that many of the education leaders did not have the skills to undertake quality assurance activities (Republic of Kenya, 2014).

The NESP highlighted the need for instructional/pedagogical leadership by head teachers. Most importantly, the NESP stated: *"The heads of institutions should concentrate on their core business of managing and delivering effective learning* and therefore should be relieved from managing non-curriculum projects like building and construction" (Republic of Kenya, 2014, p.135, emphasis added). The NESP is the first government policy document that explicitly presents the case for a separation of responsibilities between a school manager and an instructional leader.

Teachers Service Commission Act, 2012

The TSC was established under the Constitution of Kenya to register, employ, promote, and transfer teachers. It is from the ranks of teachers that the TSC appoints head teachers based mostly on seniority. In the TSC Code of Regulations, two parts highlight the extensive duties and responsibilities of head teachers: Part IV of the Code of Regulations of TSC, which deals with performance standards for teachers, lists 16 responsibilities of head teachers to ensure quality education (Teachers Service Commission, 2015, pp. 1166–1167). Part V of the Code, which deals with conditions of service, mentions 15 responsibilities for head teachers (Teachers Service Commission, 2015, pp. 1178–1179). Head teachers' role and responsibilities outlined by the TSC require the head teacher to be an instructional leader, a manager, and a community leader. However, the bulk of the work is to ensure that teaching and learning are taking place within the school. It is noteworthy that the head teachers are not trained to perform any of these tasks since most have received little or no training on instructional supervision.

The government policy documents examined in this section present a complex picture of head teachers' expected tasks. It is important to note that the head teachers' expectations have changed as the policy pronouncements and the needs of the country have evolved. Head teachers are expected to teach, supervise the curriculum implementation, supervise instruction in collaboration with SQA officers, ensure teachers and students are in class, keep financial and other school records, connect with the local community, and ensure that democratic decision-making. In summary, head teachers are expected to be instructional leaders, social workers, guidance counsellors, financial managers, and administrators.

Data analysis: Kenya 2012 Snapshot of School Management Effectiveness data

In the previous section, we examined government policy documents to understand primary school head teachers' role and responsibilities. In this section, we used the Kenya 2012 SSSME survey data to examine the tasks performed by primary head teachers. The SSME survey data was collected by the Ministry of Education and RTI International under the USAID EdData II project to evaluate school management and governance factors strongly associated with school effectiveness and learning achievement. The data used in this paper is from the Head teacher/Principal Questionnaire administered in each school visited.

There are 274 primary school head teachers in the sample. Forty-seven percent of the participants were female. The proportion of female head teachers was higher in the urban areas, 52%, compared to about 16% female in rural areas. Head teachers in the sample had an average of 7 years experience on the job.

The sample was primarily drawn from the urban areas in the Central and the Rift Valley regions of Kenya (Table 13.1). About 73% of Kenya's population resides in rural areas (UNESCO Department of Economic and Social Affairs, Population Division, 2018). Therefore, the sample is not representative of either Kenya or the country's Central and Rift Valley regions. However, the data is useful because it gives researchers a picture of what the primary school head teachers do and how much time they spend on the tasks. There are differences in rural/urban access to schooling in Kenya; rural areas have lagged as the country has developed. The disparity in development is the result of a segregated school system inherited from the British colonialists and decades of flawed policy development and implementation (Amutabi, 2003; Cooksey, Court, & Makau, 1994; Mugo et al., 2016; Nkinyangi, 1982; Sifuna, 1980; Somerset, 2009).

In the SSME sample, 57% of rural schools did not have clean water, 76% had no electricity, 27% had no girls' bathrooms, and 75% had no library. Access

Table 13.1 Overview of the geographic distribution of the Kenya 2012 Snapshot of School Management Effectiveness data

District	Urban	Rural	Total
Dagoretti	26	0	26
Embakasi	56	0	56
Kasarani	31	0	31
Langata	33	0	33
Makadara	3	0	3
Nairobi	22	0	22
Nakuru	9	19	28
Nakuru Municipality	8	0	8
Njoro	0	7	7
Rongai	0	6	6
Starehe	17	0	17
Thika	7	3	10
Thika East	0	3	3
Thika Municipality	4	0	4
Thika West	5	0	5
Westlands	15	0	15
Total	**236**	**38**	**274**

to these facilities is crucial to student learning and impacts how schools are organized and the head teacher's time use. For example, the World Health Organization (2018) reported that the school might require students attending schools without safe, clean water to bring water to school, a practice that is likely to interfere with learning. It is expected that head teachers in schools without clean water must allocate time for students and other school personnel to fetch clean water. Previous research found that leadership practices are, in part, the result of interactions between the school leader and the broader socioeconomic context (Goldring et al., 2008; Hallinger, 2018a).

Figure 13.1 shows the qualification levels of the primary school head teachers in the sample. Primary school teachers are mostly trained in Teacher Training Colleges (TTCs), where they receive a Diploma in Education after two years of study. These diploma holders are hired as P1 teachers. P2 teachers are also trained, but they enrolled in TTCs with lower secondary school pass grade; however, the P2 teacher grade was phased out by the government in 2013. The existing P2 teachers were required to take teacher proficiency courses offered by the TSC before they were promoted to P1 status. After that, P1 teachers can be promoted, on merit, to Approved Teacher Status (ATS). About 51% (142) of the head teachers in the sample were P1 teachers.

As indicated earlier, head teachers in Kenya receive no formal pre-service training in school leadership. However, in-service opportunities are available at the KEMI. About 170 head teachers (60%) in the sample reported they had received in-service training in school leadership. This means that about 40% of primary head teachers in the sample were running their schools without any pre-service or in-service training. On average, the training received by the head

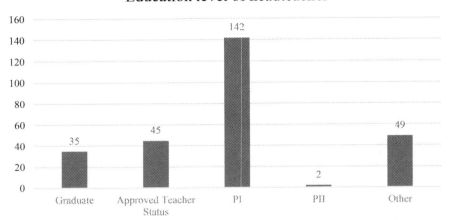

Figure 13.1 Qualification levels of primary school head teachers

teachers was about three months. The majority (55%) of the training offered was initiated by the Ministry of Education.

The head teacher questionnaire for the SSME survey documented what head teachers do. The head teachers in the sample reported they taught classes, supported instructional support, reviewed lesson plans, and worked with the parent-teacher associations. These practices are in line with the government's expectations. On average, primary head teachers taught about 13.03 hours per week. The number of hours taught varied by location; head teachers in rural areas taught an average of 17.03 hours compared to 12.32 hours for urban head teachers. Rural head teachers are likely to teach more classes because their schools are more likely to face teacher shortages due to the skewed development of education and teachers' reluctance to work in many rural areas (Amutabi, 2003; Mathooko, 2009; Nkinyangi, 1982; Sifuna, 1980).

We find that the head teachers teach multiple grade levels based on the survey data though they mostly teach the higher classes. For example, only 15% of the head teachers reported that they taught standard 1 compared to about 84% who said teaching standard 8, the highest grade level. Teaching higher grade levels may not be entirely surprising given that head teachers are chosen by seniority. Hence, they have the skill and experience that can be beneficial for teaching the higher grade levels preparing the students for the national primary school examinations.

According to the policy documents, the head teacher must ensure quality teaching and learning occur in the school. The questionnaire asked: *How many hours per week, do you provide instructional support for the teachers?* The head teachers reported they provide an average of 3.59 hours per week of instructional support. The instructional support level differed by location, 3.73 hours in urban areas and 2.78 hours in rural areas. Rural head teachers teach more hours, explaining why they spend fewer hours offering instructional support to

Evidence from the SSME survey 209

Table 13.2 Responses regarding reviewing teachers' lesson plans and classroom observation

Responsible for reviewing lesson plans		%
No one	105	38.46
Head teacher	102	37.36
Deputy head	52	19.05
Other—senior teacher/academic master	14	5.13
Total	273	100

Responsible for observing teachers in class		%
No one observes	123	44.89
Head teacher	109	39.78
Deputy head	30	10.95
Other—senior teacher/academic master	12	4.38
Total	274	100

their teachers. Although we cannot claim causality, it seemed noteworthy that rural teachers who attended in-service training spent more time (3.18 hours) on instructional support than those who did not.

To determine the head teacher's instructional support type, the following questions were asked: *Who is responsible for reviewing the teachers' lesson plans? How often are these plans reviewed? Who is responsible for observing teachers in their classrooms?* Participants were also asked how they were able to observe the teachers in their classroom per term. Table 13.2 reveals that 38% of the participants indicated no one was assigned to review the lesson plans. Additionally, about 45% of the sample participants indicated that no one was responsible for observing the teachers in the classroom. In an indication of shared responsibilities, instructional support is also provided by the deputy head teachers and other staff members.

The head teachers were also asked how they knew whether their students were progressing. According to the survey data, principals determined academic progress by observing classrooms (32%), monitoring student test scores (95%), orally evaluating students (32%), reviewing homework (56%), and reading teacher progress reports (54%).

The head teachers were also asked whether they were satisfied with reading and math performance in standards 1 and 2 in their schools. About 48.74% of urban head teachers and approximately 76.91% of rural head teachers reported that they were not satisfied at all. Again, without claiming causality, the study found that head teachers in urban areas who were not satisfied with the school performance spent 4.67 hours on instructional support compared to 2.71 hours for those who were satisfied with their school performance. In rural areas, head teachers who were not satisfied with the school performance spent 2.75 hours compared to 2.95 hours for those who were satisfied.

Finally, the questionnaire was also used to gain insights into the schools' work ethic through items like: *How many teachers were absent yesterday? How many teachers arrived after the start of classes yesterday?* The results were cause for concern: Respondents indicated that about 46% of the teachers were absent the day before; about 69% in rural areas and 43% in urban areas. Also, principals noted that about 25% of teachers arrived after the start of classes; about 40% in rural areas and 33% in urban areas. According to the policy documents, it is the head teacher's responsibility to ensure that teachers attend and teach their classes (Teachers Service Commission, 2015).

From the SSME data, we find that most primary school head teachers have received little to no pre-service or in-service training on school leadership. The average urban head teacher will spend about 12 hours teaching and about 4 hours on instructional support; we can assume they spend the rest of the work week (24 hours) on administrative work. The average rural head teacher spends about 17 hours teaching and about 3 hours providing instructional support. While we know that observing teachers in the classroom and providing feedback are useful tools that can improve the quality of instruction in the school (Bambrick-Santoyo, 2012), we find that for about 40% of the schools was no one assigned to this critical task.

Conclusion

The study aimed to understand what the government expects from primary school head teachers and how these head teachers use their time. Leadership is a social activity. Hence we cannot ignore the socio-cultural, economic, and political forces that shape practice. Understanding these forces is especially pertinent in a field dominated by research from the Western countries (Hallinger, 2018a, 2018b). The policy environment in Kenya has evolved as government priorities have changed. The Sessional Paper No. 1 of 2005 presented the education system as a highly centralized bureaucracy. Under the sessional paper, primary school head teachers were viewed as education managers responsible for schools' day-to-day operations. The SSME data findings support the notion of head teachers as managers because they spend less than 10% of their time providing instructional support to their teachers and less than 30% teaching.

The 2013 Basic Education Act was part of the new constitution with a devolved form of government to push toward increased accountability and democratic decision-making. The Act established a Board of Management that would share management responsibilities with the head teachers. Beyond practicing distributed leadership, head teachers are expected to be instructional leaders (section 66 and 70), social workers (section 40), guidance counsellors (section 59), financial managers (section 59), and administrators (section 59).

The National Education Sector Plan emphasized the need to develop instructional/pedagogical leadership. The Sessional Paper No. 14 of 2012 noted, an institution "stands or falls by its head" (Republic of Kenya, 2012b, p. 69). As a result, this sessional paper presented six key responsibilities for head teachers: curriculum and policy implementation, resource allocation, instructional supervision, promoting positive school climate, community relations, and teaching. In the TSC Code of Regulations, there are 16 responsibilities of head teachers to ensure quality education. Head teachers' role and responsibilities outlined by the TSC require the head teacher to be an instructional/pedagogical leader, a manager, and a community leader.

Head teacher time use and practices are influenced by the context in which they work (Hallinger, 2018a). As previous research demonstrates, it is crucial to understand the context if we are to make sense of head teachers' time use. Hallinger (2018a) points out that we need to broaden our lens to be more mindful of context to understand head teachers and how they use their time and why. For example, rural areas in Kenya lack many essential services, making it hard to attract qualified teachers. Therefore, it seems plausible that head teachers spend more time teaching and less time on instructional support.

This study represents an initial step toward increasing the research base on educational leadership in Africa, a region with limited educational leadership research (Hallinger, 2018b). For researchers and policy makers to understand the time use of head teachers, we must understand the contextual nuances that impact how these leaders use their time. Hallinger (2018a, 2018b) utilized a framework that highlights the importance of understanding how the broader context affects how the head teachers view their role and shape their behavior and actions. This study begins the conversation on how political and school contexts can impact head teachers' time use. In the case of Kenya, previous research has examined the impact of the political context on the education system (Amutabi, 2003; Mugo et al., 2016; Nkinyangi, 1982; Sifuna, 1980), but there has been no substantive research on how the political/national context shapes the behavior and practices of school leaders. Given the limited research available on Africa, the next steps should include research investigating how head teachers within the African context can bring about change or improve schooling.

References

Altheide, D. L., & Schneider, C. J. (2013). *Qualitative media analysis. Qualitative research methods*, Vol. 38. Thousand Oaks, CA: Sage Publications.

Amutabi, M. N. (2003). Political interference in the running of education in post-independence Kenya: A critical retrospection. *International Journal of Educational Development*, 23(2), 127–144.

Asuga, G. N., Eacott, S., & Scevak, J. (2015). School leadership preparation and development in Kenya: Evaluating performance impact and return on leadership development investment. *International Journal of Educational Management*, 29(3), 355–367.

Avenstrup, R., Liang, X., & Nellemann, S. (2004). *Kenya, Lesotho, Malawi and Uganda: Universal Primary Education and Poverty Reduction*. World Bank. Retrieved from http://web.worldbank.org/archive/website00819C/WEB/PDF/EAST_AFR.PDF.

Bambrick-Santoyo, P. (2012). *Leverage leadership: A practical guide to building exceptional schools*. San Francisco, CA: Jossey-Bass.

Brown, L., & Conrad, D. A. (2007). School leadership in Trinidad and Tobago: The challenge of context. *Comparative Education Review*, 51(2), 181–201.

Bruns, B., Filmer, D., & Patrinos, H. A. (2011). *Making schools work: New evidence on accountability reforms*. Washington, DC: The World Bank.

Bush, T., & Oduro, G. K. (2006). New principals in Africa: Preparation, induction and practice. *Journal of Educational Administration, 44*(4), 359–375.

Chapman, D. W., & Burchfield, S. A. (1994). How headmasters perceive their role: A case study in Botswana. *International Review of Education, 40*(6), 401–419.

Cooksey, B., Court, D., & Makau, B. (1994). Education for self reliance and harambee. In Joel D. Barkan (Ed.), *Beyond Capitalism vs. socialism in Kenya and Tanzania.* Boulder, CO: Lynne Reinner.

De Grauwe, A. (2001). *School supervision in four African countries.* Paris: UNESCO/International Institute for Educational Planning.

Duflo, E., Dupas, P., & Kremer, M. (2011). Peer effects, teacher incentives, and the impact of tracking: Evidence from a randomized evaluation in Kenya. *American Economic Review, 101*(5), 1739–1774.

Fuller, B. (1987). What factors raise achievement in the third world? *Review of Educational Research, 57*, 255–292.

Glassman, D., & Sullivan, P. (2008). *Governance, management, and accountability in secondary education in Sub-Saharan Africa.* Secondary Education in Africa (SEIA) Thematic Study No. 3. Washington, DC: World Bank.

Glewwe, P., Kremer, M., & Moulin, S. (2009). Many children left behind? Textbooks and test scores in Kenya. *American Economic Journal: Applied Economics, 1*(1), 112–135.

Goldring, E., Huff, J., May, H., & Camburn, E. (2008). School context and individual characteristics: What influences principal practice? *Journal of Educational Administration, 46*(3), 332–352.

Hallinger, P. (2018a). Bringing context out of the shadows of leadership. *Educational Management Administration & Leadership, 46*(1), 5–24.

Hallinger, P. (2018b). Surfacing a hidden literature: A systematic review of research on educational leadership and management in Africa. *Educational Management Administration & Leadership, 46*(3), 362–384.

Hallinger, P., & Heck, R. H. (1998). Exploring the principal's contribution to school effectiveness: 1980–1995. *School Effectiveness & School Improvement, 9*(2), 157.

Harber, C., & Davies, L. (1997) *School management and effectiveness in developing countries.* London: Cassell.

Horng, E., Klasik, D., & Loeb, S. (2010). Principal's time use and school effectiveness. *American Journal of Education, 116*(4), 491–523.

Kenya Institute of Curriculum Development. (2017). *Basic Education Curriculum Framework.* Kenya Institute of Curriculum Development, Nairobi. Retrieved from https://kicd.ac.ke/curriculum-reform/basic-education-curriculum-framework/.

King'oina, J. O., Ngaruiya, B. N., & Mobegi, F.O. (2017) The role of boards of management as a determinant of pupils' academic performance in public primary schools in Marani Sub-County, Kenya. *International Journal of Scientific Research and Innovative Technology, 4*(6).

Kitavi, M. W. (1995). The induction of beginning school principals in Kenya. Ph.D. Dissertation, Potchefstroomse Universiteit, South Africa.

Kitavi, M. W., & van der Westhuizen, P. C. (1997). Problems facing beginning principals in developing countries: A study of beginning principals in Kenya. *International Journal of Educational Development, 17*(3), 251–263.

Kremer, M., & Holla, A. (2009). Improving education in the developing world: What have we learned from randomized evaluations? *Annual Review of Economics, 1*, 513–542.

Lee, M. S., & Hallinger, P. (2012). Exploring the impact of national context on principals' time use: Economic development, societal culture, and educational system. *School Effectiveness and School Improvement, 23*(4), 461–482.

Leithwood, K. (1994). Leadership for school restructuring. *Educational Administration Quarterly, 30*(4), 498–518.

Lungu, G. F. (1983). Some critical issues in the training of educational administrators for the developing countries of Africa, *International Journal of Educational Development*, 3, 85–96

Mathooko, M. (2009). Actualising free primary education in Kenya for sustainable development. *The Journal of Pan African Studies, 2*(8), 151–153.

Mugo, J. B., Moyi, P. M., & Kiminza, O. (2016). The challenge of access, quality and equity: Education in Kenya, 1963 to 2015. In I. I. Munene & S. Ruto (Eds.), *Achieving education for all: dilemmas in system-wide reforms and learning outcomes in Africa*. Lanham, MD: Lexington Books.

Njogu, I. N. (2003). The role of inspectorate in maintaining education standards and the problems encountered. A case of Nyandarua district, Central Province Kenya. *Unpublished M.Ed Project, Kenyatta University*. Nairobi, Kenya.

Nkinyangi, J. A. (1982). Access to primary education in Kenya: The contradictions of public policy. *Comparative Education Review, 26*(2), 199–217.

Okaya, T. M. (2015). School board governance in urban low-socio economic setting: A case study of public primary schools in Kibera, Kenya (Doctoral thesis, Australian Catholic University). Retrieved from https://doi.org/10.4226/66/5a9cbdacb0b9b.

Oplatka, I. (2004). The principalship in developing countries: Context, characteristics and reality. *Comparative Education, 40*(3), 427–448.

Plank, D. N. (1987). School administration and school reform in Botswana. *International Journal of Education Development, 7*(2), 119–126.

Republic of Kenya. (1964). Kenya Education Commission Report, Part 1 (Ominde Report). Nairobi: Government Printer.

Republic of Kenya. (1976). Report of the National Committee on educational objectives and policies (Gachathi Report). Nairobi: Government Printer.

Republic of Kenya. (1981). *Second university in Kenya: Report of the working party*. Mackay Report. Nairobi: Government Printer.

Republic of Kenya. (1988). Report of the Presidential Committee on Manpower Development for the Next Decade and Beyond (Kamunge Report). Nairobi: Government Printer.

Republic of Kenya. (1999). Kenya Commission of Inquiry into Education System of Kenya: Totally Integrated Quality Education and Training, TIQET: Report of the Commission of Inquiry into the Education System of Kenya (Koech Report). Nairobi: Government Printer.

Republic of Kenya. (2005a). Sessional Paper number 1 of 2005—A Policy Framework for Education, Training and Research. Meeting the challenges of education, training and research in the 21st century. Nairobi: Government Printer.

Republic of Kenya. (2005b). Kenya Education Sector Support Programme 2005–2010. Delivering quality education and training to all Kenyans. Nairobi: Government Printer.

Republic of Kenya. (2008a). The Development of Education: National Education Sector Report 2008. Nairobi: Government Printer.

Republic of Kenya. (2008b). Final Report on the Kenya Education Management Capacity Assessment (KEMACA). Nairobi: Government Printer.

Republic of Kenya. (2008c). *Ministry of education strategic plan 2008–2012*. Nairobi: Government Printers.

Republic of Kenya. (2012a). *Towards a globally competitive quality education for sustainable development*. Report of the Taskforce on the Re-alignment of the Education Sector to the Constitution of Kenya 2010. Nairobi: Ministry of Education.

Republic of Kenya. (2012b). *Sessional paper number 14 of 2012 on reforming education andtraining sectors in Kenya*. Nairobi: Government Printer.

Republic of Kenya. (2013). *The Basic Education Act, No. 14 of 2013*. Nairobi: Government Printer.

Republic of Kenya. (2014). National Education Sector Plan. Volume One: Basic Education Programme Rationale and Approach 2013/2014–2017/2018. Nairobi: Government Printer.

RTI (2012). *Snapshot of School Management Effectiveness Frequently Asked Questions (FAQs)*. Retrieved from https://globalreadingnetwork.net/eddata/ssme-faqs.

Sifuna, D. N. (1980). *Short essays on education in Kenya*. Nairobi: Kenya Literature Bureau.

Sifuna, D. N. (1990). *Development of education in Africa: The Kenyan experience*. Nairobi: Initiatives Limited.

Somerset, A. (2009). Universalising primary education in Kenya: The elusive goal. *Comparative Education, 45*, 233–250.

Teachers Service Commission. (2015). *Code of Regulations for Teachers, 2015*. Nairobi: Government Printer. Retrieved from https://www.tsc.go.ke/index.php/media-centre/downloads/category/54-codes-of-regulation#.

Teachers Service Commission. (2016). Performance contract between Teachers Service *Commission and the Principal/Head teacher*. Retrieved from https://www.tsc.go.ke/index.php/downloads/finish/47-perfomance-management-for-head teachers/3449-performance-contract-for-head teachers-principals.

UNESCO. (2011). *The hidden crisis: Armed conflict and education*. EFA Global Monitoring Report 2011. Oxford: Oxford University Press.

United Nations, Department of Economic and Social Affairs, Population Division. (2018). *World urbanization prospects: The 2018 Revision*.. Retrieved from https://esa.un.org/unpd/wup/Country-Profiles/.

Uwezo, (2014). *Are our children learning? Literacy and numeracy in Kenya*. Nairobi: Twaweza East Africa.

Vespoor, A. M. (2008). *At the crossroads: Choices for secondary education in sub-Saharan Africa*. Washington, DC: The World Bank.

Waters, T., Marzano, R. J., & McNulty, B. (2003). *Balanced leadership: What 30 years of research tells us about the effect of leadership on student achievement*. Aurora, CO: Mid-Continent Research for Education and Learning.

World Bank. (1988). *Education in Sub-Saharan African policies of adjustment, revitalisation and expansion*. Washington, DC: World Bank.p

World Health Organization. (2018). *Drinking water, sanitation and schools. Global baseline report 2018*. New York. Retrieved from https://data.unicef.org/wp-content/uploads/2018/08/JMP-WASH-in-Schools-WEB.pdf.

14 Emotional workload and time use in principalship
Insights from Israeli educational leaders

Izhar Oplatka

Introduction

Since the 1990s many educational systems have experienced large-scale neo-liberal reforms such as school-based management, standardization of teaching and learning processes and outcomes, marketization, school choice, and the like (Gibton, 2013; Oplatka, 2007). These reforms have led, among other things, to the proliferation and diversification of principals' tasks and spheres of responsibility ranging from simple paperwork, through budgeting and teacher appraisal, to external relations and marketing (Philips, Sen, & McNamee, 2007; Saidun, Mohd, & Borhandden-Musha, 2015).

Usually, employee workload has been constructed and explored in terms of pressure, stress, and amount of work. Basically, employee workload refers to "having high amounts of work, having to work fast, and working under time pressure" (Ilies, Huth, Ryan, & Dimotakis, 2015, pp. 2–3) and is generally defined as "a job demand or stressor that represents a consumption of energy in terms of time and psychological resources" (Goh, Ilies, & Wilson, 2015, p. 67). Workload may be either quantitative or qualitative. The former is created when the employee is requested to perform many tasks in a given unit of time, while the latter is created when the employee is required to perform complex and difficult tasks (Cooper & Marshall, 1976).

In a large qualitative study of the perceived components, factors, and outcomes of principal workload from the subjective perspectives of Israeli principals, another type of workload was identified—emotional workload. Surprisingly, while there has been increased empirical attention to emotion in educational leadership (Berkovich & Eyal, 2015), very few studies have addressed the issue of emotional workload despite its relevance in our time of accountability in educational systems worldwide. Thus, the research questions underpinning this contribution were twofold: (1) How do principals use their time at work? (2) What are the characteristics of emotional workload and its determinants in principalship?

This study may increase our theoretical understanding of the concept of emotional workload and contribute, in turn, both to the emergent literature about emotion in educational leadership and to that about principal's time use.

The research on emotion in educational leadership

Life in schools is complex, partly because emotion is integral to the processes of teaching and learning. Therefore, school leaders need to manage emotionally as well as rationally. In this sense, leadership is a combination of cognition and emotion that are equally important in guiding, facilitating, or inhibiting leadership capability (Harris, 2004). The social activities of schools coupled with the major place of teacher-student and principal-teacher interactions produce and reflect emotions, passions, feelings, and so forth (Crawford, 2007).

Education researchers, however, put forward the view that leadership is also an emotional practice involving intensive personal interactions that are publicly displayed (Berkovich & Eyal, 2015; Yamamoto, Gardiner, & Tenuto, 2014). Thus, emotion and leadership are interrelated as part of human experience in different social arenas. Yet, this view, as Harris (2004) indicated, is mainly normative, tending to focus on what leaders should be doing rather than on the actual emotional labor of their work. Thus, the emotional practice and processes of school principals remain relatively under-explored.

Past research has identified a wide variety of emotions and feelings among school leaders, including passion, empathy, excitement, satisfaction, intuition, relief, joy, trust, adrenaline rush, and caring (Beatty, 2000; Yamamoto et al., 2014). Awareness and appropriate utilization of emotion guide leaders in self-understanding and can strengthen relationships with others, which in turn contribute to growth and improved communication (Tenuto, Gardiner, & Yamamoto, 2016). Irish principals overwhelmingly agree that they have to use their emotional intelligence, in the broadest sense, to achieve "whole school" mediated change. They care for and care about their teachers and see relationship building as a key task in the establishment of a collegial culture driving school transformation activity (Redmond, 2016).

In addition, several publications focus on negative emotions of school leaders, such as fear of failure (Gronn, 2003), a sense of emotional "woundedness" (Johnson, Aiken, & Steggerda, 2005), anxiety, fear, pain, demoralization, anger, frustration, despair, dissatisfaction, distress (Blackmore, 2004; James & Vince, 2001), disempowerment, threatened self and disillusionment with the system (Beatty, 2000). Female principals found themselves split between social scripts that perceive the display of negative emotions as non-feminine (Blackmore, 2004).

Congruent with the literature about emotion regulation (e.g., Gross, 1998) and emotional labor (e.g., Rafaeli, 2013), school principals have to manage and regulate their emotions frequently, at least in part because teaching, as the core technology of school, is considered to be an emotional practice (Beatty, 2000; Crawford, 2007). Oplatka (2017) found that Israeli school principals are allowed, even encouraged to display—under specific circumstances—empathy and attentiveness, compassion, and happiness, and caring, and that there are two emotions they are expected to suppress publicly—anger and fear. In fact, school principals benefit when they are able to manage emotion and act with integrity and purpose in their day-to-day events as leaders on the front line (Yamamoto et al., 2014).

Likewise, educational leaders also tend to help other school members regulate their emotions (Crawford, 2007), mainly in the era of accountability, standardization, and inter-school competition in many educational systems. For example, Australian principals increasingly had to manage teachers' sense of alienation and anger arising from a dissonance between what they referred to as their "real work" and the type of work required by new educational reforms initiated by their government (Blackmore, 2004). Similarly, Boyatzis (2012) pointed to the importance of supervisors engaging in self-reflective activity and using emotion in leadership. The leaders simultaneously seek to listen, reflect on how others might feel, and to infer and understand through empathetic caring how the other person feels. Through this self-reflective activity, the leaders strengthen their own capacity to manage and use emotion, and also reinforce connections with others.

Method

The current study adopted the qualitative paradigm that is suitable when the research aims at exploring.

Context

Although gradually changing, the Israeli government is the provider of education for almost everyone, and education is geared toward matriculation exams that usually take place at the end of high school and are necessary to gain entrance into higher education institutions. The spirits of globalization and privatization have brought about some changes in the Israeli educational systems since the early 2000s. The Ministry of Education (MOE) has begun to encourage schools to specialize and offer unique subjects out of a predetermined list of subjects taught for matriculation exams. In addition, many schools have increasingly become autonomous and self-managed, providing some freedom for school staff to build a vision and mission for their schools, based on their values, communal needs, and the ethnic characteristics of their students.

Participants

Fifty interviews were conducted with elementary and secondary school principals. All of them were tenured employees from three public educational systems in Israel—the State Educational System, the Religious State Educational System, and the Arab Educational System. Eighteen male and 32 female principals participated in this study, a number that represents, by and large, the ratio of men to women in principalship in Israel. Most of the men are high-school principals (N = 13) while most of the women run elementary schools (N = 24). The age range of the principals was 37–69 (average 49.76) and the range of years in post was 2–16 (9 were 1–3 years in post, 16 were 4–8 years, 15 were 9–12 years, and 10 were 13 years and above). Thirty-four principals manage schools in the State

Educational System, six run schools in the Religious State Educational System, and eight run schools in the Arab Educational System. Twenty-five principals manage elementary schools, 3 junior highs, and 22 high schools (includes both junior and high schools in one building). The schools' size in which they work ranges from 354 to 1,823 pupils. Their pupils belong to the upper middle class (n = 8), middle class (n = 28), and working class (n = 14).

Participant selection

Due to the need to focus on a homogenous group of subjects in a qualitative inquiry that aims at profoundly understanding a certain phenomenon (Marshall & Rossman, 2016), research staff approached supervisors, educational counselors, and other informants (either heads of department or schoolteachers) and asked them to recommend principals with two years or more experience in principalship, who are considered to work in highly competitive or stressful school environments (e.g., high pressure from parents, newly mandated changes), and, consequently, face high levels of workload. It was believed that principals meeting the criteria indicated above are more likely to face a challenging workload in their work and therefore could provide us with knowledge about this kind of personal state in principalship.

Procedure

Semi-structured interviews were used to gain insights into the interviewees' subjective conceptualizations of principal workload using an interview guide designed to provide a certain amount of coherence across the various interviews (Marshall & Rossman, 2016). In the first part of the interview, the principal was asked to depict his/her role-perception, daily schedule, and workload. To assure the principal experienced some level of overload, he/she was asked to provide personal interpretations of workload coupled with examples from his/her work life. Principals who claimed emphatically not to experience overload were not included in the study.

Next came questions about the principal's feelings when required to perform a wide variety of role tasks followed by questions about the sources and outcomes of a heavy workload in the principal's post. At the end of the interview, the principal was asked to provide the interviewer with coping strategies he/she uses to curtail the levels of workload. Note that in order to limit the risk of any kind of "social desirability," the interviewer refrained from discussing the topic of workload in positive or negative terms.

The manual analysis of the interview data followed the four stages described by Marshall and Rossman (2016): "organizing the data," "generating categories, themes and patterns," "testing any emergent hypothesis," and "searching for alternative explanations." This analysis aimed to identify central themes in the data, searching for recurrent experiences, feelings and attitudes, so as to be able to code, reduce, and connect different categories into central themes.

The coding was guided by the principles of "comparative analysis" (Strauss & Corbin, 1998), which includes the comparison of any coded element in terms of emergent categories and subcategories.

The author, as principal researcher, analyzed the entire data set independently and a research assistant and a "critical friend" examined the results of this analysis independently (Strauss & Corbin, 1998). The research team then met to compare their analyses, to discuss contradictory interpretations that arose, and to search for disconfirming evidence (Marshall & Rossman, 2016).

Findings

The findings shed light both on the principal's time use and on the principal's emotional work.

The principal's time use during the day

When the principal's time use was discussed, most of the interviewees indicated that most of their time is devoted to school routine while meetings and events organized by stakeholders (e.g., the supervisors, the municipality) receive less attention. The principals said they worked "all day, all day," "when I eat and sleep I don't work," and "all the time, you could see me walking in the school, managing meetings, conversation … all the time." This is reflected in the voice of a secondary school principal (Male, 10):

> Interviewer: If I observed you at work, when would I see you working?
> Principal: 24 hours a day. Only when I sleep, I don't work. The school's work never ends … you have to initiate and advance projects, to mobilize resources, to be in contact with external sources … I start my working day at 7 am and end it only when I go to sleep, I think about the school all the time, I don't feel any pressure, but I experience everything that's happening here …

The principals depicted their workday in terms of "a meeting after meeting, a problem after problem" and "you can't catch up the multiple tasks … the teachers go home and you stay [in the school] …"

The principal's described their workdays as commencing early in the morning and often ending late in the evening. Most of the principals indicated arriving at their school around 7 am and leaving around 4 pm. But they also listed many occasions (staff meetings, visits, parents' meetings, parties) where they left the school later, around 7 pm. This is echoed in the subsequent quote:

> You could see me working from 7:30am until 8pm. Today I leave the school at 10pm. I have to attend the education committee of the city council and I have tonight parents' meeting … four times a week I have meetings afternoon. There are more comfortable days in which I leave at 5pm, never

> before ... now it's 3pm, the middle of the day for me, I have so much paper work, and afternoon is the best time for me, after all the others have left ...
> (Male, secondary school, 5)

Most principals are engaged with various tasks right from the start of their workday, such as meeting the janitor, talking with middle managers, meeting with parents, checking emails, giving some orders to the administrative staff, filling forms, and meeting pupils who might have arrived early as well. However, the mornings vary across principals, as manifested in the following citations:

> I get to my office, get phone calls from missing teachers and look for substitute teachers, read emails ... staff meetings, phone calls from outside the school, sudden visits of parents, handle violence ...
> (Male, secondary school, 3)

> I get to the school in morning, ask my secretary to do some tasks. At 7:30am I stand near the school's gate and greet the kids...I walk in the corridors, open doors and say good morning to classes ...
> (Female, secondary school, 2)

During the rest of the day, principals indicated that they participated in many meetings in and out of the school, observed classes, talked with teachers privately, "felt" the atmosphere, and the like. In the afternoon, administrative work often took a lot of time including tasks like answering emails, signing letters, and talking with officials from the education district and in the local education authority. Many principals explained that they continued working at home. Thus, it is unsurprising that many of them mentioned a high emotional workload.

The meanings of emotional workload

The principals constructed their emotional workload in terms of nuisance, worry, thoughts, and emotions, emphasizing that "I can't hold it anymore," or "I take everything to heart." The interviewees distinguished between quantitative workload and emotional workload in their job:

> ... Emotional workload is when you are inundated by significant things, unable to respond to them, many things are stuck, a kind of workload you can't remove, release, or dismantle ...
> (Elementary school female principal, 1)

> An emotional workload is not the same kind of workload, not at all. A lack of time is natural part of my job, this is a fact. You have to navigate between many responsibilities. This is a matter of choice, you choose what to carry on and what not ... The emotional workload is something else, a more difficult thing many times that needs internal work, personal work, [this is] not simple at all
> (Secondary school female principal, 8)

In fact, emotional workload is related to something that is beyond paper work, staff management, or the planning of annually events, all of which factors affecting principals' quantitative workload. Emotional workload seems to be related to the problems principals would like to solve or to many issues they would like to promote, but are not always able to do due to limited resources or forensic constraints, such as children in dysfunctional families or abused children. Unsurprisingly, then, this type of workload is related to emotions and feelings and is composed of a sense of concern, emotional coping with other school members, a failure to treat children with special difficulties, personal crises of teachers and students, and coping with children from dysfunctional families.

A sense of concern/nuisance

The interviewees connected between emotional work and their daily concerns about varied issues. For example, they were worried during the winter about the need to find many substitute teachers, care for student safety in school trips, and angry about governmental exams. A high-school male principal (5) described his sense of concern explicitly:

> The emotional workload stems from a fear that in such a big system … I feel I absorb or should be sensitive to every difficulty. To be sensitive to a difficulty means to be inclusive … to be inclusive is like having a repository in your body that becomes empty because of many emotional difficulties, so you need to enlarge the repository all the time, and this is a huge emotional difficulty …

Another high-school female principal (10) added:

> … [Emotional workload] is a kind of losing control, because sometimes it doesn't matter how much you care about student safety, sometimes things happen. You know how many principals paid a personal price and also in their job because of things like that.

The interviewees appeared to be worried, first and foremost, about the many spheres of responsibility resting on their shoulders, sometimes in areas they have never been trained for or in matters where their direct control is weak (e.g., the principal has legal responsibility over the school building even in the afternoon after the school day is over). This is echoed in the following quote:

> Interviewer: What is 'emotional workload' in your opinion?
> Principal: First, from the view of my responsibility, this is a very heavy emotional workload, issues of student; for example, you know that if there is a hole in the fence surrounding the school … this is your responsibility. Emotional workload stems from the fact that you are responsible for many people, you have to handle the welfare of teachers, to be attentive to their needs, to direct them
> (Elementary school female principal, 2)

From the principal's point of view, it seemed apparent that the emotional workload was derived, by and large, from the principal's responsibility over the safety of students and teachers in times of school trips, personal crises, student activity in the school yard, and the like. Likewise, the workload was perceived to be emotional rather than quantitative because the principal made crucial decisions about the life of people in the present and future, a matter of life and death. Thus, as principals were requested to make many decisions related to the future of students or the life of teachers, they felt heavy emotional workloads, as an elementary school female principal (10) noted:

> ... Sometimes this is an emotional, not quantitative workload; decisions that you make in cases of life and death. We are talking about children, I have to think a lot about them in many decisions we make, because of many events that take place in the school day, because I'm the one who has the responsibility over all the things here. So at the end of the day I feel breathless!

Emotional coping with school members

Another aspect of emotional workload in principalship refers to the principal's emotional coping with teachers and parents. This kind of coping is not expressed merely in terms of time required to interact with a school's members, but in emotional terms. This includes emotion display, emotion suppression, emotional inclusion, and the like, as reflected from the next quote:

> ... I think we all have the strengths, the physical strength – you sleep at night, wake up, so if it was only a technical issue, only many tasks to perform, so it would have been very simple. In my view, emotional coping is the real difficulty. An angry teacher in the teacher lounge, for example, creates a heavy emotional workload for the principal. An unsatisfied parent, students with difficulties or distress, these are very overwhelming things emotionally ... the emotional workload is with you all the time, even when you leave the school, your office, it is with you all the time and you should give solutions. You are pretty lonely in this role ...
> (Elementary school female principal, 8)

The emotional workload was expressed by feelings of suffocation, discomfort, worry, and over-involvement in emotion-stimulating events, or as one high-school male principal (10) said, "it is overwhelming, I can feel the workload in my bones, in all my body systems ..."

Instances of emotional coping appeared by and large during principal-parent interactions. The parents often demanded fast solutions the principal could not provide, leading to mistrust and resentment, and in turn, to heavy emotional workloads among principals. For example, an elementary school male principal (8) talked about a mother who demanded to see her son's teacher at the end of the school day, although she was told the teacher had to leave school in a hurry to take her child to the pediatrician. The mother's insistence to meet the teacher and her aggressiveness toward the principal led the principal ask her to leave the school building. This event is perceived by the principal as part of his emotional workload:

> ... This is part of my emotional workload. A person is cheeky because the principal ought to give him an answer? We should remember we have to provide parents with answers, but they can't be aggressive, I have never been aggressive with parents, but have always tried to touch their heart. For example, this mother, I tried to touch her feeling, told her to respect the school first, the staff ...

Interestingly, the emotional workload seemed to be related to principal-teacher relationships as well. The principals reported coping with emotional issues deriving from unethical behaviors of some teachers, such as a teacher who preferred to take her son to the clinic in the morning instead of the afternoon, a middle manager who sowed dissent regarding the principal's views on education, teacher absenteeism, and teachers who did not respect their children and put them to shame. The perceived impact of teacher misbehavior on principals' emotional workload is manifested in the subsequent quote:

> ... I'm a very pragmatic person. There are rules, there is work to do. But a teacher may come to me saying 'I'm sorry but I must arrive late tomorrow morning, my son has a medical checkup and my husband isn't at home.' I can't tell her no, and I have to 'forget' this hour ... female teachers with young children have many requests related to their children or their marital conditions, and this is very stressful to me, it kills me. On one hand, I want to be practical and professional, but on the other hand, I must be human, so here is the dilemma; to respond positively to the teacher's request or not, what about the students in the school, what about the teacher as a person, but I'm a person too, and what should I say to the supervisor, so this is my emotional workload
>
> (Elementary school male principal, 5)

The emotional workload seemed to be connected to moral dilemmas faced by principals in their interactions with teachers, especially when professional values contradicted emotions of compassion, caring, and empathy.

A failure to promote students with special needs/difficulties

The emotional workload also appeared to be connected to students with special needs and difficulties or to students from disadvantaged families. Sometimes, the emotional workload stemmed from a principal's inability to meet the needs of students with special needs due to a lack of resources or inadequate professional skills. Under such circumstances, the emotional workload was connected to the principal's failure in promoting students' achievements in the examinations, as echoed in the following quote:

> Look, emotional workload is expressed in my case when unpleasant things do happen, like children hit by another child. The level of violence here is very low but when a child is beaten by another child it increases my emotional workload; I have to cope with parents that say my son was struck and this is intolerant, and I know it's intolerant, it is very grave and we will do everything we can that it won't happen again. I feel emotional workload when a child is out of the class in the school yard instead of the class. We met his parents, built a special program for him, we had a daily table to follow his attendance, we encouraged him, and despite all we did, he is out of the class. This makes me feel emotional workload
> (Elementary school male principal, 4)

The need to find unique solutions to students in distress or to students with varied difficulties was described by several principals to cause a heavy emotional workload, predominantly because no easy solutions seemed in sight and none of the principals could be sure that a particular solution would result in the desired consequences. The difficulties in making a decision about the right way to solve challenges of inclusion were outlined by the interviewees to be a part of their emotional workload.

Particularly striking was the emotional workload that arose when principals had no other choice but to expel students with extreme misbehavior or with very low achievements and move them to another school. The emotional workload was related by the interviewees to their concern about these students' future and their uncertain success in the adult world. This workload was reflected in the words of a high-school male principal (14):

> ... When we have to dismiss a student, I mean to send him out to another school, this causes me heavy emotional workload, it is very hard to me, because usually I know that statistically most of the students we dismiss or those who drop out voluntarily, we almost never dismiss students, don't study anymore. We know they go to work or to the streets, so what am I doing with him?

Personal crises of teachers or students

In some cases, the emotional workload was related to personal crises faced by teachers or students that needed some consideration from the principal. The crisis could be a severe illness of a teacher, a family member, sudden resignation of a teacher and the need to find a substitute as soon as possible, sexual abuse of a student by a family member, anxiety for a child residing a violent neighborhood, and the like. The following quotes by two principals illustrate this issue:

> I face horrible emotional workloads ... I had a student in the school with a very complex family who told me something horrifying about his stepfather who lives with him, something terrifying, and I reported to the authorities. Then after you report, a youth investigator arrives here and sits with the student alone ... I'm responsible for the safety of my students from violent families, you know they are violent, aggressive, and you know that if you share what you know with the parents, something can happen to the child. So, you have to make the right decision all the time, to involve the parents, not to involve them ...
>
> (Elementary school female principal, 10)

> I feel many emotional workloads here, when you see a girl calling her home teacher after she came home and saw that her mother had left a suicide letter and was sleeping in bed with the box of her pill empty. This is an emotional workload, you see, this is simply horrible, terrifying, she got to the room with her friend from the class and now the friend also needs mental support ...
>
> (High school female principal, 2)

In some cases, personal crises of teachers could also be relevant to emotional workload of principals, such as teachers who coped with their son's cancer or with their daughter's problems of infertility. In such cases, principals were empathic toward the distress of their teachers while at the same time under pressure to run the school effectively despite the absence of their teachers.

Coping with children from disadvantaged families

Whereas coping with personal crises of staff and students was relatively temporary, coping with the distress of students from unprivileged families could last many months and constituted a significant aspect of the principal's emotional workload. A high-school female principal (10) indicated that "the emotional workload is to see poverty, meagerness, to see kids with no home, and this is very difficult to me." The distress that principals faced included a criminal father who didn't let school staff treat his son adequately, parents who could not pay for school trips, a female student who attended school irregularly because she helped her parents make a living, a drunken father who hit his children at home, students who came to school without textbooks and notebooks, students who were beaten or injured by their violent parents, and so forth.

> Look, I can give you an extremist example of emotional workload. Last year we had a very difficult student whose behavioral disturbances had influenced the whole school. He was very violent and we realized it stems from a severe distress, and we understood his family is very complex and hides many things from us. One day, there was something with one of his parents who didn't show up in school, so he started crying and screaming 'I wish

my parents would die,' and I said, how can you say such a thing, they are your parents, and he told me, 'you don't understand anything, you know what my parents do to me.' I felt my tears are falling on my face, I entered my office and said that if someone dares to say anything about this child without realizing what he has gone thorough, I will tell him to get out of here ... you simply can't ignore the distress of a child in our school ... this is an emotional workload you can't do anything to change because you know that bad things happen in his family

(Elementary school female principal, 2)

The principals elaborated a lot on their coping mechanisms with student distress and how it influenced their mood and self. An elementary school female principal indicated, "this is so tiresome, I come back home all in." These feelings were part of their emotional workload, which differed from other forms of workloads in the workplace as it could stay with them well into their leisure time.

Discussion

Although our analysis of the "emotional workload" represents an initial attempt to grasp this term and use it in a study, a number of insights can be provided. First, despite the difficulty to distinguish between characteristics of emotional workload and its determinants in a small-scale qualitative study, it seems from our interviewees' accounts that emotional workload includes aspects such as concern, pain, suffocation, discomfort, distress, worry, sadness, nuisance, emotional coping, and internal difficulties. While some of these aspects have been reported by principals worldwide (e.g., Beatty, 2000; Berkovich & Eyal, 2015; Johnson et al., 2005), the emotional workload is likely to reflect a collection of undesired emotions and work attitudes. In the view of our interviewees, emotional workload is distinguishable from quantitative workload, the type of workload usually explored in the research on employee workload (e.g., Goh et al., 2015).

Second, emotional workload in principalship is related primarily to a host of responsibilities in principalship characterizing many educational systems worldwide (Philips et al., 2007; Saidun et al., 2015), especially with respect to student safety and well-being and to the principal's need to cope emotionally with teachers and parents. This kind of coping includes emotion display, emotion suppression, emotional inclusion, and listening, all of which elements of emotion management and regulation reported in past research on principal emotion (e.g., Crawford, 2007; Oplatka, 2017) that make it necessary for principals to face various moral dilemmas and personal energy-depletion.

Likewise, emotional workload appears also when the principal faces undesired events and conditions such as a failure to promote a student with special needs, a teacher's personal crisis, and severe difficulties among students (e.g., violence in their family, sexual harassment). Put differently, due to a principal's limited ability to solve a student's distress or a teacher's crisis by common means in school, he/she can remain frustrated, nervous, and worried without changing the overwhelming situation. In common with principals worldwide (e.g., Oplatka, 2017; Redmond, 2016), the principals simply care for their students and teachers and feel empathy and compassion toward their distress. But at the same they are aware of their limited ability to alter a possibly deplorable situation or to help teachers and students in distress to manage their undesirable emotion appropriately. Unsurprisingly, then, they may feel heavy emotional workload.

Third, principals reported experiencing emotional workload 24 hours a day due to their ultimate responsibility over the teachers' and students' safety and well-being. In this sense, they exposed a latent form of principal time use that consists of worry, sadness, never-ending thoughts about school members in troubles during workday, leisure time, and even during their nights. Therefore, any further research on principal time use should not be limited to observable data but rather needs in-depth interviews to unearth the time principals devote to human problems and educational issues under the surface, i.e., in their mind.

What was absent in the principals' accounts are negative emotions indicated in the literature about principal emotion, such as anxiety, fear, demoralization, anger, despair, dissatisfaction disempowerment, threatened self and disillusionment with the system (Beatty, 2000; Blackmore, 2004; James & Vince, 2001). This could mean, in some sense, that emotional workload is perceived as not modifying the general mood or emotion of principals, i.e., that it is unlikely to bring about deep emotional changes in the person. Thus, although feeling a heavy emotional workload, the principals in our study do not necessarily feel threatened by it nor do they experience any deterioration in their general mood.

The current study is limited by scope; therefore, subsequent research on emotional workload in diverse educational systems is warranted. Future research should begin to inquire into how emotional workload is constructed by principals and other educational leaders in different countries. Clearly much research is needed around the determinants and consequences of this type of workload as well as around the strategies used by principals to cope with this workload effectively.

References

Beatty, B. R. (2000). The emotions of educational leadership: Breaking the silence. *International Journal of Leadership in Education*, 3(4), 331–357.

Berkovich, I., & Eyal, O. (2015). Educational leaders and emotions: An international review of empirical evidence 1992–2012. *Review of Educational Research*, 85(1), 129–167.

Blackmore, J. (2004). Leading as emotional management work in high risk times: The counterintuitive impulses of performativity and passion. *School Leadership and Management*, 24(4), 439–459.

Boyatzis, R. (2012). Neuroscience and the link between inspirational leadership and resonant relationships. *Ivey Business Journal*, 76, 26–28.

Cooper, C. L., & Marshall, J. (1976). Occupational sources of stress. *Journal of Occupational Psychology*, 49, 11–28.

Crawford, M. (2007). Emotional coherence in primary school headship. *Educational Management, Administration and Leadership*, 35(4), 521–534.

Gibton, D. (2013). *Law, education, politics, fairness: England's extreme legislation for education reform*. London: Institute of Education Press.

Goh, Z., Ilies, R., & Wilson, K. S. (2015). Supportive supervisors improve employees' daily lives: The role supervisors play in the impact of daily workload on life satisfaction via work–family conflict. *Journal of Vocational Behavior, 89*, 65–73.

Gronn, P. (2003). *The new work of educational leaders: Changing leadership practice in an era of school reform*. London: Paul Chapman Publishing.

Gross, J. J. (1998). The emerging field of emotion regulation: An integrative review. *Review of General Psychology, 2*(3), 271–299.

Harris, B. (2004). Leading by heart. *School Leadership and Management, 24*(4), 391–404.

Ilies, R., Huth, M., Ryan, A. M., & Dimotakis, N. (2015, April 27). Explaining the links between workload, distress, and work–family conflict among school employees: Physical, cognitive, and emotional fatigue. *Journal of Educational Psychology*. Advance online publication. http://dx.doi.org/10.1037/edu0000029.

James, C., & Vince, R. (2001). Developing the leadership capability of headteachers. *Educational Management, Administration & Leadership, 29*(3), 307–317.

Johnson, R. G., Aiken, J. A., & Steggerda, R. (2005). Emotions and educational leadership: Narratives from the inside. *Planning and Changing, 36*(3&4), 235–252.

Marshall, C., & Rossman, G. (2016). *Designing Qualitative Research* (5th ed.). Thousand Oaks, CA: Sage Publications.

Oplatka, I. (2007). The place of the 'open house' in the school choice process: Insights from Canadian parents, children and teachers. *Urban Education, 42*(2), 163–184.

Oplatka, I. (2017). Empathy regulation among Israeli school principals: Expression and suppression of major emotions in educational leadership. *Journal of School Leadership, 27*(1), 94–118.

Philips, A., Sen, D., & McNamee, R. (2007). Prevalence and causes of self-reported work-related stress in head teachers. *Occupational Medicine, 57*(5), 367–376.

Rafaeli, A. (2013). Reflecting on emotional labor as a social meme. In A. A. Grandey, J. M. Diefendorff, & D. E. Rupp (eds.), *Emotional labor in the 21st century* (pp. 294–299). New York, NY: Routledge.

Redmonds, M. (2016). *Affective attunement: emotion and collaboration: A study of Ireland's voluntary secondary school principals*. Dublin: The Joint Managerial Body, Emmet House.

Saidun, R., Mohd, L., & Borhandden-Musha, M. (2015). Problems faced by novice principals in Malaysia: An exploration study. *Mediterranean Journal of Social Sciences, 6*(4), 562–569.

Strauss, A. L., & Corbin, J. (1998). *Basics of qualitative research: techniques and procedures for developing grounded theory* (2nd ed.). Thousand Oaks, CA: Sage.

Tenuto, P. W., Gardiner, M. E., & Yamamoto, J. K. (2016). Leaders on the front line—managing emotion for ethical decision making: A teaching case study for supervision of school personnel. *Journal of Cases in Educational Leadership, 19*(3), 11–26.

Yamamoto, J. K., Gardiner, M. E., & Tenuto, P. L. (2014). Emotion in leadership: Secondary school administrators' perceptions of critical incidents. *Educational Management, Administration & Leadership, 42*(2), 165–183.

Index

Note: *Italicised* folios indicate figures and **bold** indicate tables in the text.

addressing methodological limits 17
"add value" to the organization 28
adequate yearly progress (AYP) 14
administration 12, 15; activities 25; colonial government 202; finance and 159, 161; leadership responsibilities 88; management and 159; organization and 175; strategic framework for school 173
administrative burden 147–148
administrative tasks 4, 12, 59, 127, 141, 144, 160, 172–173, 175, 191; *see also* tasks
Africa 1–2
agentic control assumption 26, 29–30, 40–41
Al-Jammal, K. 191
American Educational Research Association (AERA) 1, 5, 18
American Time Use Survey 10
analysis: cluster 9; correlation 31, 102; cross-national and/or cross-cultural 13, 16–17; data 65, 97, 203–210; discriminant 31; emotional workload 5, 226; exploratory factor 98, 100; hierarchical linear model (HLM) 82; MTMM 35–36; primary school head teachers in Kenya 202–203; quantitative 9, 69; research 202–203; time-series 14; universal unit of 10; workplace 176
analytical scope of principals' work life 17–18
ANOVA model 82
Approved Teacher Status (ATS) 207
Armstrong, P. W. 165
Aronica, L. 77
Asia 1–2, 14
Asia Experience (China) program 135

assumption: agentic control 26, 29–30, 40–41; dimensionality 26, 30–31; equal weighting 26, 31–33; exchangeable instruments 26, 35–36; generality 27, 38; ignorable facets of measurement 26, 33–35; job performance 26, 28; leadership 26–27; object of measurement 26, 28–29; in principals' time-use research 26–38; ratio level of measurement 26, 31; replicability 26, 37
Astor, R. A. 76
attending to parents 194, 198
augmented, total role concept (TRC) *130*, 131, 134–135
Australia 127, 133; *see also* principals discretionary time use in Australia
Australian Principal Occupational Health, Safety and Wellbeing Survey: 2018 Data, The 127, 147, 149
Australia's Time Use Survey 10
Austria 84, 175

Baltimore 113
Barnes, C. A. 51
Barrèrre, A. 175
Basic Education Act (2013) 203–204
Bass, B. M. 129
Bates, G. 60
Bauman, A. 10
behaviors: address school safety and problem 77; instruction-related 25; leadership 9, 16–17, 27, 31, 88–89; managerial 22, 29, 35; measuring 46; social 11; well-being and 78; work 24
being visible 195
Bennis, W. 129, 132
Berman, J. 60

230 *Index*

Bill 13 Anti-Bullying 102
Bill 212 Safe Schools Act 102
Bittman, M. 10
Blendinger, J. 63
Botha, R. J. 188
Boyatzis, R. 217
Bradburn, N. M. 45, 47, 55
Braun, V. 192
Bristow, M. 98, 127
Broward County 113
Brown, K. S. 192
Buenviaje, J. 14, 18
burden: administrative 147–148; minimizing 45; principal time-use measurement strategies 54–56; respondent 3, 33, 44–45, 56
Burns, J. M. 129
Bush, T. 129, 158

Caldwell, B. J. 133
Camburn, E. 25, 28–32, 34–36, 41n2, 51, 53, 60, 62
Canada 18, 191 *see also* time use by principals in Ontario
catholic primary school principals *146*
central office demands 120–121
Centre for Contemporary Learning 135
challenges: capabilities of researchers 61; to leadership 47, 128, 136; measurement assumptions in principals' time-use research 26–38; of student absences 77; work-related 174
Chambers, J. 15
China 14
Chung, K. A. 16, 90
Clarke, V. 192
Cleveland 113
cluster analysis 9; *see also* analysis
Cobanoglu, C. 54
cognitive dissonance 132
Coleman, A. 98
Collins, J. C. 129
command and control (CaC) 142–147, 152–153
communication: email 149; modes of 100–102; principal time-use measurement strategies 48; between researchers 45; written 46
comparative school leadership 76, 90
compliance 25, 110, 113, 121, 147–148, 152
concordats 172
conflicting understandings of instructional leadership 105–106

Constitution of Kenya 203–205
contracutalism 152
Cook, T. D. 51
coping strategies 179–180, 218
coping with children from disadvantaged families 225–226
Copland, M. A. 164
core, total role concept (TRC) *130*, 131, 134
Council of the Great City Schools 111
Covey, S. R 128
creating dynamic culture and leading 197–198
credibility scale 56
Cronbach's *alpha* 32
cross-national and/or cross-cultural explorations of principal time use 13, 16–17
Cross-National Exploration of Principals' Time Use (research conference) 1
Cuban, L. 129
curriculum management 197
Cycyota, C. S. 46

data: analysis 15, 97, 203–210; familiarising self with 192; international assessment 10, 15, 17; longitudinal 61; sample and 113–114; self-report activity log 9
data collection: mode 48–49; opportunities 68–69; research 65; scoring and interpretation 24–38
day-today instruction 15
decentralization 158, 163, 201
defining and naming themes 193
degree of privacy 48
Departmental Heads (DHs) 187
departments of education (DoEs) 142–143, 152
dependent variable 79, 82–83, 88
description of sample 97
Des Moines 113
dimensionality assumption 26, 30–31
Di Natale, E. 133
disadvantaged families 223, 225–226
diversifying sampling strategies 69
Doherty, J. 134
doughnut principle 132
Drake, T. A. 68
Drysdale, L. 128, 133
Duncheon, J. C. 188
Dwyer, D. 13, 77

Eacott, S. 10–11, 128
East Asia 16
Educational Administration Quarterly (EAQ) 17, 43, *44*
educational leadership 171–176; research on emotion in 216–217; time-use data on 40
educational leaders' use of time in Switzerland 171–182; coping strategies 179–180; educational leadership 171–176; hiring and professional responsibilities 173–174; limited capacity for leadership 178–179; principalship 172–173; research on school leadership in 174–176; results 178–181; study background 176–178; Swiss education system 171–176; training and professional development 181
Educational Reform Act 1988 158
education research 11, 22
Education Standards and Quality Assurance Council (ESQAC) 204–205
"effort" factor 55–56
email 18, 69, 96, 100, 104, 114–115, 127, 144, 148–149, 179
emotion: in educational leadership 216–217; negative 216, 227; of seminar participants 177; undesirable 226
emotional coping with school members 222–223
emotional workload 220–226
empirical evidence, principal time use in England 161–163
end of day (EOD) log 53
England *see* principals time use in England
English, M. 61
English school system 158–159, 165
equal weighting assumption 26, 31–33; *see also* assumption
ESM *see* experience sampling method
Europe 1–2
evaluating teachers 15–16, 78, 191
exchangeable instruments assumption 26, 35–36
expand observation periods 69–70
expectations, total role concept (TRC) *130*, 131, 134
experience sampling method (ESM) 9, 24, 32–33, 35, 48, 53, 56, 61–62
exploratory factor analysis 97–98, 100
external relations 12, 15, 23–25, 191–192, 215

failure to promote students with special needs/difficulties 223–224
familiarising self with data 192; *see also* data
finances 19n1, 23, 159, 165, 167, 174
financial cost 3, 44, 53–54
fostering relationships 12, 127, 191
framework: data collection 1, 16–17, 90; G theory 33; policy guiding work of school principal 188; principal time-use measurement strategies 44–45, *45*; TRC 130
France 135

Gantt, H. 126
Gantt chart 126
Gardner, W. L. 61
Gates Foundation 15
generality assumption 27, 38; *see also* assumption
Generalizability (G) theory 33–36
generating initial themes 192
Geneva 174
Gentilucci, J. 76
Germany 135, 175
Gershuny, J. 10
Ghamrawi, N. 191
Gilbreth, F. 126
Gilbreth, L. 126
Global Educational Reform Movement (GERM) 152–153
Goldring, E. 12, 15, 19n1, 25, 29–32, 35–38, 41, 69, 191
Goode, H. 133–134
government policy documents on role of teachers in Kenya 203–206
Great Britain 10
Greller, S. L. 12–13, 14
Grissom, J. A. 15, 25, 27, 29, 61–62, 68, 187, 191
Gronn, P. 53
Groves, R. M. 47, 54
Gurr, D. 127

Hallinger, P. 12–13, 15, 62, 76, 79, 82, 86–88, 97, 211
Handy, C. 129, 132
Harris, B. 216
Harrison, D. A. 46
Hauseman, D. C. 47
Hayden, J. M. 54
Heck, R. H. 13
Heifetz, R. 129
Herman, R. 60

Herrington, C. 76, 87
high-school female principal 221, 225
hiring and professional responsibilities 173–174
Hochbein, C. 69, 127, 192
Hofstede's power distance index (PDI) 82
home-school involvement **80–81**, 82
Honig, M. I. 110
Horng, E. L. 12, 15, 25, 41n1, 60–61, 191
Huang, T. 192
Huber, S. G. 175
Huberman, A. M. 192
Huff, J. 25, 30, 32, 35–38, 41n2
Hunt, B. R. 12, 60, 192
Hunt, E. 192
hybridization 165

identifying data collection opportunities 68–69; *see also* data collection
idling in the office 195
ignorable facets of measurement assumption 26, 33–35; *see also* assumption
Illinois 192
immigrant students: percentage of 79
implications for research 39–41
India 84
Indonesia 84
information and communication technology (ICT) 18
inspiring principal 195–198
instruction 15; classroom 16, 114; instruction-related activities 25, 191; instruction-related tasks 25; leadership 105; quality in school 210; supervising 61, 206; teachers 12–13, 111, 116
instructional leaders 99, 105, 110, 191, 204, 206, 210
instructional leadership 12, 14–16, 98, **99**; activities 23; classroom teachers 100; conceptualizations 3; conflicting understandings of 105–106; instruction-related behaviors 25; leadership behaviors 88; management responsibilities 99; scores 36; time spent on 24, 31, 37; time-use measure of 34
instructional program 15, 23, 25, 116
Intensive Partnership (IP) for Effective Teaching Program 15
intentional differentiation of time with principals 117–120
interface activity noise 144, 146
interfacing 144
internal relations (relations with teachers and students) 12–13, 15, 25

international assessment data 78–79
International Association for the Evaluation of Educational Achievement (IEA) 78, 82
International Monetary Fund (IMF) 82
International Successful School Principalship Project (ISSPP) 126, 132–133
Ireson, G. 98
Irlicht, B. 133
Israeli educational leaders *see* principalship
Italy 135
item-response-theory (IRT) 32–33

Jantzi, D. 105
job demands and resources theory (JD-R) 141
job performance 25–26, 28
job resources 141–142
job stress 187
joint work 110

Kenya *see* primary school head teachers in Kenya
Kenya Education Management Institute (KEMI) 202
Kenya Education Staff Institute (KESI) 202
key performance indicators (KPIs) 143
Klasik, D. 12
Klostermann, B. K. 192
Kmetz, J. T. 59
knowledge equals power 142
Kotter, J. 129
Kuwait 84

lack of time to devote to teaching and learning 148
Laplace estimation 82–83
Lavigne, H. J. 12–14, 16
leadership 175; assumption 26–27; behaviors 9, 16–17, 27, 31, 88–89; challenges to 47, 128, 136; comparative school 76, 90; domains in time use research 11–15; instruction 105; limited capacity for 178–179; management and 104–105, 126–137, *130*, *132*, *136*; responsibilities 88; school business 159–164; school research 15; transactional 105, 129; transformational 12, 105, 129; *see also* educational leadership; instructional leadership
Lee, J. 14

Lee, M. 11–15, 62, 76, 79, 82, 86–88, 97–98
Leithwood, K. 105, 129
lessons from districts 122–123
Levitt, T. 130
limited capacity for leadership 178–179; *see also* leadership
Lipham, J. M. 129
Little's MCAR test 82
Loeb, S. 12, 187
Long Beach 113
Lortie, D. C. 75, 77
Lungu, G. F. 202

macro-level characteristics (level-2) 82
Mahone, A. S. 69
management and leadership *see* leadership
managing student discipline 12, 25
managing time 197
Marathon, M. 196
Marshall, C. 218
Martinko, M. J. 61
Master, B. 187
May, H. 15, 25, 30, 32, 35–38, 41n2, 61–62, 127
MCAR test (Little) 82
McPeake, J. A. 14
measurement assumptions in principals' time-use research 22–41; challenges 26–38; data collection, scoring and interpretation 24–38; implications for research 39–41; problem 23–24
measures and analytical strategies 79–83; dependent variable 82–83; macro-level characteristics (level-2) 82; organizational level characteristics (level-1) 79–82
Mertkan, S. 164
Miami 60
Miami-Dade County Public Schools 66
Middle East 1–2
Miles, M. B. 192
Ministry of Education (MOE) 206, 217
Minneapolis 113
Mintzberg, H. A. 22, 95
Miskel, C. G. 16, 90
Model Principal Supervisor Professional Standards 111
modernization 159
modes of communication 100–102
Morris, E. 160

multi-trait, multimethod (MTMM) correlation matrix 35–36
Mulvaney Hoyer, K. 69
Muta, C. 76

National Centre for School Leadership (NCSL) 160–161
National Education Sector Plan (NESP) 2013–2018 205, 210
National Standards of Excellence for Headteachers 158
negative school climate 79, **80–81**
neoliberalism 141–151
Nettles, S. 76, 79, 87
New Labour 160
New Public Management (NPM) 142, 153, 172
Ni, Y. 69
Nigeria 188
No Child Left Behind (NCLB) 14, 66
North America 1–2, 84
Norway 84

object of measurement assumption 26, 28–29
Obrist, S. 175
observation periods 62–64, **66–67**, 67, 68
observed work activity analysis 9
Oceania 1–2
OECD 172
O'Neil, C. 15
online survey 96–97
Ontario Leadership Framework 105
Ontario Principals' Council (OPC) 96
Oplatka, I. 216
organizational barriers 111, 120–121
organizational culture 12
organizational level characteristics (level-1) 79–82, **80–81**
organizational management 4, 15, 95, 105–106, 158–160, 162, 164
outward facing 158–159

Papua New Guinea 135
Parent Engagement Policy 102
Parents in Partnership 102
Perrenoud, O. 177
personal crises of teachers or students 224–225
perspective of data provider 49–51
perspiring principals 193–195
Peters, T. 129
phenomenon measured 46–47

phenomenon sampling 51–52
Philippines 14
Plank, D. N. 202
Poisson hierarchical linear model (HLM) 79, 82, **85**
policies influencing principals time 102–104
Policy on the South African Standards for Principalship 188
Pollock, K. 18, 47
population, principal time-use measurement strategies 45–46
post-heroic leaders 134
potential, total role concept (TRC) *130*, 131, 134–135
power distance index (PDI) (Hofstede) 82
PricewaterhouseCoopers 159
primary school head teachers in Kenya 201–211; analysis 202–203; data analysis 203–210; data sources 202–203; government policy documents on role of 203–206; primary school leadership in Kenya 201–202; qualification levels of *208*; research 202–203; school management effectiveness 206–210
primus inter pares 175
principal(s): efficiency 141–151; gender, years of work, and age 98; goal and task prioritization 10; health and wellbeing strategy **150**; leadership practice 25; professional development 13–14; spending their time 98–100; supervisor initiative 111–112; time use 60–62, *145*, 219–220; work life 17–18
Principal Health and Well-being Services 149–151
Principal Health and Wellbeing Studies (report) 143
principals direct interaction with individual students 75–90; comparative school leadership 90; implications 89–90; international assessment data 78–79; limitations 88–89; measures and analytical strategies 79–83; results 83–86; 34 societies 86–87; student outcomes 89–90; time spent 86; within-society variance 87–88
principals discretionary time use in Australia 141–153; administrative burden 147–148; case study 141; command and control (CaC) 142–147; compliance 148; email 148; knowledge equals power 142; lack of time to devote to teaching and learning 148; neoliberalism 141–151; principal efficiency 141–151; service delivery model (SDM) 148–151; sheer quantity of work 147; time and motion study 142–147; time usage 141–153
principalship 172–173, 215–227; context 217; coping with children from disadvantaged families 225–226; emotional coping with school members 222–223; emotional workload 220–226; failure to promote students with special needs/difficulties 223–224; findings 219–226; method 217–219; participants 217–218; personal crises of teachers or students 224–225; principal's time use during the day 219–220; procedure 218–219; research on emotion in educational leadership 216–217; sense of concern/nuisance 221–222
principals time use in England 157–167; empirical evidence 161–163; reconfiguration of principal role 163–164; role within the English school system 158–159; school business leadership 159–164; values conflict and 164–166
principals time-use measurement strategies 43–56; burden 54–56; communication 48; data collection mode 48–49; degree of privacy 48; financial cost 53–54; framework 44–45, *45*; perspective of data provider 49–51; phenomenon measured 46–47; phenomenon sampling 51–52; population 45–46; researcher involvement 49; validity 52–53
Principal Supervisor Initiative (PSI) 111–114, 116–117, 119–120, 122–124
producing the report 193
professional development (PD) 14–15, 98, **99**, 181
Progin, L. 176–177
programme for international student assessment (PISA) 172
Progress in International Reading Literacy Study (PIRLS) 2, 12–13, 15, 78, 86, 88, 97–98
Pruchno, R. A. 54
public school principals 12–13
Purchasing Power Parities (PPPs) 82

Qian, H. 14
quality of time spent by supervisors with principals *116*, 116–117
Qualtrics (web survey tool) 54

quantitative analysis 9, 69; *see also* analysis
quantity of time spent by supervisors with principals 114–115, *115*

ratio level of measurement assumption 26, 31
reconfiguration of principal role 163–164
recruitment 15, 55
reflective interview 9, 17
reform 15–16, 157–160, 162, 201–202, 205, 215, 217
Regulation 274/12 Hiring Practice 102
Reimagining Special Education Through Arts Education and Therapy (conference) 135
replicability assumption 26, 37
report production 193
research 59–70; data collection 65; diversifying sampling strategies 69; emotion in educational leadership 216–217; expand observation periods 69–70; identifying data collection opportunities 68–69; methodology 62–64; observation periods 67; primary school head teachers in Kenya 202–203; recommendations 68–70; results 64–67; roles and responsibilities of principals 59–60; on school leadership 174–176; school level 66, **66**; school locale 65–66, **66**; synthesis 67–68; time-use findings/methodologies 60–62
researcher involvement 49
reviewing themes 193
Reyes, I. 15
Riley, P. 69
Robinson, K. 77
Robinson, V. 90
roles and responsibilities of principals 59–60; *see also* principal(s)
Rossman, G. 218
rotated component matrix **99**
RTI International 202, 206
Russia 10

sampling 96–97; diversifying strategies 69; error 37; heterogeneous 62; instrument 46; phenomenon 47, 51–52; snowball 62; structure 63, **64**, 68; technique 63
SBM Demonstration Project Programme 161
scheduled meetings 193–194
school business leader (SBL) 157, 159–164, 167n1, 167n3

school business manager (SBM) 167n1
school climate 79, 210; *see also* negative school climate
School Governing Body (SGB) 187
school leadership research 15
school level 66, **66**, 68, 173
school-level SES 79
school locale 65–66, **66**
school location 82
school management 24, 98, 99, **99**, 101–102, 106, 171, 187, 206, **207**
School Management Team (SMT) 187
school principals in South Africa 187–198; findings 193–198; inspiring principal 195–198; literature 188–192; methodology 192–193; perspiring principals 193–195; policy framework 188; purpose **189–190**
school resources 79, 86, 88
school safety 76–77, 79, 88–90, 104
Schools and Staffing Survey (SASS) 12, 14, 69
school size 28, 79
searching for themes 193
Sebastian, J. 29–31, 34–35, 47, 50
self-care 196
self familiarising with data 192
self-imposed limits 132
self-report activity 9, 17
semi-structured interviews 218
sense of concern/nuisance 221–222
Sergiovanni, T. J. 129
service delivery model (SDM) 142–143, 148–151, 153
Sessional Paper No. 1 of 2005 203, 210
Sessional Paper No. 14 of 2012 204–205
Shadish, W. R. 38
Shakman, K. 12–13, 14
sheer quantity of work 147
Shrimpton, J. 133
Simons, J. 192
Snapshot of School Management Effectiveness (SSME) 202, 206–210, **207**
social behavior 11
social conduct 11
social theory 27
34 societies (education systems) **80–81**, 86–87
South Africa 84 *see also* school principals in South Africa
South Korea 16, 90
Southworth, G. 160–161
Spain 84

spans of control 120
Sparks, D. 69
Spillane, J. P. 12, 27–31, 34–35, 53, 60, 127, 164, 192
Standards and Quality Assurance (SQA) 204–206
Starratt, R. 129
Steinbach, C. 105
Stewart, J. 165
Stitziel Pareja, A. 28
structural separation 165
structured observation 9, 12, 22, 24, 32–33, 35–36, 39, 41, 60
student affairs 12, 98, **99**
student outcomes 89–90
students with special needs/difficulties 223–224
Sudman, S. 56
Sun, M. 69
supervising students 12
supervisors 110–124; ability 122–123; barriers 121–122; data and sample 113–114; flexibility and discretion 123; lessons from the districts 122–123; principal supervisor initiative 111–112; quality of time with principals *116*, 116–117, 123; quantity of time with principals 114–115, *115*, 123; time allocation 114; time spent 114–117; time use 112–113, 117–122; tools 123; vision 122
Supovitz, J. A. 15, 61
Survey Monkey (web survey tool) 54
Swiss Conference of Cantonal Ministers of Education (EDK) 172–174
Switzerland: education system 171–176; *see also* educational leaders' use of time in Switzerland

Taskforce on the Alignment of the Education Sector 204
tasks 24; accountability 144; administrative 4, 12, 59, 127, 141, 144, 160, 172–173, 175, 191; curriculum 127; instruction-related 25; job incumbents 25; leadership 28, 78; management-related 99; managerial 3; operational 116; unrelated 3
Taylor, F. W. 10, 126
Taylor, S. 187
(neo-)Taylorism 11
Teachers Service Commission Act (2012) 205–206

Teacher Training Colleges (TTCs) 207
teaching and learning 195
teaching-oriented supervisors 110
Teisl, M. F. 54
theoretical interpretation 25
therapeutic activities 18
Thurler, G. 175
Tiernery, W. G. 188
time allocation of supervisors 114
time and motion study 142–147
time management 4, 29, 122–123, 128, 146, 171, 180–182, 197
time spent 97–98, *101*, 114–117
time usage/use 112–113, 141–153; barriers 120–122; supporting supervisor 122–123; unintentional variation in 120–122; variation in 117–122
time use by principals in Ontario 95–107; conflicting understandings of instructional leadership 105–106; data analysis 97; description of sample 97; findings 97–104; leading and managing 104–105; methodology 96–97; modes of communication 100–102; online survey 96; policies influencing principals time 102–104; principals gender, years of work, and age 98; principals spending their time 98–100; sampling 96–97; time principals spent at work 97–98
time use research 9–18; future directions of principal 15–18; leadership domains in 11–15; theoretical perspectives of 10–11
TIMSS *see* Trends in International Mathematics and Science Study
total product concept 130
total role concept (TRC) 128–135, *130*, *132*; augmented *130*, 131, 134–135; conceptual ideas 132; core *130*, 131, 134; described 130–131; expectations *130*, 131, 134; leadership and management 128–132; methodology 132–133; potential *130*, 131, 134–135; principals 133–135
Towne, H. 126
training and professional development 181
transactional leadership 105, 129
transformational leadership 12, 105, 129
Trends in International Mathematics and Science Study (TIMSS) 2, 15, 78
Tschannen-Moran, M. 152
Tudor, R. 134

unintentional variation in time use 120–122
United States 10, 38, 63, 68, 77, 111, 176, 192; instructional leaders 110; Intensive Partnership (IP) for Effective Teaching Program 15; public school principals 12–13
University of Manchester 161
unscheduled meetings 193–194
urgent important matrix 180

validity: argument 23; construct 51; convergent 24; of data 48; measurement 3, 17, 78; predictive 40; principal time-use measurement strategies 52–53
values: business 157; conflict 4, 163–166; school community 135; social 136
Vanderbeck, S. C. 69
variation in time use 117–122
Vaud 174

Victor, A. A. 188
vision crafting 196–197

Walker, A. 14
Wallace Foundation 111
Wang, A. 15
Weick, K. E. 188
White, B. R. 192
Willower, D. J. 59
Windlinger, R. 175
Wolcott, H. F. 60
Wood, C. 163–164
workforce remodeling 159
workloads 147, 159, 226; *see also* emotional workload
workshops 14, 128, 193–194
World Health Organization 207

Ylimaki, R. 133

Zweig, J. 12–13, 14